TOMMY AT WAR

TOMMY
AT WAR

1914–1918
THE SOLDIERS' OWN STORIES

JOHN SADLER &
ROSIE SERDIVILLE

The Robson Press

First published in Great Britain in 2013 by
The Robson Press (an imprint of Biteback Publishing Ltd)
Westminster Tower
3 Albert Embankment
London SE1 7SP
Copyright © John Sadler and Rosie Serdiville 2013

ISBN 978-1-84954-514-3

10 9 8 7 6 5 4 3 2 1

A CIP catalogue record for this book is available from the British Library.

Set in Garamond and Futura

Printed and bound in Great Britain by
CPI Group (UK) Ltd, Croydon CR0 4YY

This one is for Silvie and for Gerry. Inspirations both.

YOUR KING WANTS YOU!
YOUR COUNTRY WANTS YOU!
YOUR CHUMS WANT YOU!
– Colonel Gilbert O. Spence, 5th Battalion Durham Light Infantry

At every Great War memorial service, the soldier is referred to as though patriotism had been the chief influence that had made him join the army and ultimately die in action. To the ex-serviceman who has had his eyes opened to the lies and deceptions of the Great War, how sad and ignorant it all is, he knows that practically all the pious outpourings over their dead comrades and comrades' enemies are based on a false thesis.

The majority of the rank and file of the 'Contemptibles' joined the army for many various reasons other than that of patriotism; unemployment, home troubles and petty evils were the best recruiting sergeants in pre-war days and, when the war came, the spirit of adventure was the main influence, backed by every possible means of enticement and coercion. If the psychology of the un-conscripted Great War British soldier could ever be written, patriotism would be the least of impulses and hard instinct of men of fighting temperament at the top.

The truth about the non-commissioned soldier, who fought in the Great War, is a thing to be ashamed of, instead of being blessed and glorified as a virtue by those who are far removed from the foul realities of it.
– Sergeant Charles H. Moss, 18th (Pals) Battalion DLI (c.1924)

Naturally, the common people don't want war, but after all it is the leaders of the country who determine policy and it is always a simple matter to drag people along … voice or no voice, the people can always be brought to the bidding of the leaders. This is easy. All you have to do is tell them they are being attacked and denounce the pacifists for lack of patriotism and for exposing the country to danger. It works the same in every country.
– Reich-Marshal Hermann Goering (at Nuremberg)

CONTENTS

ABOUT THE AUTHORS

John has had an enduring fascination with the Great War since childhood, when men of his grandfather's generation who had served were in their sixties and seventies. His paternal grandfather, a lifelong pacifist, had been amongst that relatively small group of conscientious objectors who refused to take up arms. Their cases, like those of the 'shot at dawns', remain controversial. His grandfather was imprisoned in Richmond Castle and, at times, force-fed. The experience had a lasting effect upon his health.

Despite this anti-war pedigree, John's life has been spent studying conflict. He has walked the ground of the Western Front on countless occasions, from rain-drenched, leaden soil in Flanders, through mining villages in Artois to the chalk uplands of the Somme and the rolling terrain of Verdun. Some years ago, when a few veterans were still sufficiently spry to visit the small and lovely city of Ypres, he encountered with a school group one survivor, there with his family. The young people had the privilege, denied to future school parties, of talking with one who was actually there, a living link with those featured at 'In Flanders Fields', the museum they'd just visited. The old man had acted as battalion runner, a highly risky job. Many of his comrades had been killed or injured. When one of the young asked him, 'Why did you do it?' he simply replied, 'It was my duty'. I doubt anyone could summarise the generation of 1914 any better.

Rosie's angle of approach is rather different. Part of the 'second wave' of the Women's Movement back in the 1970s, she began to puzzle over those suffragettes who put their campaign on hold in 1914. It did not mesh with the anti-war mood of the new generation. The situation turned out to be more complex (they always are).

We make no apologies if this book appears to adopt a rather northern-centric view. The county regiments of the north contributed more battalions than any others and suffered accordingly. A previous book, *Dunkirk to Belsen*, covered the fighting man's experience in World War Two and this volume, in part, is intended as a companion. Ours is also a British account, viewing the conflict from Tommy's side of the wire. This does not denigrate the immense sacrifice of our allies in the war or that of our enemy, who proved a brave, honourable and remarkably tenacious foe.

ACKNOWLEDGEMENTS

Over the years we have learned a great deal, partly from contact with others in the field and partly from published and media sources. Anyone of our generation who has studied the Great War owes a debt to John Terraine, not just for his numerous published works but for his groundbreaking TV series, aired from the late summer of 1964 and which remains unsurpassed.

Amongst those other writers whose work has greatly expanded our own understanding and fuelled our enthusiasm we must number Martin Middlebrook's *First Day of the Somme*. It must be one of the most influential texts in terms of how many view military history. Alistair Horne's haunting account of Verdun remains by far the best. Alan Clerk, Peter Hart, Lyn MacDonald, Peter Ellis and numerous others deserve their place in the list. Amongst those whose personal empathy and knowledge have been invaluable we must cite Steve Shannon, Dr Barry Matthews, Dr Ian Matthews, Graham Trueman, Trevor Sheehan, Paul Thompson, Captain R. Sadler of the Royal Engineers and Captain S. Meadows of 2nd Gurkhas.

This book could not have been written without the generous assistance of a number of organisations and individuals, particular thanks are due to: Roberta Goldwater of *A Soldier's Life* and colleagues at Tyne and Wear Archives and Museums; Tony Goddard of the Border Regiment Museum at Carlisle; Ian Martin of the King's Own Scottish Borderers Museum, Berwick-upon-Tweed; Trustees of the Green Howards Museum, Richmond; Trustees

of the Durham Light Infantry Museum and Art Gallery; staff of
Durham County Record Office; staff of Northumberland County
Archives at Woodhorn; the Trustees of the Fusiliers Museum of
Northumberland, Alnwick; colleagues at the North East Centre
for Lifelong Learning at the University of Sunderland; staff at
the Literary and Philosophical Library, Newcastle; Anna Flowers
and colleagues at Central Libraries, Newcastle and Gateshead,
Clayport Library Durham, Northumberland Libraries at Morpeth,
Alnwick, Blyth, Hexham and Cramlington; to Glenn Baume
and colleagues of the Heugh Gun Battery Trust Limited. We are
also indebted to Lindsey and Colin Durward of Blyth Battery,
Blyth, Northumberland; Peter Hart and the staff of the Imperial
War Museum Sound Archive; Richard Groocock at the National
Archive; Amy Cameron of National Army Museum; archive staff
of the Defence Academy of the United Kingdom at Shrivenham;
David Fletcher of the Tank Museum, Bovington; Rod Mackenzie
of the Argyll and Sutherland Highlanders Museum; Thomas
B. Smyth of the Black Watch Museum; Paul Evans of the Royal
Artillery Museum; curator and staff of the Royal Engineers
Museum and Archives, Chatham; Peter Barton of La Boisselle
Study Group; John Stelling, Anthony Hall and Henry Ross of
North War Museum Project; Tony Ball of the Western Front
Association; Jennifer Laidler for her grandfather's memoir; J. R.
Keighley for his poem *One Hundred Years*, Samantha Kelly for
original verse; Jan and Michael Crawley; Morag Miller and family;
Mr and Mrs Cookson of Meldon Hall; Silvie Fisch; Gerry and
Helen Tomlinson; Liz Clarke for bouncing ideas around so happily;
The Women's Library. Special thanks are due to Kate Hordern, our
indefatigable agent and to Jeremy Robson of The Robson Press for
another successful collaboration.

Thanks must also be given to the staffs of various Great War
museums and memorials across the breadth of the Western Front
who have provided willing and friendly assistance over the years –
'In Flanders Fields', Ypres; the Memorial Museum Passchendaele
at Zonnebeke; Tyne Cot Cemetery Visitor Centre; Hooge Crater

Museum; the Trench of Death, Diksmuide; Newfoundland Park Visitor Centre; 'Ocean Villas' WWI and WWII Museum; Ulster Tower; Thiepval Visitor Centre; Museum of the South African Forces, Delville Wood; Historial de la Grande Guerre, Peronne; Somme 1916 Trench Museum, Albert; Vimy Memorial Park; Notre Dame de Lorette and the Wellington Tunnels, Arras.

Every effort has been made to trace copyright holders for those individuals whose diaries and correspondence we have used, held in the archives listed above. We would be grateful for any information which might help to trace those whose identities or addresses are not currently known.

We acknowledge the following books from which extracts have been taken. *Fanny Went to War* by Pat Beauchamp (London: John Murray, 1919), *Women Wanted: the Story Written in Blood Red Letters on the Horizon of the Great World War* by Mabel Potter Daggett (G. H. Doran, 1918), *Diary of a Nursing Sister on the Western Front 1914–1915*, attributed to K. E. Luard (William Blackwood, 1915). We apologise to anyone who inadvertently has not been acknowledged.

Odd punctuation, phrasing, spelling and grammar have not been corrected if they are those of the original authors – though we have offered translations of some dialect words. As ever, the present authors remain responsible for all other errors and omissions.

Rosie Serdiville and John Sadler
Northumberland
Autumn 2012

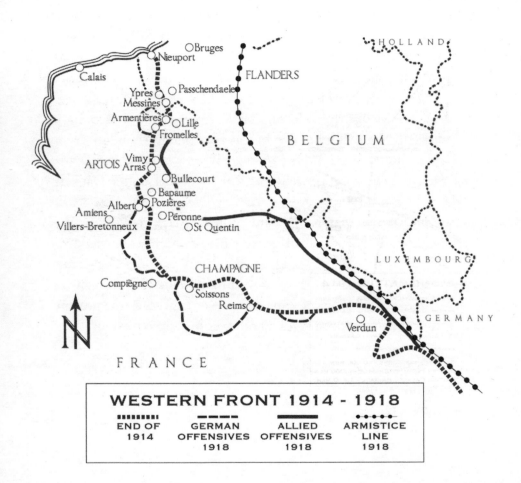

HOLLAND

Bruges

Nieuport

Calais

FLANDERS

Ypres

Passchendaele

Messines

BELGIUM

Armentières

Lille

Fromelles

Vimy

ARTOIS

Arras

Bullecourt

Bapaume

Pozières

Albert

Amiens

Péronne

Villers-Bretonneux

St Quentin

LUXEMBOURG

CHAMPAGNE

Compiègne

Soissons

Reims

GERMANY

Verdun

N

FRANCE

WESTERN FRONT 1914 - 1918

| END OF 1914 | GERMAN OFFENSIVES 1918 | ALLIED OFFENSIVES 1918 | ARMISTICE LINE 1918 |

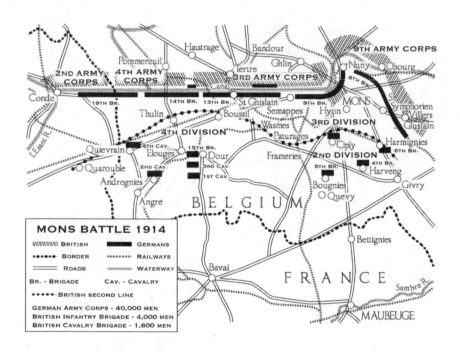

MONS BATTLE 1914

▧▧▧	BRITISH	▬▬	GERMANS
••••	BORDER	+++++	RAILWAYS
═══	ROADS	≈≈≈	WATERWAY
BR. - BRIGADE		CAV. - CAVALRY	
••••• BRITISH SECOND LINE			

GERMAN ARMY CORPS - 40,000 MEN
BRITISH INFANTRY BRIGADE - 4,000 MEN
BRITISH CAVALRY BRIGADE - 1,600 MEN

3: 1ST BATTLE OF YPRES, 19 OCTOBER–22 NOVEMBER 1914

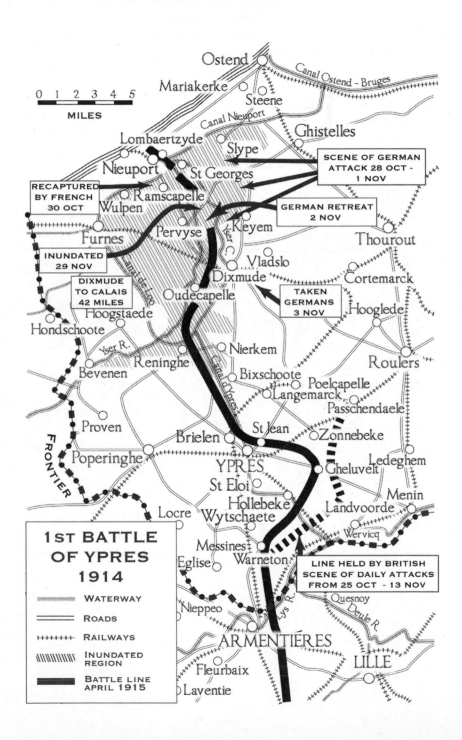

0 1 2 3 4 5
MILES

Ostend

Mariakerke

Steene

Canal Ostend - Bruges

Canal Nieuport

Ghistelles

Lombaertzyde

Slype

SCENE OF GERMAN ATTACK 28 OCT - 1 NOV

Nieuport

St Georges

RECAPTURED BY FRENCH 30 OCT

Ramscapelle

Wulpen

Pervyse

Kleyem

GERMAN RETREAT 2 NOV

Furnes

Iser C.

Thourout

INUNDATED 29 NOV

Vladslo

DIXMUDE TO CALAIS 42 MILES

Oudecapelle

Dixmude

Cortemarck

Canal de Loo

TAKEN GERMANS 3 NOV

Hooglede

Hoogstaede

Hondschoote

Yser R.

Nierkem

Roulers

Reninghe

Bixschoote

Bevenen

Canal of Ypres

Poelcapelle

Langemarck

Passchendaele

Proven

Brielen

St Jean

Zonnebeke

Ledeghem

Poperinghe

YPRES

Gheluvelt

FRONTIER

St Eloi

Menin

Hollebeke

Landvoorde

Locre

Wytschaete

Wervicq

1ST BATTLE OF YPRES 1914

Messines

Eglise

Warneton

LINE HELD BY BRITISH SCENE OF DAILY ATTACKS FROM 25 OCT - 13 NOV

~~~~~~~~ WATERWAY

———— ROADS

++++++ RAILWAYS

//////// INUNDATED REGION

▬▬▬▬ BATTLE LINE APRIL 1915

Nieppeo

Lys R.

Quesnoy

Deule R.

ARMENTIÉRES

LILLE

Fleurbaix

Laventie

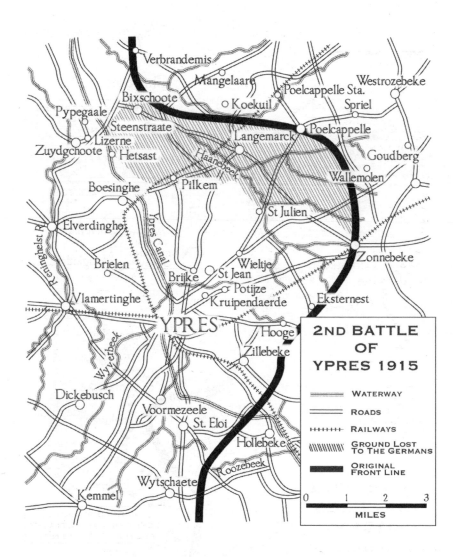

2ND BATTLE
OF
YPRES 1915

▓▓▓▓▓	WATERWAY
══════	ROADS
┼┼┼┼┼┼	RAILWAYS
▨▨▨▨▨	GROUND LOST TO THE GERMANS
████	ORIGINAL FRONT LINE

0   1   2   3

MILES

5: THE BATTLE OF THE SOMME, 1916

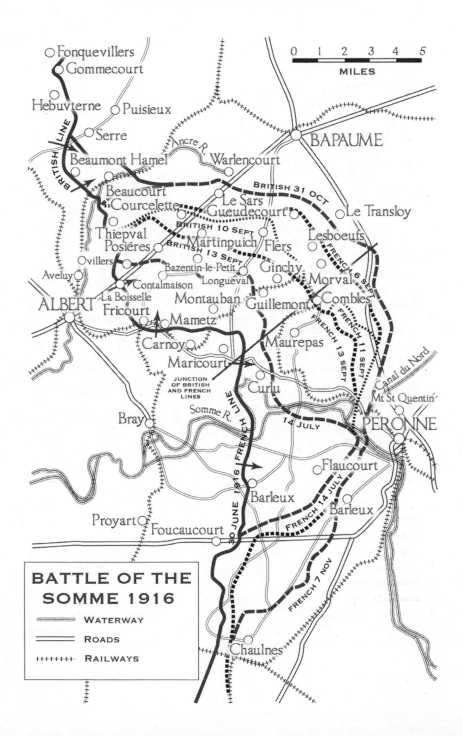

Fonquevillers
Gommecourt
Hebuterne
Puisieux
Serre
BRITISH LINE
Beaumont Hamel
Ancre R.
Warlencourt
BAPAUME
0 1 2 3 4 5
MILES
Beaucourt
Courcelette
Le Sars
Gueudecourt
BRITISH 31 OCT
Le Transloy
Thiepval
Posiéres
BRITISH 10 SEPT
Martinpuich
Flers
Lesboeufs
BRITISH 13 SEPT
FRENCH 6 SEPT
Ovillers
Bazentin-le-Petit
Ginchy
Morval
Aveluy
Contalmaison
Longueval
La Boisselle
Montauban
Guillemont
Combles
ALBERT
Fricourt
Mametz
Maurepas
FRENCH 11 SEPT
FRENCH 13 SEPT
Carnoy
Maricourt
JUNCTION OF BRITISH AND FRENCH LINES
Curlu
Canal du Nord
Somme R.
FRENCH LINE
14 JULY
Mt St Quentin
Bray
30 JUNE 1916 FRENCH LINE
PERONNE
Flaucourt
Barleux
Barleux
FRENCH 14 JULY
Proyart
Foucaucourt
FRENCH 7 NOV
Chaulnes

BATTLE OF THE SOMME 1916

- ≡≡≡ WATERWAY
- ── ROADS
- ┼┼┼┼┼┼┼ RAILWAYS

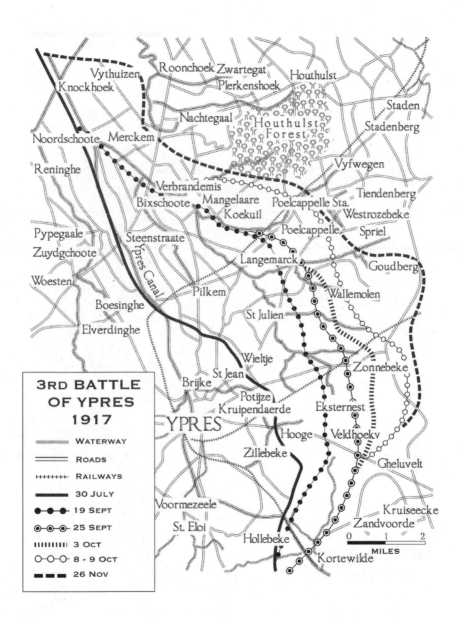

3RD BATTLE OF YPRES 1917

▓▓▓▓	WATERWAY
▬▬▬	ROADS
┼┼┼┼┼	RAILWAYS
▬▬▬	30 JULY
●━●━●	19 SEPT
◉━◉━◉	25 SEPT
▐▐▐▐▐	3 OCT
○━○━○	8 - 9 OCT
▄▄ ▄▄	26 NOV

Vythuizen
Knockhoek
Roonchoek Zwartegat
Plerkenshoek
Houthulst
Staden
Stadenberg
Nachtegaal
Houthulst Forest
Noordschoote Merckem
Vyfwegen
Reninghe
Verbrandemis
Tiendenberg
Bixschoote Mangelaare
Poelcappelle Sta.
Westrozebeke
Koekuil
Pypegaale
Steenstraate
Poelcappelle
Spriel
Zuydgchoote
Langemarck
Goudberg
Woesten
Pilkem
Wallemolen
Boesinghe
St Julien
Elverdinghe
Ypres Canal
Wieltje
Zonnebeke
Brijke
St Jean
Eksternest
Potijze
Kruipendaerde
Veldhoekv
YPRES
Hooge
Gheluvelt
Zillebeke
Voormezeele
Kruiseecke
St. Eloi
Zandvoorde
Hollebeke
Kortewilde

0   1   2
MILES

INTRODUCTION

'No Conscription'

Would you show your love for freedom?
Would you stand for truth and right?
Would you take the path of wisdom?
Then be ready for the fight!

[Chorus] For we won't have conscription,
We all hate conscription,
We don't want conscription
So we'll all be volunteers.

Would you keep your homes in safety?
And protect the fatherland?
Have your commerce prosper greatly,
On the sea and on the land.

[Chorus]

Have we foes across the water?
Who must be kept at bay?
If we value freedom's charter,
We'll be ready e-en than they.

[Chorus]

But should the foe ever threaten,
Or but touch our silver strand,
We will drown him in the ocean,
By the aid of God's right hand!

[Chorus][1]

One of Marlborough's redcoats toiling on the road to Blenheim in 1704 might have had little or no difficulty in recognising his great-grandson marching in the rain towards the ridge of Mont St Jean under Wellington over a century later. Both wore the famous red coat. They marched or rode as armies had through distant centuries. They wheeled and drilled, delivered their platoon volleys in a very similar manner. Both carried a smooth-bore flintlock musket that might just kill their man at fifty yards. Yet Wellington's infantryman, 'that article', as his commander described him, might have found far greater difficulty in recognising his own great-grandson, slogging along the hot *pavé* towards Mons in 1914. *Tommy* was clad in stiff khaki. He carried the Short Magazine Lee-Enfield (SMLE) bolt-action repeating rifle, deadly at a dozen times the distance of its predecessor. Much of his travel was undertaken by rail and the ubiquitous tin meant he could fight all year round and still be fed. None of this promised an easier life. Indeed, his would very likely be harder, more terrifying and very much shorter.

Every year Remembrance Day on 11 November becomes an ever more self-conscious event, almost Disneyfied in a slush of sentimentality. No future generation now will be able to listen to the voices of those who served first-hand as the last known survivors have died. This marks a watershed; now the conflict passes beyond immediate consciousness, out of the memory of parents and grandparents. It grows increasingly remote. There is a duty and a compulsion to keep these voices alive. Whether Tommy Atkins was a 'lion led by donkeys' or whether the generals were thwarted by advances in technology which rendered a well-held trench line unbreakable is not the subject matter of this book. The core of this new work is the words of those who were there, the experience of war and of battle as they saw it.

The opening battles in which the British Expeditionary Force (BEF) was pitched against enormous odds were fought at Mons and Le Cateau in a fast-moving war of manoeuvre, quite unlike the stalemate which set in during the autumn of 1914. Wrong-footed and exposed, the BEF fought some masterly, if costly, actions and played its part in General Joffre's counterstroke on the Marne. 'Papa Joffre' first saw service during the Franco-Prussian war of 1870. He had spent most of his career in the colonies as a military engineer before being appointed commander-in-chief of the French Army in 1911. The BEF now advanced into Belgium in what would become known as the 'Race for the Sea' which ended in the ferocity of 1st Ypres in October. This battle and those of 1915 drastically reduced the ranks of regular formations and handed the baton, in part, to Kitchener's 'New Service' Battalions.

After stalemate in 1915 came the colossal slaughter at Verdun and then the Somme, a battle which cost Britain and the Empire more dead than the entire course of World War Two. In 1917 the British learned how to crack the linear German defences and scored some great successes before German resilience and new defensive systems drowned all hopes in Flanders mud. For spring 1918, the Kaiser's generals unleashed a series of blistering offensives which came close to breaking the Allied Forces. Close but not close enough and the tide inexorably turned, the victory won at enormous cost.

This is very much a participant's account, Anglo- or 'Tommy'-centric if you like. We have relied heavily on memoirs, diaries, correspondence and previous interviews with survivors. The narrative will focus almost entirely upon the role of British formations, the movements and dispositions of our French allies and German adversaries will be provided in essential outline. Much will be said about BEF recruitment, training, arms and accoutrement, the ethos of the British regular soldier (average age: twenty-eight) in 1914, and the Territorial and Kitchener battalions.

As a battlefield guide, one of us has walked the ground and examined the action with a variety of groups, from students to serving MOD personnel and officers. Readers will, hopefully, feel they have been transported to the scene of the actions which they will relive through the eyes of those who were there. They will glean an understanding of what it's like to march twenty miles a day, in summer heat, over unyielding *pavé* in wool uniform and heavy webbing.

New small arms, accurate and deadly, were not the only lethal hazards on the battlefield. Field guns were quick firers, throwing high-explosive shells over long distances with fearful accuracy. Hiram Maxim had heeded a colleague's exhortation that, if he wanted to make money, he should invent a means whereby European armies could slaughter each other with greater ease. He obliged and the machine gun, with a range of 2,000 yards and a rate of fire of some 600 rounds per minute, would change the nature of the battlefield forever.

This new volume, coming in the wake of so many others, is not intended as a definitive history. It is rather a narrative of individual experiences intended to provide the reader with as close an impression as might be had of what it was like to serve in the war. Not just in the inferno of the front but in the lines, in rear echelons, on the home front. If, by the end, the reader is sobered, chastened and humbled then this effort will not have been wasted.

> For gold the merchant ploughs the main;
> The farmer ploughs the manor;
> But glory is the soldier's prize,
> The soldier's wealth is honour.
>
> The brave, fair soldier ne'er despise,
> Nor count him as a stranger
> Remember, he's his country's stay
> In day and hour of danger!
> – 'Bobby' Burns, 11 February 1917[2]

ONE

YOUR COUNTRY NEEDS YOU, 1914

Shall we forget them?
They who marched with smiles away,
When dawned the long-expected day,
Of German making
High were their heads and firm their lips,
As they trod the street to the waiting ships,
Then eastwards taking.

Shall we forget them?
Men of blood who gave up life
In a noble cause in day of strife,
And to glory trod.
Or, in the days to come shall our children tell
The story of those who fighting fell?
For England and for God!
– J. Cooke[3]

'The Noodles'

On 16 August 1819, British cavalry turned their sabres against protestors and put numerous of them ruthlessly to the sword. The Peterloo Massacre outraged public opinion and yet gentlemen of property felt that revolutionary trends were undermining the fabric of society, threatening to shake the established, God-given order of things. Something had to be done.

Raising local mounted forces, drawn from the tenantry and

affinities of local magnates, landed and industrial, was considered the best means whereby those of substance might 'render effectual aid to the civil power in case of disturbance'. The Duke of Northumberland, a man of very great estate, had called a meeting of county magistrates in October of that year. Within two months, the Northumberland and Newcastle Volunteer Corps of Cavalry was raised. For the most part, it comprised 'gentlemen of great respectability, such as merchants, brokers and tradesmen, together with officials of the collieries, and tenantry and retainers of the landed proprietors'.[4]

For obvious reasons the Yeomanry were regarded as tools of oppression and these well-groomed class warriors were soon dubbed 'the Noodles'. The origin of the term is uncertain but it may be derived from 'macaroni', which was an eighteenth-century term for a dandy. 'Blue bummed bumblers / Cock-tail tumblers / Fireside soldiers / Dorn't gan te waar'.[5] Oddly, in mining areas of Northumberland, everyday colliers volunteered. The lure of working with horses outweighed any disaffection. The Ashington troop was soon amongst the smartest. There was stiff competition between troops: gentlemen need to dress up. With their smart, tailored uniforms, they took on a very dandified air. If this was training for war, it smacked of romance and derring-do, of stiff parades 'of jewelled hilts / for daggers in plaid socks; of smart salutes / And care of arms; and leave; and pay arrears / Esprit de corps; and hints for young recruits'.[6]

Reviews were glittering affairs, everything shone when the regiment was reviewed on the Town Moor by the Duke of Northumberland, who wore the full uniform of a Lord Lieutenant, shining with the insignia of the Order of the Garter. All the stars of local Edwardian society turned out; none more splendid than the Duchess herself. Highlight of the social calendar was an annual grand ball in Newcastle's Assembly Rooms, held every year through the nineteenth century from 1828: 'In all, 343 ladies and gentlemen, who included nearly the whole of the gentry of the neighbourhood',[7] attended, and the event was interrupted only once by an uncivil outbreak of the new plague, 'King Cholera', whose ravages discourteously took no heed of civil society.

Service in the militia had traditionally been far less glamorous and decidedly unpopular. Limited forms of conscription in the eighteenth century, during the Seven Years War (1756–63), had led to riots; one of which at Hexham in 1761 ended in bloodshed with forty-odd deaths as panicky North Yorkshire militia opened fire on a hostile crowd. Those fears over possible French aggression in the late 1850s had led to the raising of Rifle Volunteers, altogether more fashionable than unwilling and workaday militia but, unlike their mounted contemporaries in the Yeomanry, unwaged. Inevitable rivalries arose:

'The Noodle an' Rifleman's Dispute'

The Noodles thor a' gentlemen,
Respected to be sure,
They nivor like the rifle curs,
Fixed ramrods of the Moor; the riflemen black-legged us a',
Undermined wor daily pay,
But smash, aw'll fight him for a quart
Then for war lads, clear the way.
– Joe Wilson[8]

South Africa changed all that. Those irritating but remarkably effective Boer riflemen inflicted a series of costly and humiliating defeats on Imperial forces. To beat these hardy farmers-cum-guerrillas in their own country would require far more fast-moving light cavalry than the Army had available. So, the Noodles went to war. Many rushed to volunteer, gentlemen of means and estate subscribed generously so that 355 local horsemen formed three full squadrons of Imperial Yeomanry. This was triple the number originally hoped for. Now there was real fighting in a very real war and the part-time soldiers performed creditably.

Viscount Haldane, Secretary of State for War from 1905 to 1912, had taken on board the lessons of the Boer War. Determined to prepare for both potential Imperial and European conflicts, he implemented a series of measures which included the establishment of British Expeditionary and Territorial forces. His reforms of 1908 abolished old distinctions between Rifle Volunteers and Yeomanry. The Noodles were now the Northumberland Hussar Yeomanry. These measures, though long overdue, were not entirely popular. Rates of pay came down and country gentlemen, who had been used to doing things very much their own way, suddenly found themselves altogether more accountable to that great Whitehall behemoth: the War Office. All the new Territorial units from Northumberland, Durham and North Yorkshire were to form part of the newly created Northumbrian Division, commanded by General R. S. S. Baden-Powell, hero of Mafeking and founder of the Scouting Movement. Territorial divisions were intended for homeland defence though many in the ranks chose to volunteer for overseas service.

Even as dark and stormy clouds began to mass over Europe, this Edwardian twilight seemed set to endure. Tradition garnished with the laurels of Empire, boosted by centuries of Imperial expansion, fuelled by unparalleled industrial might. Annual camps stretched through sixteen languorous days of summer. Riding and manoeuvre, saddle soap and champagne. Uniforms elegantly tailored to show the rider to best advantage, to impress ladies with coquettish smiles and parasols, in dazzling white:

> A feature of these annual camps was the regimental sports, which were made the occasion not only of an attractive display of horsemanship, in which keen competition was witnessed, but of social gatherings in which friends joined officers and men in a pleasurable outing.[9]

A shining twilight before the apocalypse, a world that writers such as Ford Madox Ford would capture in prose, perhaps never better than in his *Parade's End*.

It was during this epoch, when the Queen Empress ruled nearly a quarter of the earth's inhabitants, that the Royal Military

Tournament got underway, a chivalric tribute to the Spartan fighting qualities of British soldiers and sailors. Officers duelled with
sabres and hacked imaginary foes, represented by melons, from
horseback in a ritual dubbed 'cleaving the Turk's head'. Political
correctness (of the sort correct for its time) was making an early
appearance: manly displays or martial prowess were to be lauded

> without encouraging the display of those brutal and degrading
> passions, which induce a couple of vagabonds, with a dislike for
> work, to batter each other with their fists for a wager, till one or
> the other can no longer stand upright.[10]

The brewing conflict would be a very different type of engagement.
It was to be industrial warfare on a scale and intensity never experienced before or even imagined. Technology had vastly increased
the killing power of both artillery and small arms. The new quick-
firers,[†] would move the guns to prime slot as arbiters on the field.
Tommy could fire twelve to fifteen aimed rounds per minute from
his Short Magazine Lee Enfield (SMLE).[‡] Steamships could transport him over oceans in a fraction of the time sail would have taken.

Railways could move him, his horses, equipment, rations, fodder
and ammunition over great distances on land. Tinned food, that
most commonplace of commodities, ensured he could be fed and
sustained year-round in trenches. Machine guns could spew out
500–600 rounds per minute and kill at 2,000 yards. The war itself

---

† An artillery innovation from the 1890s. 'Quick-firers' were distinguished from
  earlier ordnance in that they were fitted with buffers to limit recoil, the breech
  was adapted to allow rapid re-loading and shell and propellant were combined
  in cartridge form. Consequently, in the early twentieth century, the killing
  power or artillery increased exponentially.

‡ The Short Magazine Lee Enfield (SMLE) was the standard British service rifle of
  the era, called 'short' because of the barrel length being shorter than the earlier
  'Long' Lee-Enfield which did service in the Boer War and with which many
  Territorial units were still armed in 1914. The SMLE was intended both for cavalry
  and infantry, firing ten rounds of .303 ball cartridge. The weapon reached its final
  pre-war variant, the Mark III, in 1907 and confounded its critics, doing good service
  throughout the conflict and, depending on circumstance for decades afterwards.

would witness exponential development in the role of aircraft and in the introduction of new, even more terrible weapons. Tanks, poison gas and flamethrowers would add fresh dimensions of horror. It would prove a very unlovely war.

When, in that August of 1914, war was declared, the Noodles were commanded by Lord Ridley of Blagdon – though he was already a sick man (he died in 1916). At this point 'A' Squadron was in billets on Gosforth Racecourse; 'B' Squadron somewhat distant at Castle Eden in East Durham and 'C' Squadron in south-east Northumberland. All three were soon concentrated at the Racecourse before, on 11 September, being ordered down to Hampshire under Major (then Lieutenant-Colonel) Cookson of Meldon Hall (formerly of the Lifeguards) in mid-Northumberland. They were destined for Belgium and the war as divisional cavalry.

They were going to war. Those halcyon days of festive pomp, of war imagined, would become a distant memory.

Countdown; Summer 1914

'Spirit of the New Army'

Fear death?
I would hate that death bandaged my eyes and forbore
And bade me creep past,
No! Let me taste the whole of it, fare like my peers
The heroes of old,
Bear the brunt, in a minute pay gladly life's arrears,
Of pain and darkness and cold;
For sudden the worst turns the best to the brave,
The black minute's at end
And the elements rage, the fiend-voices that rage
Shall dwindle, shall blend,
Small change shall become first a peace out of pain
Then a light...
– Anon.[11]

On 28 June 1914, in the unheard of Bosnian city of Sarajevo, a tuber-
cular teenage terrorist named Gavrilo Princip fired two opportunistic
and fatal shots at the heir to the Austro-Hungarian throne and his
consort. He could have had no idea of the whirlwind his actions would
unleash. Seeds of conflict had been sown over forty years previously
when Prussia, burgeoning into a united Germany, trampled France,
humiliatingly, unexpectedly and comprehensively and relieved her of
both Alsace and Lorraine. Desire for revenge burned fiercely in the
breast of every Frenchman with red blood in his veins.

In the course of those four decades, Imperial Germany, which had
come late to the ideal of nationalism and the scramble for empire,
blossomed and boomed. Her industry came to rival that of Britain,
a concept almost inconceivable in 1871. Once the canny touch of
the ageing Bismarck had been prised free, Kaiser Wilhelm II with
a generation of gilded hawks, flush with power and might, steamed
headlong into fresh confrontation. Hostility with Austria was forgotten as France and Russia drew together. This was ominous, for a war
on two fronts, both east and west, was not to Germany's advantage.

The Kaiser's provocative championing of the Boers and his desire
to challenge the Royal Navy's hitherto unchallenged dominance in
the North Sea, led to a worsening in relations. France and Britain
came to an entente in 1904 and this was extended to include Tsarist
Russia a mere three years later. Britain's growing fear of German
intentions outweighed established fears of the Bear's claws feeling
towards India. Battle lines were being drawn and those lines hardened
as a series of diplomatic crises threatened to trigger a conflagration.

If Germany had to fight on both flanks, she must deal swiftly
with one opponent to then concentrate upon the other. Russia was
the larger demon and fears of Asiatic hordes sweeping westwards
a recurrent nightmare. Count von Schlieffen gave his name to a
strategic plan which proposed an immediate knockout blow in the
west to deal swiftly with France before concentrating upon Russia,
perceived as far slower to mobilise. Russia's own industrial miracle,
unforeseen by Schlieffen, indicated to the German General Staff
that, by 1917, her capacity would have expanded so prodigiously as

to remove any prospect of victory. The whole European polity, by summer 1914, was a tinderbox requiring only a single spark.

The killing of Franz Ferdinand inspired little mourning by his own side. Indeed, conspiracy theorists might suggest his death was precisely what had been hoped for to provide a cast iron *casus belli*. There comes a point when the slide into war cannot be halted. The troop trains having departed cannot be recalled. He who mobilises fastest can land the first, very probably decisive, blow. High command cannot simply wait upon events and hope for a diplomatic outcome. If one side begins to mobilise, the other must do likewise or else be left unready and hopelessly exposed. Vast conscript armies cannot be summoned and marshalled overnight.

Britain's fear of the Kaiser's unchecked ambitions and the competition to slide more armoured leviathans, Dreadnoughts, into the waves, had prompted an understanding with France, which did not extend quite so far as a full alliance. Both Britain and Prussia had guaranteed Belgian neutrality by treaty in 1839. That neutrality was to be an early casualty once Count von Schlieffen's plan was put into operation. This proposed a massive mailed fist crashing through the crust of French defences in the north while their own main effort battered futilely in the east, then sweeping south and east, around Paris on both flanks and herding the French together for a serious hammering. It is said that the Count, on his deathbed, begged his successors not, at any cost, to weaken the thrust that would sweep west of Paris, thus guarding his left flank. Happily for the Allies, this advice was to be ignored.

'Is There Anyone I've Forgot?'

Kaiser Wilhelm said to his Chancellor one day,
I have got a new game I'm going to play,
I am de best ruler in de world today
I vill send out ultimatums!

Of course I vill be ruler of every land
Almighty Gott is my second-in-command

When I go to heave, he vill sit on my right hand,
Or I vill send him an ultimatum!
– Anon.[12]

War was not unpopular – far from it. Those eager young legions that would flock to heed Kitchener's famous call were keen to sample their share of martial glory. The very young fretted they might be left behind and that it would be all over before they had a chance to join their older brothers in khaki. This generation had no idea what awaited them. Britain had not fought a major war in any European theatre since the Crimea, a salutary lesson in itself.

In 1900 Anglo-Scots residents on Tyneside had waxed enthusiastic over the idea of a kilted Volunteer Rifle Corps. In these relatively untrammelled times, the War Office response was dismissive, citing the disparity in numbers between infantry and cavalry units already in existence. On 8 September 1914 this proposal for a Tyneside Scottish battalion was dusted off.

'The Call of the Pipes'

The Fiery cross is out, now
There's a beacon on each hill,
The Scottish pipes are sounding,
'Tis the slogan wild and shrill.[13]

With such a change in circumstances, the War Office initially proved more accommodating and recruiting was allowed to proceed. Those north-easterners who could or would claim Scottish ancestry were fewer in number than those of Irish origin. Recruiting in September 1914 was steady if not spectacular. When the Tyneside Scottish Committee met on 14 September, members were made aware that there would be a deficit in their recruiting budget which either they or the public, through subscription, would have to make good. One sticking point was that the War Office was not disposed to allow distinctive uniform, no kilts or plaid socks. The battalion would wear standard Fusiliers' kit. Locally, this caused consternation:

> The London Scottish don the kilt and also the Liverpool Scottish so why shouldn't the Tynesiders do the same. I am sure the adoption of so distinguishing a dress would bring in a better class of recruit. Only a Scotsman knows the feeling of national pride awakened by the sight of the kilt.[14]

Rather more dishearteningly, the War Office, in a letter dated 18 September, changed tack on the formation of the unit and now rejected the idea. A similar ban was laid on the raising of the Tyneside Irish. There is a suggestion that Kitchener had doubts about the formation of units which were 'quasi-nationalist' in character, possibly a legacy of the situation in Ireland. The position was again transformed in October when Lord Haldane himself visited Newcastle. On the 10th he addressed crowds in two local theatres where he announced a complete reversal of the earlier prohibitive stance: 'We are going to give you a Scottish Battalion here. We are giving every encouragement to the Irish, who are a splendid fighting race to make their battalions together...'[15]

In due course the Tynesiders would form both a Scottish and Irish Brigade. The motto of the former would be 'harder than hammers'. They would earn it.

> Get a feather te yer bonnet and the kilt abain yer knee
> And list bonnie laddie and cam awa' wi' me.[16]

'It Will All Be Over By Christmas'; August 1914

> I joined up not through any sense of patriotism but as a means of getting out of the pit. I was a hand putter and the men were hewing in a two-foot seam.
> – Lance-Corporal J. G. Barron, 21st Battalion Northumberland Fusiliers[17]

When Major Morant, commanding the Durham Light Infantry depot, received an urgent telegram at 8 p.m. on 4 August – 'mobilise, stop acknowledge' – he was, despite, the terse wording, unsure. Did this mean a general mobilisation? Morant asked 3rd Battalion's adjutant, who was in the mess that evening, if he was sending call-up notices out to the Special Reserve. 'He said no, he was awaiting another telegram … I said I was certain this was the signal for general Mobilisation and that action as regards the Special Reserve should be taken.'[18]

By the early hours of next morning 'every reservist's kit was complete and in order'. War had come. In addition to regular battalions and reservists, Haldane's plan had been that county Territorial Associations would be responsible for any large expansion in army numbers. True to their task, these immediately began to recruit and were, at the outset, so successful that by November 1914 not only had all shortfalls been made good but recruiting was some 25 per cent over capacity.

Kitchener had other ideas. Partly, he was unconvinced by the part-time soldiers. He realised, perhaps uniquely, that the war would be both long and hard. He proposed to raise seventy new divisions to bolster the six regular and fourteen Territorial. The great man was aware that the existing county system could not hope to build armed forces which might have to compete with the Kaiser's conscripted hordes. Raising a 'New Army' from the general populace was a mammoth undertaking. First call was for six divisions and went out on 7 August. He hoped to raise 100,000 men and this call (K1) was soon followed by K2 & K3 on 11 and 13 September respectively, aimed at raising a further dozen divisions.

As a consequence the County Associations found themselves competing with the War Office, though, by the end of 1914, the overall strength of the Territorials had doubled. On 15 September 1914, these 'Terriers' were called upon to volunteer for active service abroad.[†]

---

† Territorials were often referred to as 'Terriers' or Saturday-night soldiers. Maybe it was a reference to their pre-war part-time status or perhaps it had something to do with the nature of their recruitment. Saturday evenings in the pub, with your mates egging you on: something to do, a bit of a laugh.

They would be amateurs no more. Thereafter, recruitment was in the hands of local cross-party committees. On 15 January 1915 in Durham, a Bantam battalion was formed for men who sought to enlist, of good physique but below the minimum regulation height of 5ft 3in. The first battalion had been raised in Birkenhead during the autumn of 1914 and the concept soon spread. Many men from the poorer industrial areas of the north, ill-nourished and stunted, came forward.

Herbert Waugh from Newcastle was very much a Saturday-night soldier, an aspiring professional who had joined the rather smart 6th 'City' Battalion of the Northumberland Fusiliers:

> All battalions of infantry were and are very much alike. They were composed of the same type of men, who dressed alike, were armed in the same way, trained in the same way, and fought and suffered in the same places and in almost exactly the same circumstances.
>
> Throughout that August Bank Holiday weekend, there had been incredible headlines in the newspapers and then, one midnight a special postman delivered a small, blue form which intimated that the Battalion would parade in St George's Drill Hall at six o'clock the following morning.[19]

They were still there waiting at noon. The CSM 'whose South African Medal ribbons lent great weight to his words' was heard to prophesy, 'this is too big a thing to last, it will all be over in three weeks'. So much for the voice of experience.

'A' Company were known as the 'collar and cuff' brigade as recruits were drawn from the ranks of clerks and professionals based on Newcastle's Quayside. From the drill hall they were marched to Tilley's New Rooms where their first dinner comprised a large slab of meat served on a bed of newspaper, accompanied by dry hunks of bread – 'I am sure the firm of Tilley will deplore their association, however accidental, with catering of this character.'[20]

Those of the 'collar and cuff' brigade enjoyed a relatively calm if somewhat tedious first winter in khaki. Their time, as days shortened, was spent digging trenches at Backworth and with guard duties at Blyth, which as a thriving port was thought to merit the Germans' hostile intent (none came). Battalion 'pub crawls' enlivened cold, dark winter days and nights spent in billets in mining hamlets. The weekend warriors discovered that the nation's martial fury had so swelled that they were no longer caricatures in uniform but heroes in khaki, even though they had yet to fire a shot in anger.

> I heard the bugles callin' an' join I felt I must,
> Now I wish I'd let them, go on blowin' till they bust!
> – Anon.[21]

The TA was now 'guarding the shores of old England while Jack is busy on the sea'. When the call to volunteer for overseas service went out, all flocked. The pressure was subtle but considerable. As the battalion paraded, officers called for all who were willing to serve abroad to 'slope arms'. Everyone did. Many a loyal toast followed in the fleshpots and alehouses of the metropolis. Those who returned after hours adopted a cunning ruse of arriving not quietly but in the fanfare of a private motor-taxi having affixed a red ribbon around their caps – the badge of a staff officer, clearly on important regimental business. Then, it was back to digging trenches.[22] Herbert Waugh would develop a theory about the stages of a soldiers' life which did not incorporate this initial enthusiasm:

> The footsoldier is a professional dawn-watcher; he has been so since Hadrian's legionaries peered northwards from the crags at Housesteads. This is the hour of fate. There are three stages in the life of an ex-soldier: (1) the 'fed up and let's forget it' stage (2) the annual reunion stage and (3) the arm-chair and grandchildren stage.[23]

Waugh was writing some sixteen years after the end of the war. Winter was enlivened by airship raids, the dreaded Zeppelins 'a cigar-shaped shadow'. Despite much drama and standing-to, punctuated by the odd angry shot, these monsters passed overhead without incident.

Some enthusiastic statistician has calculated the average duration of an infantry subaltern's sojourn at the front … as a
matter of two or three weeks. We were untried, unbroken. We
had a fresh nerve, health and youth. There was an end of term
spirit about.

Hours of boring oratory from senior officers and padres were made
memorable only by one sermon on the eve of battle:

Many of us who are standing here will not live to see the end of
this war, and those who do will be martyrs to rheumatism before
they are forty![24]

As the battalion marched away from their homes in north-east
England they sang 'Tipperary', 'Who's Your Lady Friend' and,
predictably, 'Blaydon Races'.

Wash me in the water where you wash your dirty daughter
And I shall be whiter than the whitewash on the wall.[25]

How Britain Went to War

Almighty Lord God, the Father and Protector of all that trust
in thee, we commend to thy fatherly goodness the men who
through perils of war are serving this nation, beseeching thee to
take into thine own hand both them and the cause wherein the
King and country send them. Be thou their strength when they
are set in the midst of so many and great dangers. Make all bold
through death or life to put their trust in thee, who art the only
giver of victory and can save by many or by few; through Jesus
Christ our Lord – Amen.
– Form of Intercession 1914

It has been said, and not without truth, that Britain fielded four
armies in the war. Firstly, the original regular army and reserves which

formed the BEF in 1914 immortalised as 'the Old Contemptibles'.[†]
Secondly, the Territorial Battalions, thirdly, Kitchener's New Army
Battalions and, finally, the conscript army of 1917–18. The core
tactical unit throughout was the battalion (typically 750–1,000
men). This was commanded by a Colonel, essentially an honorary
position. Actual day-to-day command vested in the Lieutenant-
Colonel. As a rough rule, some 10 per cent of battalion strength
was kept in reserve, left out of the battle (LOOB), as a core around
which to rebuild if the unit was badly cut up. All too often this
pragmatic prophecy would indeed come to pass.

Below Lieutenant-Colonel, the Major was the next most senior
officer. He normally commanded the 150-strong HQ Company. Then
'A', 'B', 'C' and 'D' Companies were each commanded by captains, all
at similar notional strength. The Company was then divided into four
sub-units or platoons; a HQ platoon, commanded by a Lieutenant
with a non-commissioned officer (NCO) and four privates (or 'rifleman' in a rifle unit); then four other platoons, numbered 1–4, led
usually by a Second-Lieutenant (subaltern), with four NCOs and
thirty-two privates. The platoon itself was broken down into sections,
the smallest tactical unit each of eight men and an NCO.

Crucially, the infantry battalion in 1914 possessed only two
Vickers Medium Machine guns.[‡] From 1915 firepower was significantly enhanced by the introduction of lighter automatic weapons,
such as the Lewis Gun.[§] Latterly, the medium machine-gunners
were transferred to the Machine Gun Corps and the number of

---

† The expression is said to have derived from the Kaiser's dismissive observation
that the BEF was nothing but a 'contemptible little army'.

‡ The Vickers, manufactured by Vickers-Armstrong on Tyneside, was a .303
calibre, belt-fed, water-cooled weapon with a cyclic rate of, say, 500 rounds
per minute, which was famed for its reliability and robustness. It required
a crew of eight, a full section: one firer, one loader and the rest to carry the
weapons, tools and ammunition.

§ The Lewis Automatic Machine Gun remained in service from 1914 to 1953. It was
a .303, drum-fed light MG which used a 47-round box with a cyclic rate of 500
rounds per minute. At 28lb in weight it was far more portable than the Vickers and
had a marked effect on British infantry tactics. One of the authors can recall seeing
a Lewis Gun still in service with Bosnian-Serb Forces during the civil war in 1995.

Lewis Guns available was increased from four per battalion to four times that number and double that again after the Somme.

Initially, in 1914, four battalions, under a Brigadier-General, formed a brigade and three brigades a division. This larger unit was commanded by a Major-General and possessed its own signallers, medical staff, engineers and gunners. Some three or perhaps four divisions would be formed into an army corps, led this time by a Lieutenant-General. A number of corps, say four to six, would constitute an Army. Britain would have five armies deployed on the Western Front with total ration strength of over a million men.

When Herbert Waugh, blooded and wounded at St Julien in the Ypres Salient in 1915, finally returned from war he would be sounding an altogether more sombre note:

Do you remember (you at the street corner or you in your private office), the thaw near Peronne which turned dry trenches into miniature canals, the march up to Arras in the snow, when someone burst a blood vessel and died by the roadside, the promulgation of a court martial before daybreak near a Belgian farmhouse, followed by a volley in the next field and, within two hours, a newly filled grave in the field beyond?

Do you remember that peculiar smell which had only one mean-ing; the miles of duckboard track, with horrid caricatures floating in the slime beneath? Do you remember the March retreat in 1917 when the unit strolled thirty miles across country in seven days, half asleep, defending a road here and a wood there. Do you remember when, on one parade, the battalion numbered two officers and less than 20 men, when the French shot some of us (quite by accident) and our own gunners (again by accident) shot others?[26]

From Mons to the Aisne

'Wor Contemptible British Army'

Three cheers for wor brave Tommies, wherever they may be,

Likewise to wor allies which lie beyond the seas;
They've fitten well together, nyen kin that deny
They went away determined, to conquer or to die.
                              – Chas Anderson[27]

On 4 August leading elements of German forces had moved into Belgium. Three full army groups were to squeeze through the relatively narrow plain west of the Ardennes and sweep down through France, while a further trio of the Kaiser's armies, deployed on their left, would contain French attacks. Should the French obligingly move into Alsace-Lorraine, those precious territories stripped in the wake of defeat in 1871, then they would be duly crushed between the 'hammer and the anvil'.

Schlieffen's plan called for boldness. Fortunately for the Allies, his successor Helmuth von Moltke was not bold and had modified the original plan, creating fundamental flaws which would undermine its effectiveness. Nevertheless, Belgium was rapidly overrun and Belgian civilians learned very soon the price of resistance. General Joffre did not believe the threat from the north could develop. In fact he felt the Germans were obliging him by weakening their forces to the east. From 20–24 August, the Battle of the Frontiers raged and the French, for all their dash and élan, suffered terribly. Joffre lost over 200,000 men in that first frightful month, some 10 per cent of his mobilised strength.

General Sir John French led 100,000 men of the BEF, divided into two corps, each with two divisions. Sir Douglas Haig commanded 1st Corps. Dour and uncommunicative, the prudish Scot was scandalised by French's numerous affairs. Sir James Grierson was to command 2nd Corps but natural causes removed him before the Germans had a chance. French hoped for Sir Herbert Plumer as his successor but got Sir Horace Smith-Dorrien instead. Relations between French and his new subordinate were frosty in the extreme. Kitchener appears to have considered that the latter's considerable experience and sound judgement might be a useful counterweight to Sir John's Hussar temperament. It was not to prove a happy partnership.

One of those who marched up the dusty *pavé* to Mons was
J. B. W. Pennyman, from Ormesby Hall near Middlesbrough. He
served as a machine-gun officer (MGO) in 2nd Battalion KOSB
(King's Own Scottish Borderers), from the start of hostilities
till being wounded on the Aisne in October 1914. The Battalion
embarked from Dublin on 13 August 1914:

Left Dublin on the Bibby Liner 'Gloucestershire' – expecting a
hostile demonstration from the citizens but none occurred.

14 August: We passed quite close to the Cornish coast. I'm sure
there was a general though not expressed idea that for each man
this might be his last sight of England. We were packed very tight
and the ship and each regiment messed in the saloon. At Havre,
teams of London dockers were already in situ.

17 August: Left camp at 04.00 hours, entrained at 06.00. We
all, officers and men, performed our ablutions and shaved at the
station. Breakfast was at 07.00 hours and we left two hours later,
still having no idea of our destination. We were in a passenger train
and reasonably comfortable, arriving at Rouen about midday. We
were cheered by the French who were begging souvenirs; half the
men gave away their badges. Everyman we saw in the fields first
pretended to twist his moustache up to his eyes and then to cut
his throat to show by what means the Kaiser should die! About
22.00 or 23.00 hours we passed through Amiens.

22 August: We crossed into Belgium today. The inhabitants had
heard we were starving and all classes loaded us with fruit (mostly
unripe), cigarettes, tobacco, matches and wine. It was an awful
job getting the battalion along through these towns and I shall
never forget it … we might have been marching through the
slums of Glasgow, except for the language of the people. At about
17.00 hours we arrived at the Mons-Conde Canal, where we took
up our posts for the night. I put my guns in a little sandbag fort

which I built on the lock abutment with the guns trained straight down the canal.

23 August: We were not attacked early on so I looked around for a better location for my guns. A line of houses stood on the opposite side of the canal and it seemed the only place I could get any field of fire would be from the second floor of the highest house. I knew we should have to leave on the arrival of the first shell.[28]

The section hacked loopholes through the walls and piled sandbags so the guns could fully cover the lock and its approaches. By late morning things were beginning to hot up.

A, B & C companies were lining the meadows in front facing half-right. We could see the Boche deploying around 900 yards in front [see map 2]. They were beginning to filter into woods across the canal in front of our position and were engaged by A & C companies. A group of Boche, possibly an MG section, were spotted in front and we laid out four of them with our first traverse. We then took on any Germans we saw in the open and did considerable damage. This was our first experience of killing people. It was rather horrible but satisfying.

   Our infantry were heavily engaged and taking casualties. D company was attempting to winkle the Germans out of the wood. Suddenly I saw the front edge of the wood lined with Germans and surmised that they were going to try and rush D company, so I concentrated the full fire from both guns on the fringes of the wood and the Germans retreated.

Their eyrie was now a prime target:

Gilmartin asked me whether our sandbags were bullet proof and, as he spoke, one bullet just came through and dropped on the floor. It was really red hot. Soon the fire on us became so hot indeed that bullets started coming through the walls.

It was time to move.

> I went along the line seeking a good fire position; shells were by
> now pounding the houses. The colonel was walking calmly up
> and down sucking on his old pipe and not caring a damn. By
> 18.00 hours we had orders to withdraw, on orderly retirement
> covered by the YLI [Yorkshire Light Infantry]. The swarm of refu-
> gees tumbling back included our hosts of the night before from
> the lock-keepers house. This was now blown to pieces.

Mons, the first British battle of the war had cost the BEF some
1,600 casualties, though the Germans had received a very bloody
nose and sustained much greater losses. The brunt of the fighting
had fallen on Smith-Dorrien's 2nd Corps. Haig had come up on
his right during the day. With his Gallic allies on his right pulling
back, French ordered a retreat.

> 24 August: We retreated to Wasmes, took up a good defensive site
> overlooking the KOSB position. The country in front was nothing
> but a collection of coal mines with enormous heaps of slag. There
> was a terrific artillery duel all over. Again, we retired, constantly
> under heavy shell fire. Our limber lost a wheel in a most exposed
> position and we had to lift it free and shoulder some of the contents.

Constantly the MG section was obliged to halt and take up a
rearguard position, exhausting work in high summer heat. Though
covered by a British howitzer battery, the German guns reached out
unending talons of fire. Shortage of transport was becoming acute.

> I went back into the village and was told there wasn't a cart avail-
> able. A wretched refugee woman came along leading a pony and
> cart. There was nothing for it but to commandeer this. It was most
> heartbreaking but it had to be done. The pony was the most miser-
> able creature I ever saw so we christened him 'EEP, EEP Ouray'
> which is what all the country folk cheered when they saw us.

As the division continued its retreat, back the long weary miles over which they'd earlier advanced, they drew on towards Le Cateau. It was harvest time. Heat lay heavy as a thick blanket, caking men and animals in mingled sweat and dust. Le Cateau was in fact a larger battle than Mons. Smith-Dorrien wished to deliver what he termed 'a stopping blow' to halt the Germans and allow his corps to fall back unmolested by close pursuit. Although the BEF saw off a number of German attacks and then continued its withdrawal in good order, the day was dearly bought; some 7,812 men and thirty-eight guns were lost.

> 26 August: At 16.30 hours we relieved another regiment in some trenches … well dug and well sited, but only very short, holding a platoon at most, and very far apart. About dawn the CO and adjutant galloped round the trenches, said we had to stay on and not retire under any circumstances. I had an excellent field of fire, about 800 yards and we thought we would do some damage before we were all put out of action.

To their right front stood Le Cateau church and a crossroads. The poplar-lined Cateau–Cambrai road ran before them.

> At about 19.00 hours we saw enormous masses of German infantry deploying around three miles ahead and realised we were in for a big thing. There was much heavy shelling but little damage, the Boche advanced to within around 2,000 yards. Troops to our front, being without orders, began to retire but the colonel just stood there on his great horse till they were all back in their trenches and then he trotted back. By some miracle he wasn't hit.

As the long summer's day waned towards evening the KOSB position was becoming steadily more exposed. Enfilade fire was snapping over their heads.

> My [machine] guns had not fired all day but as other troops were

retiring so did we. I pointed out a place to the rear which we could use as an RV [rendezvous] and, at the word 'go', we just ran like wild rabbits bolting out of a burrow, men in my section each carrying two or three ammunition boxes.

Matters swiftly descended into confusion. Men became separated and valuable ammo was lost. Initially only one of the precious guns could be located. The other had to be retrieved. It is likely the gun had been left in a forward position and someone (like the poor sod who left it there) was sent back for it. Tracing the prized Vickers gun was providential: its loss would have been anathema. The army, following Wellington, refused to give up its guns. An artillery limber sufficed for ready transport and the retreat continued.

As darkness began to fall Pennyman rounded up a platoon-sized group of stragglers and marched on.

We lined a potato field and prepared to give any German Uhlans [Tommy's term for any German cavalry] a warm reception. None came and we were relieved by our own cavalry. The battalion had suffered casualties and men captured. The Colonel was wounded and captured in the retreat. I was knocked flat by a shell, though seemingly unhurt. A few days afterward, however, my attention was called to a neat little bullet hole in my Glengarry strings.

A very near miss indeed.

27 August: Our retreat continued, the men were very tired. I noticed some horrible looking carcases in the mud by the road-side. They looked so dirty and beastly that nobody had touched them but, on closer examination, I found them to be perfectly good British ration meat. So we hacked some flesh off and went on till we saw a chance of cooking them.

By the village of Beaurevoir the KOSB harvested potatoes grow-ing in the fields and later cooked a grand stew in a vast witches' cauldron which an old lady kindly provided for the task. 'All said this was the best meal they'd had since leaving Dublin!'

As the British marched out of the village, there was more cheering, rudely cut short by incoming salvoes of German shells. Next stop was the township of Ham but as fears of prowling Uhlans circulated, the exhausted borderers kept marching. On this time towards Muille, over the unyielding *pavé* with summer's full heat still blazing. 'Here the brigadier was regrouping, we had marched 35 miles from le Cateau and the men were beat to such a degree it was more like herding sheep than leading soldiers.'

> 28 August: The RV was now to be at Noyon, another 20 miles away; lots of stragglers were coming in, some marching, a lucky few in motor lorries. In that week we'd marched over a hundred miles, fought three battles and two scraps [skirmishes].

The next day, 29 August, passed with much needed rest, followed by a moonlit march in the cool of night. More hard marches followed between 29 August and 1 September and the state of the men's feet gave rise to worry: 'It is a curious fact that all the reservists' boots were too small for them, either their feet swell in Civvy Street or they swelled instead under the strain of constant marching.'

> 1 September: [Another rearguard action,] the enemy had no artillery or else it was very soon put out of action, and we gather what little artillery we had with us did tremendous execution amongst the enemy's infantry. After about two hours firing we had apparently got the better of the Germans in front of us and it was rather annoying to have to retire. After fighting all day we fell back to Silly le Loy where I was billeted in a very nice farm. Dined that night at a table and ate with knives and forks; plenty vin du pays and most exquisite brandy and liqueur rum.

Though the Schlieffen Plan appeared to be working, there were serious cracks. Von Moltke's timidity and rising crisis on the Eastern

Front, led to a thinning of the concept. With the right flank weakened, there was opportunity for a significant Allied riposte. Joffre had not lost his head and was far closer to the fighting than his opponent. His driver was in fact a star of early Formula One. Dazzling panache at the wheel enabled his commander to keep in constant touch with his front-line officers. Joffre's blow, the Battle of the Marne, achieved no breakthrough. While the Kaiser's armies did not crumble, the confidence of their commander did. The order came for the Germans to retreat – 'the miracle of the Marne'.

Now the BEF were swinging west of Paris; 'we were hoping for a siege, at least we'd get a rest!' By 4 September they had reached Coulommes, 'ate apples, drank cider, had a rest day and moved off at 23.00 hours, passed the field of Crecy'.

6 September: Our retreat was at an end, we marched back to Villeneuve, some Germans appeared in the early hours but they were falling back now and we captured some Uhlan stragglers.

7 September: Marched to Boissy … saw a strange RAMC [Royal Army Medical Corps] major having dinner with us and thought we had a new doctor [the battalion MO had been wounded in the retreat] then we found out he had been put under arrest for stopping on the line of march to buy something!

8 September: We engaged the German rearguard north-east of Doue. We were faced by German horse artillery and two cavalry regiments plus one heavy gun. The KOSB were ¾ mile in front of the British gun line and the Boche gun was plumping very large HE [heavy-explosive] shells all amongst the battalion. Miraculously we sustained no casualties.

Despite this intense weight of fire the order for the infantry to advance came through:

We had to cross the brow of a hill – about five hundred yards of perfectly open ground of which they already had the range to a tee. The battalion doubled across this in two lines, went down through a thick wood and reformed in a railway cutting at the bottom. Nothing could have bettered the German artillery's efforts and I'm sure they thought they'd wiped us out. As a matter of fact we had twelve casualties, killed and wounded. When we got through the wood we saw the River Marne in front of us. We chased their horse artillery off with MG fire then, full of fury, the MG section charged on, looking for more Boche. We passed staff cars full of senior officers looking on till we found a wood we were told was full of Boche. Like pheasant shooters we waited for the quarry to emerge but none did!

'The Big Push'

God bless wor gallant armies, on the sea and land,
Splendid deeds they have done, we hear from every hand,
In fact there's none can beat them for stability, courage and skill,
They stand predominant above all others, I trust they always will.
– Chas Anderson[29]

Thursday 10 September, the pursuit continued:

We marched all day through unsavoury German remains. I found an abandoned MG limber. It was a most beautiful little conveyance and all the fittings were A1.

11 September: I was in charge of a small group of German POWs. They were extraordinarily docile and well-behaved … all the prisoners I saw were decent looking young men, quite good class and well-nourished. Their equipment and uniforms were excellent. I saw no sign of any atrocities nor heard of any though of course these were widely reported.

Within two days the KOSB were approaching the River Aisne. Here, the fluid front would harden as the Germans dug in along

the favourable high ground beyond the river. The war of manoeuvre was nearly over. Stalemate was looming even if this was not
obvious to the combatants. As the Borderers approached the village
of Sermoise, they were held up by plunging, long-range fire. Only
at dusk did they move forward into the village:

> People were very plucky, gave us coffee and anything they had
> to eat. Our orders were to get to the river – this proved difficult
> in the late summer dark, the only bridge was under fire. The
> battalion was very tired, we'd had only an hour's sleep in the last
> twenty-four. In the confused night the MG section got lost and
> we ended up back in the village where the West Kents doctor told
> us we could now get over the bridge.

After a confused and difficult night Pennyman and his MG section
made for the bridge at first light. The river was no more than fifty
yards across, the bridge had been blown but 'the RE had made a raft
but it had a very nasty habit of sinking, and when we got there we
found three drowned men ... oddly the Boche were not contending
the crossing'. Once over, the borderers faced a difficult task.

> The village of Missy was about ½ mile ahead, the riverbank was
> thickly wooded, a belt of trees thirty yards wide sloping down to
> the water's edge. Beyond say ½ mile of parkland rising to wooded
> hills full of Boche. The West Kents were just ahead of the wood;
> but we couldn't advance and retreating meant swimming for it.
> By 08.00 hours the battalion was fully across and deployed in the
> trees. The Boche advanced into the copse some 700 yards ahead
> but our MG fire sent them running back as quick as they could.

Enemy fire soon intensified. The Germans were trying to infiltrate
the woods and a single platoon was detailed to occupy the ground.
Murderous small-arms fire forced them back:

> The river was alive with bullets. We lost a good many men. I wanted
> either to advance or retire but the West Kents colonel ordered us

to hold on. We swept the enemy ground with MG fire. One gun jammed, the first time this had happened. There was so much noise, verbal communication was almost impossible. A bullet went into the ground very close to me as I was working the other gun. I thought it might be a sniper who had caught sight of me so I moved three or four yards to our right. Next thing I remember was a sensation like a blow from a cricket ball in the chest. It knocked me clean down and I remember shouting as I fell bleeding profusely at the mouth.

I felt quite certain I was a 'gonner' but managed to get up and give some directions to the gunner; then I flopped down again. I passed out. I was wounded at about 14.00 hours but couldn't be got back till 19.00 and came to as I was being treated. I began to have a feeling of terrible cramp all over my chest and difficulty breathing. I was told my only chance was to lie perfectly still and flat and a healthy dose of morphine helped me to do this. Evacuation was difficult and protracted: we travelled in spring-less lorries to the railhead at Ouichy. The large covered entrance to the station was entirely full of wounded. Mostly pretty bad: I and four other officers were put in the ticket office where we lay all night.

The old ticket man's daughter provided for us next morning. When she saw I couldn't get up to drink, she bent down and fed me like a trained nurse. Later our stretchers were put into the familiar carriages 'Hommes 40; Chevaux 8'. Spring hooks had been fitted to hold stretchers ... a stretcher is a very cold, hard thing to lie on for the best part of a week.

Along the Aisne there was stalemate and the lines began to harden. The war of manoeuvre was very nearly over.

Psalm 144: 'Blessed be the Lord my strength who teacheth my hands to war and my fingers to fight.' A strange beginning for a psalm used as part of a Christian service, what sort of a man was this who speaks ... a bloodthirsty sabre-rattler or a man who is always 'spoiling for a fight', quarrelsome, ready to take offence, pugnacious and aggressive?
– Stanley Purvis MA, sermon, September 1960[30]

TWO

THE RACE FOR THE SEA, 1914

Old England's emblem is the Rose,
There is no other flower,
Hath half the graces that adorn,
The beauty of the bower:
And England's daughters are as fair
As any bud that blows
What son of hers who hath not loved
Some bonny English rose.

Who hath not heard on one sweet flower,
The first among the fair,
For whom the best of English hearts,
Have breathed a fervent prayer?
Oh, may it never be her lot
To lose that sweet repose
That peace of mind which blows now
The bonny English rose.

If any bold enough there be
To war against England's Isle,
They soon shall find for English hearts,
What charms hath woman's smile,
Thus nerved, the thunder of their guns,
Would teach aspiring foes,
How vain the power that defies
The bonny English rose![31]

The Western Front

As the trench line began to harden, both sides had to try and hook around an open flank. Inevitably, the response was a steady thickening of the line northwards towards the sea. The hope for both was that they could outflank the enemy and then roll up his line. Such tactics had served commanders well in the past but these huge armies of industrial age warfare were simply not agile enough. The vast coiling snake of supply, stretching so far behind, weighed too much for any lightning moves. Grand Napoleonic gambits such as the Manoeuvre of Ulm, which in 1805 had netted an entire Austrian army, were not likely to be repeated.

> You are ordered abroad as a soldier of the King to help our French comrades against the invasion of a common enemy. You have to perform a task which will need your courage, your energy, your patience. Remember that the honour of the British army depends on your individual conduct … Be invariably courteous, considerate and kind. Never do anything likely to injure or destroy property and always look upon looting as a disgraceful act.
>
> Do your duty bravely,
> Fear God,
> Honour the King.[32]

It was early in October that the BEF advanced northwards. Field Marshal Sir John French hoped he would be able to strike a blow against the Germans' exposed flank. He had already been reinforced by a further division to make good his earlier casualties. Encouraged by General Foch (the French commander who had successfully halted the Germans at Nancy and who would go on to become Supreme Allied Commander on the Western Front), Sir John believed the hinge of his successful blow would be the Belgian city of Ypres. At this point, the German high command entertained similar hopes. As the British felt their way towards Menin, they collided with large enemy forces. Flanders was about to become a major battlefield.

As late as 1926 Sir Douglas Haig expressed the pious view that:

the value of the horse and the opportunity for the horse in the future are likely to be as great as ever … aeroplanes and tanks are only accessories to the man and the horse, and I feel sure that as time goes on you will find just as much use for the horse – the well bred horse – as you have ever done in the past.[33]

This spirit of the cavalry as the arbiter of the field was summed up in verse, even in the summer of 1915 when the lessons of wire and machine guns should have been evident.

> The air is filled with loud hurrahs
> For the bold and dashing King's Hussars,
> Who on the 24th May
> To fame and glory carved their way
> Positions held, 'spite deadly fire
> Thousands saved from a funeral pyre
> 'Beyond all praise' the words were true
> They did as the 15th always do.
> Here's a motto for all – a motto for you,
> Behave as the 15th always do!
> – A. B. Crump[34]

Reality was to prove very different and far less glamorous.

The 1st Battle of Ypres

> I want to tell you now sir
> Before it's all forgot
> That we were up at Wipers
> And found it very hot
> – *Plum & Apple*, September 1915[35]

Sir John French wrote the preface to the first volume of Northumberland Hussars' regimental history. They were, he wrote, 'commanded by the Earl of Ravensworth, than whom no better sportsman ever lived. The officers were all good sportsmen ... two of them were prominent Masters of Hounds.'[36] During autumn 1914 the Noodles would be as much the hunted as hunters.

On 5 October 1914, the regiment sailed on the *Minneapolis* from Southampton for an uneventful night passage to Zeebrugge.

> The morrow broke cold and wet as we steamed slowly into harbour ... It was late in the afternoon before we set off down a long typical Belgian road toward Bruges. Our reception ... was ecstatic. At every hamlet along that poplar-lined stretch of pave the inhabitants would raise a cheer for 'les Anglais' while little urchins would clamour for buttons & badges ... pretty girls would almost drag us from our saddles to kiss us and to shake our hands.

Waving her handkerchief, a buxom young lady, shouted 'Vivent les Anglais'; Private Daglish from Morpeth replied in thick Northumbrian, 'Vary canny, hoo's yorsel?' (I'm very well, how are you?)

Captain Grant, who narrated the experience of the Noodles during the 1st Battle of Ypres, had previously served in South Africa. The Hussars were the first Territorial unit to be shipped out. By 8 a.m. on 8 October the yeomanry were in the saddle, riding as the eyes and ears of 7th Division. They hoped to fight Uhlans 'but to our disappointment encountered none. Instead we discovered how unsuitable pave roads are for cavalry, and that mounted men do only less foot-slogging than infantry when a division is moving en masse.'

Ostend proved less congenial. The streets were chaotic as stunned refugees struggled to get clear of the Teutonic horde, 'fearsome rumours as to the fate of Antwerp flew from mouth to mouth ... at this period of our soldiering we were credulous and drank them in'. It was now they realised that their task was not to assist the Belgian Army as much as to cover its withdrawal, 'to shield that heroic remnant from annihilation'. They entrained for Ghent where their

earlier rapturous welcome was replayed. The Noodles deployed
on outpost duty and, for the first time, came under enemy fire,
happily ineffectual:

I was picturing to myself Saturday night at home, and thinking
how little the boys there were dreaming of what we were doing
that night, when suddenly a succession of reports sounded in the
air. If must confess I could not determine whether they were rifle
shots or not. Just then a shadow loomed up before me, and with
an effort I spluttered out 'Halt! Who goes there?' I had my finger
on the trigger and was ready for him. I felt, I must confess, much
relieved when immediately there came the whispered assurance
'friend'. It was an infantryman, like myself, on outpost duty, and
he enquired if I had heard anything lately. 'Yes' I replied 'I think it
must have been the rumbling of transport wagons on the cobbled
road.' 'No, mate,' was his rejoinder, 'it was 15 rounds rapid.' The
battle was drawing nearer.

Ghent was being prepared for defence (10 October). The ominous
sound of explosions, signifying the destruction of bridges, barri-
cades and barbed wire entanglements spread. In spite of this the
British were about to retreat. This time their passage would not be
marked by rejoicing:

12th October: We slipped by silently and almost guiltily, the
infantry with fixed bayonets, battalion after battalion, gliding past
like phantoms … ourselves as rearguard. The march was rendered
all the slower by a battalion of exhausted French marines and
the struggling masses of refugees who congested the roads, flying
from the invader with what household effects they could save,
piled on their small, dog-drawn carts, accompanied in almost
every case by weeping children.

On unyielding cobbles the cavalry were denied the luxury of
riding for lengthy periods. To spare their horses, they were obliged

to dismount and experience the chore of marching, hard enough for infantry,

> to a cavalryman, even a veteran it is worse. Not only does he have to do his share of the marching, but there is his horse to be cared for, to be fed and watered before he can attend to his own wants and then we were not veterans. The outbreak of the war had found us civilians, many in sedentary employments, and two months of strenuous training, even when accompanied by the best will in the world, can only do something toward case-hardening.

Their guides, locals pressed into service, did not always present a reassuring image: 'A seedy-looking individual … he rode a bicycle, and presented a most dissipated appearance … to this day we are convinced he was a spy.' Confusion and suspicion invariably stalk retreating armies, even one as well drilled as the BEF. At one point, on being challenged on the road, the Noodles' officer replied 'Yeomanry on patrol' and found the cavalry had just missed blundering onto an infantry ambush set for German Uhlans, '"near thing for you old man", remarked one with a grin as we passed through them'.

Private Chrystal, a noted marksman and later sniper, was astonished when shown a squadron of French horsemen, cuirassiers, to learn these were in fact allies. 'Whey,' he exclaimed, 'I thought them b******s wor German hoolans an' I fired at the likes o' them aal day yesterday.' Not entirely *cordiale* perhaps. On 14 October the Hussars clattered into the streets of Ypres

> which the enemy had looted but which had remained untouched by shells. The following day found us early on patrol. It was during one of these patrols that Sergeant-Major Hannington brought down a Uhlan with his rifle. First blood to the regiment!

German troops were now massing in front of the British Line which was taking shape around the 'rim' of the saucer that was to be the

Ypres Salient. The defenders' trenches snaked from Messines in the south, across the Menin Road at Gheluvelt, north to Zonnebeke and St Julien, the westward hinge fixed at Langemarck and the shallow Pilckem Ridge. The attacking divisions were screened by cavalry and there were frequent jousts with probing patrols of Uhlans as the Tommies dug in. By 16 October the front had hardened. The battle would unfold as the Germans tried to dislodge the BEF from higher ground, back towards Ypres and then clear through to the Channel coast.

As ever in these manoeuvres, hapless civilians caught between snarling lines were immediate losers:

> I remember how a family, consisting of an old man (presumably a grandfather) and a young mother, with a child in her arms and two other children clinging to her skirt, were leaving their little cottage by the roadside. Their barrow, drawn by a dog, stood loaded with bedding and culinary utensils, the group presenting a most pitiable sight. The most pathetic moment came, however, when the old man sorrowfully closed the shutters, locked the door and signed to the woman to move on. It was too much for her; her feelings found vent in a flood of tears, in which the poor kiddies and the old man joined. It was a few minutes before they could compose themselves sufficiently to start off on their journey towards France and safety.

More aggressive patrolling followed. British tactical aims centred upon wresting control of Menin, even though the strength of the enemy presence was daily increasing. There was still some fluidity in the war. The Noodles and other cavalry units were actively engaged on an attack put in on 19 October. Menin proved a stage too far and intense shellfire compelled withdrawal. Oddly, by the hamlet of Ledeghem, the yeomanry found themselves fighting alongside a battalion of cyclists. The British Army deployed cyclists from the 1880s and some saw action in the Boer War. By 1914 the army possessed a Cyclist Corps. The pushbike was used not in combat, but for communications and reconnaissance, being far cheaper than horses and far easier to ride, thus the complex training of the light cavalryman was avoided. Most cyclist battalions were formed as part of the Territorial Army following Haldane's reforms; they were not committed to the Front. The regulars formed cyclist companies or platoons for communications and in a potential (very) light cavalry role. The bike did not fare well on the Western Front and the idea did not endure.

> Here took place a peculiar incident. A white-haired old man suddenly made a dash from one of the houses occupied by the enemy and, running with extraordinary agility across the field of fire, reached our lines safely. He told us of the endless columns of 'field-greys' advancing to the attack and determined to force a passage to the Channel ports. By this time infantry and a battery of horse-artillery had come to our assistance ... this was our baptism of fire as a regiment. Of many memories of that first engagement, one of the most vivid is of a company of infantry [from 2nd Battalion Queen's Regiment] rising from the miry field where they had been lying, advancing in perfect extended order, led by an officer with a stick, and then being mown down almost to a man by withering fire.

This doomed attempt to take Menin signalled the end of mobile warfare. With overwhelming numbers the Germans tightened the ring around Ypres and sought to squeeze out the BEF. The race was over. It was now a fight for bare survival.

> The armies were at grips. Aeroplane reconnaissance now took the place of cavalry and revealed the fact that enemy reinforcements were arriving in vast numbers behind a screen of cyclists and the ubiquitous Uhlans. In the face of overwhelming numbers, and in view of the weakness of our infantry, our role as cavalry ended about this time. It was no longer possible to push forward cavalry patrols beyond the line of infantry, especially as the latter were

now pinned down to the defensive and needed an unrestricted field of fire.

The Noodles were cavalry no more. If anything they resembled the original dragoons, mounted infantry.

> From this time our role was to be a general reserve for the sorely tried infantry, to be ready at any moment to dash up and fling ourselves into any gap that appeared dangerous. It was not a pleasant task, involving, as it did, many weary hours of waiting under shellfire. Frequently we would receive orders to fill a gap some miles away, but would find on arrival that it was already filled. Nothing can be more trying than prolonged waiting under arms.

22 October, with the crisis of the battle drawing near, the Hussars were roused from their weary billets in filthy dark, rain in torrents and no lights allowed. Horses tired and irritable, soaking woollen blankets, cumbersome saddles, men groping for straps and harness in the black autumn night.

> Hooge Chateau was our destination. We stood-to for the remainder of the night, and in the morning were ordered right forward to the trenches; here we made the acquaintance of 'Black Marias'[†] for the first time. They would come over in groups of four and burst with a villainous roar and clouds of yellow smoke, most unpleasant to meet as we ran, as best we could in our heavy equipment, across a sodden turnip field to the assistance of the infantry.

The footsloggers had been having a very rough time indeed.

> We found them in position in the garden of a chateau, and were immediately told to prepare it for attack. The coolness of the

---

† Slang for the explosion of a German shell, on account of the black smoke.

infantry was admirable. They had been under constant fire for
several days, were ragged, unkempt and grimy, short of rations
and ammunition; but not a man appeared to be weary of the fight.
Above the appalling din could be heard the clear, concise orders
of the officers, not less ragged than their men, but undaunted and
equal to any emergency.

After a day's fighting the Noodles were withdrawn to Hooge
Chateau, filthy, exhausted 'but with a feeling of mild elation at
having been "blooded", at having proved ourselves equal to the
occasion – a feeling akin to that of the anxious cricketer who has
successfully broken his duck's egg'.

Fate would deny them any rest. No sooner had they laid aside their
arms then these were needed. Once again the Noodles mounted and
rode towards Klein-Zillebeke where another break-in threatened.
'Trenches were begun, roads barricaded, and houses – by this time
deserted – were prepared for defence. Just as it seemed we were to be
at work all night, we were relieved.' It was back to Hooge, but

… on entering the grounds we were greeted by a burst of shrapnel right at the head of the column. This caused a momentary
stampede among the horses … luckily there were no casualties.
This may seem like an incident of slight importance, but will
serve to show how clever was the range taking on the part of
the enemy, how ubiquitous his shellfire, and points further to
probable collusion between the Germans and spies on our side
of the line. Certainly at this period the atmosphere was heavy
with suspicion. Rumours of spies, carrier pigeons and windmill
turning formed a main topic of conversation.

By 23 October German pressure was beginning to tell. The embattled line was showing signs of imminent rupture.

Under increasing pressure the infantry had been forced to give
ground, and it was just at that moment when the gap was ominously

widening that the regiment, waiting in reserve, was called on to
assist. There was a hurried rush across the miry fields, and through
a wood filled with dead and wounded, to the trenches where the
remnants of several regiments were collected. Here we remained for
several hours under very heavy rifle and shell fire, unable to retaliate
very effectively, owing to the poorness of the field of fire. But these
gallant riflemen stuck to it, their crisp, sharp fire orders never seeming to falter. Then came the crowning incident of the day. A line
of Scots Guards suddenly rose to the order 'Come on, the Scots
Guards!' echoed by Major Sidney's 'Come on, Northumberland
Hussars!' and together Guards and Hussars charged against a sway-
ing mass of grey figures and finally drove them over the hill.

Casualties, despite the severity of the fighting and intensity of
enemy fire, were relatively light, though several officers were down.
Of course, the enemy had not finished. Next day the fighting
again raged. The Germans 'came on in masses, time after time, like
crowds returning from a football match'. Rifle fire tumbled them
in hundreds and the line, though bent, still held. On 24 October,
arguably the most serious crisis developed as 2nd Battalion Royal
Warwickshires were inexorably pushed back, allowing the enemy
to infiltrate Polygon Wood† which the Noodles had so stoutly
defended the day before. Once again the cavalry, mounted infantry
as they were now, cantered up the shell-scarred line of the Menin
Road, arrow straight from Ypres.

A hurried gallop ... and an advance in open order across the usual
sticky turnip field brought us to the forefront of the battle. Too
far in fact, for raking fire from a machine gun played havoc in
the ranks, and was responsible for most of the casualties – Major
Sidney, Captain Kennard and Lieutenant Clayton, amongst
others being wounded while several men were killed. Soon, the

---

† Polygon Wood is 1½ miles north of Gheluvelt. The wood witnessed heavy
fighting in 1914 and again during 'the Battle of Polygon Wood', 26 September–
3 October, 1917.

yeomanry were lying down and maintaining a steady fire. The situation was perilous. Every available man, including the personnel of divisional headquarters, was in the line. There was no reserve. Each did the work of ten. Still those grey masses advanced to the attack and when they succeeded in getting a foothold in Polygon Wood, the battle seemed as good as lost.

It wasn't lost, though a very close run thing indeed. By mid-morning, British counter-attacks, supported by French cavalry, threw the Germans nearly out of the wood.

A battalion of Welsh Fusiliers now advanced to reinforce the line, a battalion no more than three hundred strong and officered by the Colonel, adjutant and three subalterns, of whom two were barely 'off-parade' [i.e. newly commissioned]. At this period of the battle such a battalion was relatively strong [so terrible the rate of attrition] … In the early afternoon the enemy attacked the junction of the 20th and 21st Infantry Brigades just east of Gheluvelt, and again the position seemed desperate.

This time it was the Grenadier Guards who charged and won the day though, like every respite in the Salient, casualties were high. 'We were relieved and returned to Hooge, not a few horses, alas, with empty saddles … our troubles were not over, however, for we were shelled all night and sleep was well nigh impossible.' For the Noodles a day of much-needed rest followed the fighting for Polygon Wood. Along the line, pressure never slackened. The rapid rate of fire from Tommy's SMLE convinced German observers the British were all armed with automatic weapons.

The odds against us we learned were at least eight to one with no reserves to fall back on. Some idea of the desperate nature of the fighting may be gathered from the fact that the Welsh regiment with whom we had been associated the previous day, were now reduced to fifty men with no officers. But here the marvellous

discipline of the regular army asserted itself and those magnifi-
cent men fought under the command of a lance-corporal.

For two days, 26–28 October, a brief respite as both sides drew
breath, 'the artillery fire of the Germans, though still unpleasantly
persistent, was rather less intense and pointed to a reorganisation
of the enemy for further attacks'. This lull was ominous, 'the lull
before the storm'. Some good news was to be had: the BEF's 1st
Division had accomplished prodigious slaughter by Langemarck,[†]
'piles of German dead and captured'. Cynicism would soon creep
into Tommy's reading of the daily news but not yet; 'at that time
we greedily swallowed such stories without the customary grain of
salt, and perhaps it was as well that we did so'.

Even in this lull, life remained difficult and dangerous:

> A cooked meal was plainly an impossibility, when to strike a light
> at all would have attracted an overwhelming shell fire for there
> were at this time no trenches in the proper sense of the word. A
> mere hole scraped in the ground with the entrenching tool, and
> enlarged as time or strength permitted, afforded the only means
> of protection. There were no communication trenches to give
> shelter to reliefs or ration parties.

The shelling if reduced was never-ending and sawed at men's frayed
nerves.

> Fortunately casualties were singularly few. A vivid memory is that
> of heavy shells striking the pond adjoining the farm where the
> regiment was billeted, and sending columns of water into the air.

On 29 October, the storm over the Salient burst once more, 'the
fight continuing with the greatest intensity for six days, perhaps

---

† Langemarck now houses one of the largest German war cemeteries in Belgium,
   with 44,292 bodies interred there – some 25,000 in a central mass grave.

the six most critical days of the war'. The line to the east rested
on an axis Gheluvelt–Zanvoorde; 21st Brigade had the right and
20th Brigade the left with 22nd in reserve. The next German wave
struck the vulnerable hinge between 1st Division and 20th Brigade.
The Guards were forced to give ground till desperate counter-
attacks succeeded in winning it back. Pressure then swelled on the
right where the vital crossroads junction on the ridge was taken.
The Noodles

> cooperated in the counter-attack on the left and was heavily
> engaged all day. At nightfall our line, though slightly pressed
> back, still included Gheluvelt and Zanvoorde.
>
> The attacks of the enemy were renewed on the 30th, and over-
> whelming numbers and superiority of artillery fire had their
> inevitable result. The cavalry on our right were forced to withdraw,
> thereby exposing our flank, and a murderous enfilade fire from field-
> batteries annihilated the Royal Welsh Fusiliers, who died practically
> to a man. Zanvoorde Ridge passed out of our hands, but a splendid
> piece of work on the part of our gunners, who galloped into action
> and succeeded in putting battery after battery of German artillery
> out of action, somewhat neutralised this advantage.

Raw courage could not ultimately contest this incessant storm
of steel the Germans were throwing. Sustained attacks down the
Menin Road bludgeoned a breach into Gheluvelt.

> [Saturday 31 October] will be remembered not only as the most
> severe of many days of desperate fighting, but as the most crucial
> day, perhaps, in the history of the war. Daybreak found us back
> near the firing line again, standing-by in shelter of the woods,
> now bare and splintered by the torrent of shells. Men were dozing
> off, when the Colonel's voice was suddenly heard in an order to
> mount and follow him. A gallop in open order across the shell-
> swept fields brought us near the fateful Polygon Wood, and here
> we waited with some impatience to 'draw swords'.

Overall, it appeared as though the battle was now lost:

> Transport came hurrying down the road in confusion; the heavier
> guns, at this time mainly 4.7s,[†] were being hurriedly withdrawn.
> Field batteries were hastily limbered up by exhausted gunners
> and galloped across fields, and as hastily unlimbered and wheeled
> around into action again. Here was a scene of indescribable confu-
> sion and dismay, heightened by the pitiable stream of wounded
> men who plodded painfully to the rear, unbroken, however, in
> spirit, as their shouts of 'give them hell, boys' showed.

It seemed the line could not possibly hold, as thin and taut as a
drum string, with the wailing crescendo of German shells pounding like a demonic curse. The 20th Brigade, dreadfully thinned,
nearer a battalion at best, struggled forward and again restored
the line. As the enemy faltered, the British 'performed prodigious
feats of valour with the bayonet, attacking time after time with
incomparable spirit, finally driving an enemy at least six times their
strength headlong before them into the night'.

> At the beginning of this counter attack the peculiar order had
> been passed down 'cavalry will fix bayonets' – peculiar because
> mounted troops of this period had none to fix! However, we
> did the next best thing, which was to dismount and follow our
> now-victorious infantry, hot on the heels of the retreating enemy.
> Many learnt, perhaps for the first time, that there are more agree-
> able people to meet than an excited highlander with a bayonet.

For the moment at least, the Germans had had enough. The first
of November was a relatively quiet day but no oasis of calm in
the maelstrom of the Salient could endure. Next day, the British

---

† QF 4.7-inch guns were primarily intended for coastal defence; most dated
  from the late nineteenth century and saw service on land carriages in the Boer
  War. They also served on the Western Front though were virtually obsolescent
  by 1914.

learned that Kaiser Wilhelm was to tour the German positions and add fresh heart to their faltering offensive.

Once again, 'under the fiercest attacks the 1st Division was obliged to give ground ... all available reserves failed to stem the enemy advance'. This final time it seemed as though weight of numbers must win through,

> once again the regiment was hurried forward into immediate reserve. The shelling was very heavy, heavier perhaps than ever before. But the 7th Division held firm, and attack after attack was hurled back without appreciable loss of ground.

Like a spring tide, successive breakers of German attacks threatened to sweep aside the thinned and exhausted lines but Tommy, blood-ied, battered, begrimed and exhausted, somehow held. To all intents the battle was virtually over and the BEF had come through. The price had been high. Nearly 8,000 British had been killed, more than three times as many wounded, Belgian and French casualties had also been severe and enemy losses totalled some 134,000. These Saturday-night soldiers had stood the test. Kitchener had been wrong. The Salient had been compressed to a mere eleven miles but it had not fallen, it would not fall, thought the British would be fighting from the ancient walls of Ypres itself in spring 1918.

With the Noodles to France had gone Peter the Cat. This feline auxiliary was given to Sergeant Manley as the Hussars entrained for France. Peter, who was a rather stand-aloof sort of cat, nonethe-less became regimental mascot. He travelled in modest comfort atop the ration-cart with Walter Yeomans from Longhirst in East Northumberland. Peter survived four years of service and came home safe. His regimental ribbons were renewed and he was photographed (still looking grumpy). So grumpy indeed, that he had to be tied to his perch. As befitting so distinguished a veteran, he went into honourable retirement at Meldon Hall, the home of his former CO, Lieutenant-Colonel Cookson. His career finally ended on 3 August 1924 when he failed to survive an unfortunate encounter with a falling sash window. He was buried with suitable honours in the grounds.

Another survivor was Lieutenant-Colonel Cookson's charger, Paleface. He carried his master nobly till the latter was repatriated wounded. Colonel Cookson lost track of Paleface who, at war's end, was sold off as government property. Providentially, a friend of the Colonel's attended the sale and recognised the horse by his markings. He bid and was successful. Paleface, like Peter, came home, full of honours and enjoyed a long retirement. His portrait still hangs at Meldon.

On British Soil: Hartlepool, 16 December 1914

I don't want to join the army; I don't want to go to war,
I'd rather hang around Piccadilly underground,
Living on the earnings of a high-born lady
– Anon.[37]

The small port of Hartlepool on the coast of East Durham seems an unlikely setting for a Great War battle. Nonetheless, the Headland and town would earn an unenviable distinction of being the scene of a dramatic and costly fight on the cold, mist-shrouded morning of 16 December 1914. Fear of seaborne attack had preceded the Kaiser's navy by more than a generation, though Victorian planners were more concerned with closer neighbours just over the Channel. Hostile French intentions, however imaginary, led to a rash of coastal fortifications being thrown up and two were to be erected by Hartlepool. One in the charmingly, if perhaps unfortunately, named Fairy Cove and another by the lighthouse on the ancient Headland. This town within a town juts out into the cold reaches of the North Sea whose fitful moods and constant winds drive wild-capped breakers raging against the embattled point.

The great guns roared, the fire flew,
It was a grand display;

The seagulls screamed an flapped their wings,
And flew nor' far away.
The greet roond-shot went plish for plash
Into the tortured deep;
They made the crabs and lobsters hop,
An' the fish could get nee sleep.[38]

Heugh Battery received a new lease of life in 1908 when introduction of an improved Vickers 6-inch Mark VII gun greatly added to earlier, far less telling firepower. The Victorian pile was refurbished two years later and a pair of the new cannon installed. In 1907, the smaller Lighthouse Battery, lying a short distance south on the very tip of the Headland, was also equipped with one of these newer guns. Service in South Africa followed when the part-time gunners were mobilised against the Boers. During the early years of the century, coastal defences were augmented by a Coastal Patrol comprising several light cruisers and destroyers. By the time shots were fired in December 1914, work was in hand to further strengthen defences with the construction of an Examination Battery complete with searchlights. This was not, however, ready when the German cruisers struck.

Wary of encountering the Royal Navy in a major fight, the German Home Fleet had, in 1914, adopted a more peripheral strategy involving U-boats, mine-laying and coastal raiding. In November, Great Yarmouth had been shelled, a mere pinprick, but this emboldened Admiral von Ingenohl to devise a more ambitious plan for an attack on Hartlepool, Scarborough and Whitby. These exposed east coast ports were sufficiently remote from any major concentration of British warships and the raiders would comprise only a portion of the Kaiser's squadron, the remainder lurking in wait to ambush any rash pursuers. On the night of 15 December the German cruisers made steam with Admiral von Hipper leading three powerful ships, *Seydlitz*, *Moltke* and *Blucher*, against Hartlepool. Of these the first two were newer, armed with mighty 11-inch and 5.9-inch guns, formidably armoured. *Blucher* was both smaller and more venerable though her 8.2-inch guns could still wreak significant havoc.[39]

Like latter-day corsairs these sleek, dark raiders cruised parallel to the unsuspecting coast, sliding past lights from coastal hamlets and the flare of heat from a locomotive's boiler. Fishing smacks and merchantmen were disregarded, surprise more valuable. Hartlepool and the mouth of the Tees soon lay before their guns, still silent beneath the dark cloak of winter's night. A quartet of fast destroyers sallied out to take on the invaders, still night air rent with the crash of great guns, reverberating over the waves. Three English vessels, seeing they were hopelessly outgunned, soon turned to flee behind trailing smoke. One rushed on heedless into the teeth of withering fire that brought her, wallowing, to a dead halt. Despite this one-sided fight, a pair of British torpedoes passed close by two of the raiders but without inflicting any damage.

Dawn was now creeping over the headland and at 07.30 hours a small detachment of 18th (Pals) Battalion Durham Light Infantry deployed behind a sand-bagged perimeter set up between the Heugh and Lighthouse Batteries. The infantry had turned out from their billets in the Borough Hall, hobnails striking on cobbles, an early-morning rendition of 'Tipperary' echoing through the murk. One of those who marched was Charles H. Moss, a native of Seaham who would serve throughout the war. Something of a radical, he was not unduly blinded by patriotic fervour:

I was with a specially selected detachment of the Durham Pals. After six weeks of elementary infantry training we were suddenly sent to West Hartlepool to take up coastal defence duties. I was billeted with my company in the Central Estate School where we slept on the bare boards of the classroom. It was between five o'clock and six o'clock on the morning of 16th December when we were all separately woken by the orderly corporal. We were quietly ordered to 'Fall In' in the schoolyard at once 'with no lights and no noise'. We had no idea why this was being done but it was obvious that 'the wind was up' about something. When we got 'Fell In' we were issued with old-fashioned dirty white haversacks and several khaki bandoliers of .303 ammunition. It was said the haversacks were South African War issue.[40]

In charge of the Saturday-night gunners that day was Lieutenant-Colonel Lancelot Robson, a lifelong artillery enthusiast who had commanded the guns since 1908. He'd moved his HQ from Fairy Cove into Heugh Battery and had shifted the signalling station into the lighthouse. He was aware of the risk of attack, alerted by Admiralty signal that previous evening that a sharp lookout was needed along all of the east coast at dawn the following day. Charles Moss and his comrades were now in the front line:

> The main rumour was that the Germans were going to invade England on this part of the coast and we were to provide the first line of defence. It was a cold and frosty morning with rather a thick mist out to sea, with not a ship of any sort to be seen.

Untrammelled by the brave if doomed British attempt at interception, the raiders peeled off to deliver their separate attacks. *Seydlitz* intended to steam north and engage Cemetery Battery while *Moltke* would pound Heugh. Smaller *Blucher* was to lag southwards targeting harbour installations and shipping in the port. Thick woollen skeins of winter fog drifted along the coast. The enemy warships glided like wraiths, mistaken in the gloom for British battlecruisers.

When Lieutenant-Colonel Robson finally caught sight of a grey-hulled monster sliding through the swell, he realised this did not resemble any British vessel. In the battery, Captain Trechmann, despite his Germanic-sounding name a British officer, made the key assumption that these were indeed the enemy. Swiftly, gunners Tyson and Williamson were recalled from guard duty and assigned action stations at No. 1 gun. Though men might rightly feel a tremor of anticipation, one of the Durham men gleefully observed, 'Lads, I have been waiting for this for the last eighteen bloody years, let's give 'em the works!'[41]

Lieutenant-Colonel Robson was still trying to clarify the new ships' identities by telephone to coastguards but the ominous thunder of the naval fight offshore dispelled any doubts. Robson had done well to abandon Fairy Cove and take station within Heugh Battery. Inside his cramped eyrie, all was bustle as rangefinders tracked the enemy ships. The first two would be engaged by Heugh while, at the lighthouse, Trechmann's cousin Dickie was shadowing the last of the three with his single gun.

For a long moment it seemed as though everyone was holding his breath, then, with the roar of an approaching express train, huge shells from *Seydlitz* blasted the terrace houses immediately to the rear of the lighthouse. The calm domestic scene of the Headland was instantly transformed into nightmare. Masonry and tiles tumbled in clouds of dust which seemed to envelop the battery. Robson's communications were amongst the first casualties. He found he couldn't reach Lighthouse Battery by telephone, nor even communicate with his own gunners. Nonetheless, his men were well trained and this opening German salvo was their cue to return fire. British shells, far smaller than those from the raiders' massive guns, arced out to sea. More enemy rounds crashed and glissaded off the fort's glacis, careering crazily overhead, an inferno of sound.

For a brief moment the infantry, in their sandbagged emplacement, believed the firing was all from British guns:

When I [Charles Moss] saw some flashes of fire about a mile out to sea, followed by the thunder of big guns and shriek of shells close over our heads, our fellows started cheering because the first salvo seemed to be fired out to sea which made us think it was our navy in action. We soon found out how wrong we were when we heard shells exploding in the town!

The Durhams were ordered from their flimsy redoubt out into the dunes where they deployed in open order:

I was very conscious of the heat and stench of the shells as they roared close over the top of us and also how deathly cold I had gone, the excitement must have had something to do with it.

Temporarily safe behind the rear wall of the lighthouse, two gunners, Houston and Spence, detailed as stretcher-bearers, crouched as shells fell around them. The machine gun was gone, crew dead or dying, their puny sandbagged redoubt split and scattered. Both men ran towards their comrades: one was plainly dead; another two badly hit. As they knelt by the casualties, the next salvo engulfed them, too. An officer and other DLI men now rushed up to render whatever assistance they could, one soldier, deep in shock, persisted in marching up and down the roadway like a clockwork automaton.

Dickie Trechmann had to resort to a megaphone to bellow orders as shells fell all around and his own gun barked in response. *Blucher* was 4,200 yards distant but smoke and mist obscured her. Their first two rounds fell short. Their aim had to be adjusted after each round, so thick was the blanket of fog and cordite. With the third round they scored a direct hit, sheering off part of the fore-bridge. A fourth round misfired; standard drill required the round to be left in the breech for ten minutes to avoid accidental detonation, fatal for the crew. Sergeant Douthwaite ordered the rest out while he risked extracting the shell and dumping it in water. The gun stayed in action.

Blucher's assigned roles were firstly to attack harbour installations and secondly to cover her two sister ships, either from the attentions of British torpedoes or fire from the shore. When the Lighthouse Battery shell crashed into her it destroyed subsidiary armament and killed nine crewmen. Undeterred, the raider began to close towards the shore. An agonising delay ensued for the Durham men while their blocked breech was cleared, then more of their rounds struck one of *Blucher*'s gun turrets. It was unclear if the British gunners had damaged the warship's steering gear but she appeared to come close to running aground before turning and switching fire against British cruisers now sliding out of the harbour, inflicting considerable damage on HMS *Patrol*.

Robson's guns at Heugh Battery experienced similar problems with misfires as the electrical detonation system alarmingly
malfunctioned. Moving to percussion firing the guns blazed at
the raiders, focusing their fire on *Seydlitz* in the lead. Vibration
from the guns was making the work of the rangefinders almost
impossible and Robson, while he knew his position was extremely
exposed, believed it to be his duty to remain. Consequently, he and
his assistant Captain Walsh calmly kept station with commend-
able sangfroid as battle raged around them. Robson had time to
contemplate the considerable gulf between exercises and the real
thing and decided if he should survive to see another, he'd arrange
for the battery commander to be knocked out in the opening stages.

In Lighthouse Battery the gun was constantly plagued by misfires
though this did not prevent the loaders toiling below from sending
up a constant supply of shells and explosives. These now began to
build up on the surface, potentially lethal as German rounds continued to fall. Captain Jack Farmer, struggling to clear the gun, was
only alerted to the danger when a German shell bounced directly
in front and skidded overhead. The gun was cleared and another
eight rounds fired. Half of these battered their target before *Blucher*
steamed northwards, effectively out of range. Gunners at Heugh
were still duelling with *Seydlitz's* massive broadside; at least one
enemy round came perilously close to No. 1 gun, a mere six feet in
front of Gun Captain Mallin but again it sheered over the glacis
and exploded in a field behind. Mallin and his crew were spared,
the donkey grazing harmlessly was not so fortunate. Another
round slammed home terrifyingly close to the ammunition lockers.
Providentially it was a dud.

Despite the high drama, the fight had its near-farcical moments
as the Durhams watched:

> At the height of the bombardment some fishermen were beaching
> their boat, one of them got wounded. Sergeant Heal and Corporal
> Brewerton ran down to the shore and carried the wounded man
> to a safer place. One remarkable sight was to see a train come

puffing along the embankment from old to West Hartlepool when the bombardment started. The train was in full view of the sea. When it got about halfway on its journey, the driver stopped the train. He and the fireman ran down the land side of the embankment while all the passengers also jumped or rolled down to comparative safety. There the train stood throughout the rest of the bombardment, a perfect target for the German gunners yet it did not receive one direct hit. When the shelling finished the driver and fireman got back onto the train and away it went...[42]

As *Seydlitz* steamed clear, Trechmann ordered his guns to direct their fire against *Moltke*. He also ordered the gunners to switch to high explosive (HE) and aim at the ship's super-structure, as the belt armour on the Germans' hulls rendered them safe from the 6-inch rounds. After a few fell short the British shells now began to take effect, sweating gunners cheering, 'Go on shove 'em through! Shove 'em through! Give the buggers hell!' Such enthusiasm, understandable if unprofessional, earned a swift rebuke from their officer: 'Do stop your dancing about and save your breath for your gun corrections!'[43]

The infantry was still fanned out in the dunes but without any enemy in sight: 'There was a road which led to Sunderland, quite close to where I was and I could see packs of terrified dogs running along with heads down and tails between their legs, all hell bent in getting away from the awful destruction and pandemonium.'[44] By this point, the gunners realised they were no longer being fired at. The enemy ships had switched their murderous attention to the docks and to the unprotected settlement behind. *Blucher* was blasting the shoreline immediately in front of the battery, plastering the rocks with smoke shells, attempting to blind the guns. Trechmann now decided to focus on *Blucher* and the men swapped back to armour piercing rounds. Though the shells did little damage, *Blucher* began to steam clear as the other two raiders swung around to loose more rounds towards the old Cemetery Battery site. As *Blucher* slid into sheltering fog, the other two cruisers, still under fire from Lighthouse Battery, also retreated.

Dickie Trechmann ordered his men to cease firing. The enemy was now some 9,500 yards distant. It was 08.53 hours. After the fury of battle, silence descended and sweating, smoke-grimed gunners realised they had survived. These Saturday-night soldiers had withstood their ordeal and stood by their guns. They had taken on the might of the Kaiser's navy and seen it off. As they paused and looked back over the town, they began to understand the cost. The infantry saw it too, close up:

> As we marched back to our billets we saw some of the terrific damage that the shelling had done, whole streets of houses had been wrecked. One street near the school had their front walls completely blown out, exposing the contents of the rooms as though they had suffered an earthquake.[45]

Hartlepool was ablaze. A flaming gasometer lit the morning sky like a torch held aloft for the dead. And there were many dead and many more injured, over a hundred in all; dazed survivors walking shattered streets, ruined houses bulging like split sacks, the calm day-to-day of their ordinary lives suddenly snatched away. The war had reached Britain.

Winter

After the cauldron of Ypres, the Noodles were rotated out of the line and rested for two weeks, a generous furlough by later standards:

> The enemy had been driven from Meteren but a few weeks before, the inhabitants told us; a German, in fact, had been killed nearby. But the place, like Bailleul, had hardly suffered, though it had been stripped of course, of the necessities of life, so much so that 'les Allemands ont tout, tout, tout pris'.[46]

At least the mounted infantry were issued with bayonets and there was some patrolling towards Ploegsteert. Fresh attacks were being launched against the Salient though the battle was rapidly running out of steam. Winter was approaching,

> the weather about this time took a change for the worse. Days of incessant rain were followed by snow and sleet – Flanders at its worst. How bad that can be only a seasoned campaigner knows.

The regiment moved again, this time finding themselves stuck between Armentières and Laventie. It was not a region likely to commend itself to the Northumbrians, who were more used to the rugged topography of their native shore:

> The ground is absolutely flat, unspeakably dreary and feature-less. The soil is heavy clay and under the lightest rain becomes a morass. It seems to rain most days in winter, and there is often a mist of deadly coldness. To strike water even in summer it is seldom necessary to dig more than a few feet; in winter it lies on the surface. The billets were poor. With the exception of Armentieres, which was not a mile from the line, and Estaires there were no towns; only a few mean villages, and many isolated farms, buildings of rectangular form, mostly of clay, built around midden-heaps which often meant an unpleasant fall on a dark evening.

Nor was this bleak picture enlivened by the inhabitants. 'In these farms dwelt farmers of prodigious age, who tilled the ground in the absence of the young men and some emaciated stock.' The war was in its relative infancy, the Western Front had yet to sink into the routine of trenches, month in, month out, regardless of season. That vast hinterland of supply which would spread out behind the lines into a network of biblical proportions barely existed.

> At this early stage no flaring announcement of English beer met the eye of the tired warrior trudging from the trench to his

comfortless barn. Any luxuries beyond the bare rations were hard
to come by, except in parcels from home. There were no canteens,
hence a perpetual shortage of tobacco and cigarettes and of most
extras that make life worth living even in war. There were no
Divisional concert parties, no cinemas and, at first, no baths.

As the Noodles were in general reserve, their duties were varied
but universally unedifying, the minutiae of war. After the dash and
drama of Ypres, they guarded bridges and crossroads, practised the
perfect management of horse-lines.

The orderly room staffs discovered that a war of attrition means
an endless war of forms and paper, and were probably busier than
anyone else. Meanwhile rumours of spies again revived. Patrols
were everywhere on the alert, and were ordered to acquaint themselves with the physiognomy of every inhabitant…

For the yeomanry their brief war of movement was very definitely
over. Now they would have to become used to a very different
environment, one that would come to define the Great War. As the
year drew to a close, 'Christmas came and went, with its football
matches and the informal armistice of the trenches; but in a few
days the guns were barking as merrily as ever'. From now on they
would live and fight from the trenches.

THREE

THE CRUCIBLE, 1915

It is always instructive to watch museum visitors encounter a trench mock-up for the first time. Expectations are usually confounded, if only because our mental images cannot encompass the sheer variety of environments they offered:

> First and foremost these were not the spacious and well-ordered works with which many became acquainted on the Somme and elsewhere. The very nature of the terrain precluded any system of mining excavation; water was seldom more than two or three feet below the surface even in comparatively dry seasons, so the trenches were in most places a compromise. A narrow, shallow ditch supplied the trench proper, above it to front and back were piled sandbags, usually in higgledy-piggledy manner … even if they were well laid the Boche gunner could be trusted to see that they did not long remain so. Rough traverses there were, very necessary when the Boche sniper commanded the flanks with enfilade fire.[47]

Beyond the parapet lay the wire, still in thin belts at this early stage 'and continually preyed on by enemy trench mortars and shells'. Life within was far from agreeable:

> Before the days of revetting wire and frames, of iron and timber, even of duckboards, the painfully constructed trench was at the mercy of the weather. A heavy shower even in the heat of summer would reduce the interior to a quagmire. In the height of winter,

conditions were unspeakable. An endless winding ditch, filled with glutinous mud of extraordinary tenacity, led past the support trench to the firing line proper – a rather wide, deeper ditch and consequently with the greater depth of water, not infrequently waist high. There the infantry would pass their tour of duty, harassed by enemy snipers, who seemed inevitably to command the weakest points of the system, and to a shell-fire to which their own batteries, for very lack of ammunition, were unable to respond.[48]

Within this stygian world of unceasing danger, of cold, wet and unending frozen misery there was, at this stage, little or no shelter:

… no dugouts, no mined dug-outs impervious to shell or mortar fire; not even the miserable shacks which passed for dugouts at a later stage … there was no material with which to build them, no iron, no planks, no surplus of sandbags, no surplus of men to build them. A wretched hole within the fire-bay above the level of the water, contrived often in the thickness of the parados, provided the only means of shelter, and a waterproof sheet the covering. There was no immunity from shell-fire; the parapet was not always bulletproof. Often too after heavy rainfall or a thaw, the whole structure would collapse, burying the occupants in mud and water or exposing them to enemy fire.[49]

This was no life for a cavalryman.

†

A few hints for Tommy by 'one wot knows'

My son, beware the aircraft that flies above for his nose-caps return to earth as thou walkest, and if one drop near thee, though thou say 'pooh' yet shall thy feet be cold under thee.

Tread carefully the end of the duckboard in the trench, lest haply the other end rise and smite thee. Speak fair unto the ASC that when thou returnest from leave, he may give thee lifts in his Lorries.

Better Maconochie [stew] and biscuit in rest, than chicken and Moulin Rouge in the line, at a whizz-bang shalt thou shrug thy shoulders, at two thine eyebrows raise, at three shalt thou quicken thy pace, at four peradventure thou mayest run but a 'five-nine' who can stick it?

If a man say unto you 'Leave is open, leave is open' regard him not for he is a liar, and talketh through his hat (tin). Walk not upon the Decauville Track though it is the shorter way, that the wrath of the O.C. descend not upon thy head and he dock thy leave.

Beware the barrage that creepeth and the Minen that is Werfer[†] that thy days may be long in the line. Verily, a sandbag is a comfortable thing, it buildeth up the parapet, it improveth the dugout and maketh warm the legs of man.

A simple soul accepteth twenty-five francs to the pound but a wise man insisteth on twenty-seven fifty and raiseth Cain till he gets it. From the unit to the field ambulance is easy, from thence to the CCS mayhap harder but from the CCS to the base hospital, who shall wangle it?

– Ernest Mathers 16th London Regiment QWR[50]

The streets were lined with people; it was on a Saturday,
When the local lads in their fours, to the station made their way,
It was on the seventeenth day of April, Nineteen-Fifteen,
When the band struck up that old march; 'Soldiers of the Queen'
Our ordinary drill and training was now at an end,
We had been called to the front, our country to defend.[51]

If you travel to Ypres today, you will find a beautiful Flemish city of fine avenues, dominated by the grand and lofty bulk of the cloth hall, steep, red-tiled gables, and surrounded by a mighty ring of Vauban walls, designed in the late seventeenth century with a view to keeping the English out. If you were unaware of the history of the

---

† A *minenwerfer* was a German mine thrower. The term rapidly became used as slang by the British. Tommy called the whistling shells 'minnies', hence the phrase 'moaning Minnie'.

place you could easily be forgiven for thinking the town largely unchanged over several centuries. In fact all that you behold is rebuilt, stone upon precious stone. So thorough, so unrelenting, so massive was the destruction wrought by German shells that the whole city was virtually obliterated. Churchill wanted the shattered wreck left in 1918 as a fossilised memorial. Locals, understandably, wished to rebuild. Before the autumn of 1914, few in Britain had heard of the place. The names of nearly 55,000 British and Commonwealth dead, those who have no known grave, carved lovingly into the sepulchre of the Menin Gate,[†] offer eloquent and silent testimony.

The Salient

Little did some of us think, so sudden was our doom
We could not march quick enough, this was soon found out,
From foot sack to motor bus, we were roughly bumped about,
Over the rough and rocky road, the firing line got nearer,
The clash of deadly conflict was now getting clearer.[52]

Imagine a saucer and the city of Ypres in the depression. Around a thin, barely noticeable ring of higher ground to the east and south, like a gentle rim, is the Ypres Salient. He who holds the rim dominates the saucer. By 1915, the Germans held this higher ground. The British position was horribly exposed. Wet, low-lying Flanders proved an uncomfortable and ungracious host. By the end of the 1st Battle of Ypres, the Germans held not just the high ground to the east, ending in the village of Passchendaele, a name to become synonymous with horror, but also Hill 60,[‡] two miles south-west of the ruined city and the Wytschaete-Messines ridge further south.

---

† The Menin Gate, by Sir Reginald Blomfield, was unveiled in 1927 and is the memorial to those dead who have no known grave.
‡ Hill 60 is the high ground by Zillebeke created by or constructed from spoil from a nineteenth-century railway cutting – before 1914 it was known as 'Lovers' Knoll'; thereafter it had a very different reputation and is still regarded as a war grave for so many lie entombed there.

Most historians concur that trench warfare proper began as the retreating Germans began to dig in along the Chemin des Dames Ridge in September 1914. From that point on the line swiftly began to solidify, from the North Sea to the Swiss border, some 475 miles in all. By the end of 1915 estimates suggested that for each mile of front the maze of trenches was twenty times that distance. As the war ground on this became more rather than less; the whole troglodyte network extended for some 15,000 miles.

Digging in the heavy ground of Flanders got no deeper than a couple of feet before encountering the water table. Trenches in the usual sense could simply not be dug and the line comprised a system of sandbag redoubts. The Germans referred to these as box trenches, their white zigzag scars running across the wet plain, a comfortingly easy target for their gunners. For alternative sport the artillery could batter what was left of the carefully wrought system of water defences that held the hungry sea at bay, ratcheting up the misery quotient. 'The World wasn't made in a day / And Eve didn't ride in a bus / But most of the world's in a sandbag / And the rest of it's plastered on us.'

George Hilton, 2nd Battalion KOSB, was born in 1872 and served in the ranks for eight years before being commissioned in 1900 as a 2nd lieutenant in DCLI. Very much a career soldier, he then joined KOSB as lieutenant in 1905, promoted captain in 1909 and reached the rank of major in December 1916. He first saw action during the Nile Expedition 1898 then served through the South African War.

1 January 1915: 'The system of heating the cottages here is quite economical. The stoves could be copied in England with advantage I think.' Winters in Flanders are inhospitable, cold, wet with a dank wind that whips in over the North Sea; mud freezes; keeping out the insidious cold became a priority. 2 January: 'I have written asking Hilda [his wife] for the British Warm.'[53]

Where ground permitted, the trench would be dug down some eight feet and would be about twelve wide. A shelf or firestep was built in to the forward-facing flank to form a fighting platform. Sandbags were used to form a parapet and, to the rear, a parados.

The former was generally lower than the latter so defenders' profiles would be broken up and thus less exposed to snipers. Distances between the opposing lines could be half a mile or only a matter of yards.

> 3 January: The enemy was about 22 yards distant and during the time we were changing threw up flares by means of pistols, these burn very brightly and the men had to crouch until the light burned down … we were sniped a very little during the night.

The trench sides, even in firm dry chalk upland would not stand without support. Timber and corrugated iron had to be brought in and fatigue parties kept busy hour after exhausting hour, maintaining the structure.

> 5 January: The dugouts are in a field north of a farm. It is a very large farm and a pity to see it in this condition. There is a petrol engine here just installed and it looks like being ruined … lots of tobacco out hanging up, of course it will be ruined too.

> 9 January: We marched to the trenches and I took over a trench on the left of the road. It was a perfect maze of trenches and very difficult to understand. Fryer and myself went to shelled out Smelly Pig Farm and got some straw and tried to make things comfortable.

A trench was never a purely linear feature. If it were, once penetrated, the enemy, gaining a foothold, could rake the entire length. Instead, they were built as an alternating system of projecting fire-bays and traverses (the sections which provided linkage). To attack such a trench involved 'bombing up the traverses'. An attacking section would be divided between bombers, those who threw grenades and 'bayonet' men. The former lobbed their bombs over the fire-bay and the latter rushed the traverse ready to deal with any surviving enemy who might have fight left in them, a dreadful attritional slogging match. Snipers were a constant and deadly menace.

10 January: The enemy started sniping us and when I got back to my trench I found Fryer had been shot dead. It gave me quite a nasty turn. I fear he had been looking up and had got an unlucky shot. During the day we were badly shelled and I lost two killed and one wounded.

No battalion spent the whole of its time actually in the trenches themselves. Service in the line was followed by a period in reserve, punctuated by welcome if usually all too brief spells of relative repose. As George Hilton himself observed, a poor billet often merited more censure than an ill-sited or badly finished trench: 12 January: 'The billet in the convent isn't all that could be desired. It is strange how one exclaims over a bare room when one has been in the open.' Minor inconveniences in the daily attrition of death and disease often rankled: 17 January: 'Had to do the cooking as my new servant has gone sick. Troops are not standing this bad weather.'

Death in battle was not the only hazard. Major actions were relatively rare but random shelling, sniping and sheer bad luck ensured a steady flow of casualties whenever the battalion was 'up':

18 January: We had a very bad time today, the Germans shelled all day; I lost one killed and four wounded. The minen-werfers were very busy and about thirty of them fell in and around my trenches but did little damage, beyond frightening one platoon … marched back to Danouton [the spelling of the village name, like so many in Flanders, has been amended – it now shows on the map as Danjoutin] and had one of the worst billets I have seen.

An indispensable feature of the trench-fighter's burrowing existence was the dugout. Generally this limited accommodation was reserved for officers while other ranks (ORs) had to scrape shelters or 'funk-holes' in the sides of the trench. In the rat-infested gloom of the dugout, small comforts carried great weight: 20 January: 'Saw a very neat stove today and have sent to Army & Navy Stores for one, hope it will arrive in time for our next go of trenches.' Happily it did. 4 February: 'Found my little primus stove very useful.' Out of the line periods in support or even at rest were marked by drill, parades and sport: 26 January: 'Had a company parade this morning near the asylum, something for the men to do; football match in the evening and paid out the men.'

During the third week of February the KOSB marched up to Ypres: 28 February: 'I went to 38 & 39 trenches this time. The Germans shelled us all day but only wounded one man. We had to work like niggers to get the trenches in any sort of order. The communication trench was awful.' By mid-March an attack on high ground near St Eloi was being proposed but did not proceed. They did not entirely escape the attentions of the Kaiser's increasingly potent air force. 12 April: 'Zeppelins came over last night and dropped about half a dozen bombs. We could distinctly see the thing. The bombs did no damage at all.'

Within a month, they were being readied for an attack on Hill 60. This feature was entirely man-made, a conical mound of spoil left from railway construction. The heap rises some 60 metres, forming an artificial spur to the Messines Ridge, and was the location of the first British mine of the war blown by Lieutenant White RE on 17 February 1915. March found 173rd Tunnelling Company RE digging a series of three tunnels beneath the enemy line. It was filthy, dangerous and exhausting work, our tunnellers regularly disinterring the rotting remains of French and German dead. The explosion timed for 7.05 p.m. on 17 April flung a vast column of debris into the spring skies and the British attack swept forward, killing or capturing the shocked and stunned defenders for, by 1915 standards, very modest loss.

17 April: Lay low in the communication trench and dugouts all day, in the evening the mines were exploded and I have never

seen such a sight in my life, it was indescribable. The attack came off a few minutes later and off we went to the top of the hill and worked like niggers to make it defendable. At about midnight I retired to the woods and slept for about four hours.

The KOSB were not long in reserve. Despite the swiftness of the initial British success, the Germans, as ever, put in strong and determined counter-attacks:

18 April: Had to go and reinforce as the enemy were putting in a counter-attack. It was very difficult holding on. Command of the regiment devolved on me as all the seniors were killed or wounded. Marched off around 15.00 hours – very lucky to be alive!

Any elation at such a significant success was diluted by knowledge of the blood price paid. Besides there was no respite, a major German offensive was brewing:

22 April: Had orders to occupy trenches 35 to 37 tonight. Marched off around 19.30 hours but when nearing Vlamertinge met the adjutant of the West Kents who had turned back and said the village was impassable on account of refugees. The French had given way and were running; the Germans had broken through.

In early April, the British had taken over a further five miles of French-held trenches north-east of the battered ruin of Ypres and it was here the blow fell. This, the 2nd Battle of Ypres, witnessed the first use of poison gas by the Germans on the Western Front. French colonial forces, faced with this satanic yellowish mist, broke. Canadians, deployed around St Julien, did not and fought on in a display of sublime courage for which they paid a very heavy price. Two thousand died here, over 4,000 were wounded: fighting on the parapets to get clear of the gas, mud- and urine-soaked handkerchiefs were their only protection. Violently ill, desperate for breath, they held on in the face of machine-gun fire and shrapnel until reinforcements arrived. In the wake of this break in the line, the situation in the Salient deteriorated rapidly:

> 23 April: About 14.00 hours we were ordered to stand to. We marched to the [Yser] Canal having been given orders for an attack at 16.15 hours or thereabouts. The men behaved splendidly. I finally decided I must push up to the firing line but didn't get far before I was bowled over. Broster pulled me into a ditch and I made my way to the dressing station. I was sent off to Poperinghe and from there to Boulogne.

George Hilton was wounded in the attack on Hill 60 and a bullet remained lodged in his spine for thirty years. Nonetheless, his war was not over and he returned to active service in 1916, holding a range of staff appointments certainly until 1920.

Baptism of Fire

> Men, materials and money are the immediate necessities … does the call of duty find no response in you until reinforced, let us say superseded, by the call of conscription?
>   What have you done?
>   What are you doing?
>   What are you going to do?
>   Will you help?
>   What can you do?
>   If a man of fighting age and fit – JOIN TODAY
> If too old or working in munitions, or if a woman, get at least ONE RECRUIT TODAY!
> – Extract from Lord Kitchener's speech at the Guildhall, 9 July 1915[54]

Despite the initial German successes, 2nd Ypres quickly became a slogging match. The enemy blundered forward and the Allies blundered in riposte. General Smith-Dorrien was one high-ranking casualty, not of German bullets but of Sir John French's animosity. He had been foolish enough to suggest shortening the line at Ypres and avoiding further piecemeal and bloody counter-attacks. When General Plumer, his successor, suggested the same tactics, French concurred.

These finer points of grand tactics and general politicking were not immediately evident to Herbert Waugh (the Newcastle-born Saturday-night soldier). Nor was it familiar to those other youthful Hectors who ventured across the Channel. Their expectation was that the damsels of France and Belgium would be lining up to surrender their favours. In this they would be disappointed: they were on their way to Ypres. Tommy found the forward areas devoid of females and those he met in lanes and billets to the rear proved less than glamorous … 'Such girls as he encountered wore clogs, dressed like agricultural labourers, smelt of stables and byres and looked with reserve and suspicion at anything in a khaki uniform.'[55]

The battalion colonel was a figure of awe. The fusiliers

gazed up at him as he clattered by on his great horse and asked each other if it was true that his monocle was affixed to the peak of his service cap by a hinge. One of his sayings was 'a barrage moves as a pillar of cloud by day and fire by night'. He had a marked aversion to any officer 'not quite out of the right drawer' and, on encountering an officer in the trenches who had several days' growth of beard, he was heard to enquire 'who is that officer with a face like a musical box?'

The Geordies saw their first French *poilu* on the dockside at Boulogne; he 'stood silently on guard duty, cloaked and with a long bayonet fixed to his rifle'. Northern France, the first alien shore most had visited, was 'pretty, quite flat'. Billets were found in ancient timber-framed barns, for the most part dilapidated. St George's Day 1915 was commemorated as the regiment's annual fête day, officers sported red and white roses. Marching ever nearer to the inferno, hobnails ringing on unyielding *pavé*, they passed into Belgium where streams of refugees, human detritus of war, crowded the roads.

More followed. As they neared Poperinghe, long toiling columns of wounded appeared. Men bloodied, vacant and broken, thrown out of the giant mincer of the Western Front as surely as they were now being drawn in. By Vlamertinghe, their trenches were real, wet and very cold at night. Waugh shared his billet with a friend, known as Broncho 'after a popular American western movie character'. The pair adopted the expedient of alternately using each other as a mattress, sharing body warmth. This was necessity rather than passion and permitted a measure of sleep. As for their Belgian hosts, the fastidious Waugh observed: 'Our allies serve an admirable cup of coffee but not always in a clean cup.'

Battle-scarred Ypres, unrecognisable as the pleasing and prosperous medieval city it had been, a real tragedy – shells rattled over our heads like railway trains. 'We alternately walked and ran, stumbling over obstacles whilst fragments of roofing trickled down on us.'

In rain-soaked fields, heavy, cloying earth wet and pungent, backlit by the flames of burning villages, like some travesty of northern lights, the dipping arcs of flares ahead marked the front line. Next day, moving up they saw their first dead man, heard the first frantic calls for 'stretcher-bearers'. Their home for 25 April was a 'muddy ditch' scarcely worth defining as a trench; next door, a British field battery whose constant roaring bark filled their senses.

> When this ****** war is over,
> Oh, how happy I shall be.
> When I get my civvy clothes on,
> No more soldiering for me.[56]

With every hour, the reality of the war intruded further:

> There was an ugly field to be crossed that morning, great shells plunging into all parts of it and throwing black fountains of earth house-high. We wavered for a bit until the adjutant came up;

'come along 'A' Company, they're not firing at you'; shrapnel and 'Jack Johnsons' falling all around us.

With so little cover, snipers who now began to make themselves felt: walking wounded, 'dirty, disordered and exhausted' staggered by in droves. As morning wore on, fire from the heavier guns diminished, replaced by 'an increasing tattoo of small arms'. The almost reassuring business of digging in took on a new urgency. Labours were interrupted by a wild, dishevelled officer from the front who implored them 'to go up there'. The man was clearly in shock and the Fusiliers felt they had lost 'that boy-scout-on-holiday feeling'.

The morning of 26 April was to be 6th Battalion's moment of baptism. They went over, attacking towards St Julien: 'Up the rise we began to meet machine-gun bullets in streams, rifle bullets from every angle and then the HE coal boxes or Jack Johnsons. Sixth and 7th Battalions advanced towards the outskirts of the village where week old German dead lay all around.' More digging in – 'a hundred yards away the farmer lies dead amidst his roasted cattle, dead horses everywhere'. Cards, the soldier's eternal distraction, were produced and a game commenced. They ignored the ravaged landscape, pausing only to note the, 'ruined tower of the Cloth-Hall to rear, trees vivid in the bright sunshine. The only height is the height of the tall lines of trees, and the only immensity is the immensity of the skies.'

Broncho, the Hollywood lookalike, 'an athletic public schoolboy, already qualified as a solicitor' who had drafted Waugh's will, told his friend '"I've said goodbye to all the old life at home", so sure of he was of his presentiment of impeding death, all too soon fulfilled; he was from Benton but never saw Benton again.'

The attack against St Julien was hastily planned, ground not reconnoitred. Men moved forward beneath a full weight of kit, greatcoats included, much of which was jettisoned. They carried the older Long Lee Enfield, heads covered by their field caps, no 'steel bowlers (metal helmets) yet'. Many officers still carried pre-war private purchase rifles, originally intended for rather less dangerous sport. 'A brigade staff officer, red hat and all, galloped up to our company commander in tremendous haste, reined in his horse, shouted brief and urgent orders, pointed ahead with out-flung arm and rode off as quickly as he had come.' These Saturday-night soldiers advanced towards contact 'and on we went, clerks, artisans and labourers led by solicitors, chartered account-ants and land-agents, all dressed up in khaki'.

'The enemy played his complete orchestra, HE, Machine-gun and rifle fire.' The Fusiliers passed over the forward line, held by a Scottish unit, filing through a gap in the British wire and into no man's land.

> I remember P dropped his pipe, and popped back to pick it
> up – the enemy were invisible, lining the hedges in front, just
> like a sham attack in training. We were ordered to fire and to fix
> bayonets, advancing in rushes. All around the great black cones of
> blown up earth that rose out of the green plain, the whip-crack of
> bullets passing overhead and the little throbs as they hit the turf
> … during a moment's lull the sound of a lark in full song above.

As the City Battalion struggled forward into the wall of enemy fire, Waugh was hit, 'a dull and heavy thump, a blow, and [I] imagined for a minute I'd been struck by a flying stone'. He lay out on the field with other wounded and dead nearby: 'Z asked me to give a message to his mother in Byker.' Despite his own wounds Waugh complied. Three months later, on returning to duty at the city's drill hall, he was astonished to see the same man very much alive, though walking with a stick.

Waugh was able to make his own way back to the regimental aid post, crammed into a disused stretch of trench. Another wounded comrade whose personal camera had somehow survived the fight offered to take photos – 'battle into bank holiday'. Having been patched up and still on his feet, Waugh was advised to make his way back into the ruins of what had been St Jean. Sporadic shell-ing continued, rounds crashing amongst the waving trees, not yet reduced to skeletal matchsticks. 'If I were you,' the MO cautioned as he set off, 'I'd avoid the trees there, it's by the cemetery and they're shelling it.' Having no wish to add to the graveyard population, Waugh took a more circuitous route to relative safety.

At a field ambulance station he was fed with warm, sweet tea and Tommy's universal remedy, bread and marmalade. Irritatingly, there was no butter – happily a soldier from the Highland Light Infantry obliged from his personal supply, 'the present from Margate variety; "you'll be going home and I'm not" his benefactor confided'. The tin of butter was small and handy. He kept it with him throughout the entire war.

Even so his tribulations were not yet ended. A hazardous series of lifts by various conveyances conveyed him to Vlamertinghe. Painted images of long dead saints flickered by candlelight as they gazed benignly down on scores of British wounded in an overcrowded church, huddled on chairs, prone on stretchers. When the survivors of 149 Brigade were relieved next day, they'd lost their commanding officer (Brigadier-General Riddell), forty-two officers and 1,912 other ranks, roughly two-thirds of their total strength. They were the first of the Territorials to go into action as a full brigade. Kitchener had been wrong again: these unlikely soldiers had not faltered and had paid the full, terrible price of their blood passage.

Despite such enormous losses, there was always gallows humour for the downhearted: 'When ye get hyem [home] te Newburn gan ower [go over] te Ryton and ye'll find an undertaker called X. Buy yerself a black hat and get yerself apprenticed to him. Ye're far ower-cheerful for this job.'

Attrition

We dispersed off the buses at a place called Poperinghe,
And marched in deadly silence to a place called Vlamertinghe.
In the darkness wearily, we stumbled and plodded on,
To find some suitable resting place, to rest our limbs upon;
We were to have had shelter, in some huts that were found,
But luck was against us, we lay on open ground.[57]

Captain Robert Collingwood 'Bobbie' Roddam was the only son of Lieutenant-Colonel Roddam from Roddam Hall, North Northumberland. He had, for three years before the outbreak of war, been learning and working in the Ceylonese tea trade, latterly as a *Sinne Durai* (tea broker). His military connection went back to the pre-war Territorials. He'd joined the 7th Battalion Northumberland Fusiliers in August 1908 before transferring to the 3rd Special Reserve, at that point commanded by his father. Returning from Ceylon and the Tyspane Tea Company 'to do his bit' he moved again, this time to the 1st Battalion. His early career had been spent in Barclays bank, Berwick branch and he was noted as a keen golfer.[58]

Roddam had qualified as a musketry instructor before the war and was promoted to captain on 25 March 1915. At this point his father was commanding 15th Battalion. Bobbie's CO in recommending him for promotion wrote (23 March 1915): 'Roddam is in every way fit for promotion to the rank of captain and should be promoted at the first opportunity. He is of course not qualified by examination but he has shown marked ability in the field.' A captaincy was something of a double-edged sword. Company commanders were first in the attack along with subalterns, their daily workload and responsibility was greater and, conversely, their chances of winning a medal were less. Bobbie was clearly made of the right stuff: 'Over and over again he has been in very nasty situations and every time he has come out smiling and kept his end up wonderfully.'

On 31 May he earned a mention in Despatches, the most basic award for gallantry. This had, nonetheless, been well earned. Writing to Bobbie's father some time later, the younger Roddam's CO noted that, on 28 February, in the line near St Eloi, Bobbie's platoon had been heavily mortared and stonked by rifle grenades. Casualties were mounting, the men unsettled. Bobbie kept his head and, while reassuring the men, acted as a FOO (forward observation officer) for British guns which were eventually able to target the enemy fire. His own diary entry is typically laconic: 'Got an awful doing of trench mortars. I hope we never get another – spent all day telephoning and observing for our artillery.'

Worse was to follow. On 14 April the enemy exploded a large mine ahead of the platoon's trench and the resultant giant blast buried men in dugouts and collapsed part of the parapet. Bobbie could barely muster a dozen fit NCOs and men but swiftly got these dazed survivors into action and repelled the German attack which followed: 'Keeping a cool head and doing the right thing stopped the enemy from occupying our front trenches.' Again, Roddam's own diary merely notes that a large mine was exploded at 23.30 hours.

When the battalion attacked near Hooge on 16 June, Bobbie, with his subaltern Hugh Scrutton, led the company. A telegraph dated 21 June subsequently informed his parents that the WO 'deeply regrets to inform you that Captain R. C. H. Roddam Northumberland Fusiliers was killed in action on 16th June. Lord Kitchener expresses his sympathies.' With such curt notice the Roddams learned, like countless other families, of the death of their only son. Deeper knowledge was not guaranteed to offer greater solace. Bobbie's CO wrote to Colonel Roddam advising Bobbie had died early on during the successful attack and gave a note of his place of temporary interment, marked like tens of thousands of others by a wooden cross.

Second Lieutenant Scrutton, himself badly wounded in the attack, though he continued to direct his men till his several wounds finally felled him, wrote 'I feel as though I have lost a life-long friend'. Scrutton was awarded the MC for his actions on that day. Bobbie had earlier been recommended for the same decoration which was gazetted on the day news of his death arrived. When one opens the file of correspondence in the Northumberland County Archive it is impossible not to feel immediacy; the papers include a stack of letters of condolence written by friends and relations and the tributes from Bobbie's comrades are glowing.

Writing to Roddam's mother in 1917, Sergeant W. P. Carlin of 'B' Company gave more details of her son's last moments. He suffered a severe head wound but was recovered alive from the field and stretchered back to the communication trench. One of the bearers was himself killed and Carlin attempted to carry Bobbie who, in his delirium, was thrashing about. Eventually he was carried as far as the advanced dressing station where, after twenty minutes, he died. The letter does not say but it is likely that Bobbie was merely sedated and put quietly aside. Triage was necessary at the ADS (Advanced Dressing Station); so great was the flow of broken and maimed bodies that only viable cases could be treated.

Breaking the Deadlock

> We've served with you for near a year
> And shared your woes and joys
> We shall miss your lengthy shadow
> And so will all the boys
> But when we're digging trenches, Jim
> We shall always think of you.
> Instead of digging four feet six,
> We'll dig them six foot two!
> – *Plum & Apple*, October 1915[†59]

In the early weeks of 1915 a split had opened between the 'westerners' who perceived that the war would be lost and won on the Western Front and those who favoured a more peripheral or 'eastern' strategy. This was tried and tested and the easterners possessed impressive advocates in Churchill and Lloyd George. Kitchener wrote to French on 1 January indicating the easterners might get their way. The 'Little' Field Marshal was aghast; weakening the Western Front to create nothing more than a holding garrison would, in his view be disastrous. Of course the easterners got their way. The tragedy at Gallipoli became the graveyard of their hopes.[‡]

---

† This poem was written about Lieutenant James Barker Bradford of the remarkable Bradford brothers, two of whom won the VC. Neither they nor James survived the war.

‡ The Gallipoli campaign, a massive misjudgement, lasted from 25 April 1915 to 9 January 1916 and cost the Allies 220,000 casualties for no gains.

For Britons, the notion of a head-to-head confrontation with a formidable adversary in the main theatre of battle was inconsistent with tried precedent. The Seven Years War and Napoleonic campaigns had been won by avoiding such dreaded attrition. Expansion of the army and the need to provide vast new supplies of arms and ordnance strained capacity beyond endurance. Anti-German feeling was rampant at home and having a Master-General of the Ordnance called Sir Stanley von Donop created a difficulty of its own.

British attempts to break the deadlock of the trenches comprised attacks at Neuve Chapelle (10–13 March), at Aubers Ridge on 9 May and a fresh attempt at Festubert between 10 and 25 May. French offensives in Artois also failed at dreadful cost. Despite some gains, all of these largely stalled with heavy losses. Massive firepower was not complemented by advanced communications. Telephone wires were soon cut and battalion runners struggling through a hell of ruined trenches and shell-lashed no man's land could not hope to provide commanders with fluid and accurate action reports. Ground gained was soon lost to counter attacks. Allied operations were temporarily derailed when the Germans attacked at Ypres, a see-saw slogging match of positions lost and re-taken, only to be lost again. Despite this murderous baptism, many Saturday-night soldiers still managed to churn the horror into verse. Sergeant J. Wilkes, a signaller serving with the DLI, penned a mini-*Iliad*:

> The news went round like magic; the Huns were breaking through,
>> The news kindled up the flame that was rising in our veins,
>>> To stop the Germans' gallop, we had to hold the reins;
>> It was now breaking daylight, and awful sights were seen,
>> With hundreds of wounded soldiers returning from St Jean.
>> Yes, wounded were returning, all had the same old cry,
> 'Good luck to you, Durham lads, but you're going up to die'.
> Our tired out limbs were now forgot, we meant to make our name,
>> If we are going up there to die, we are going to die game;
>>> Rain came down in torrents, and with shot and shell.
>> It was to us no other than a raging, living Hell.[60]

Cavalry, the essence of exploitation, could no longer be effectively deployed. Whatever criticisms could be and have been launched against Allied generals, the fact remains that the deadlock could simply not, at this stage in the war, be broken. French attacks in Artois fared even worse and at terrible cost. When the British attack at Aubers Ridge foundered as did the French offensive, broken against the deepening fortress of the German defence, the relative weakness of Allied artillery was starkly highlighted. Lack of ammunition, in terms of type, quantity and quality, became a temporary *cause célèbre* and the 'shell scandal' brought Asquith's tottering ministry to its knees, ushering in the wartime coalition. Lloyd George took up responsibility for munitions. Nonetheless, lack of shells contributed to the British failure at Festubert.

Despite these repeated disappointments and the immense tide of casualties, French and Joffre, when they met at Chantilly on 24 June, remained wedded to further action along the Western Front. In this they were correct. The war would not be won on other peripheral fronts but the price of victory would be very high indeed. Joffre pushed for an attack by Haig's 1st Army at Loos, the British having now extended their own lines eastwards into the dense mining belt of Artois. A setting fit for *Germinal,* dense, bleak patchwork of collieries and huddled townships, slagheaps erupting over the largely flat ground like satanic sores. Haig was not impressed by the 'most unfavourable ground'. French shared his subordinate's concerns. 'Papa' Joffre was insistent and received unexpected support from Kitchener himself, committed on account of the Russians' deteriorating position in the east to do whatever must be done to aid the French, even though heavy losses became inevitable.

From 25 September to the night of 13/14 October the battle of Loos consumed 43,000 British casualties. Despite prodigies of valour, none more Homeric than Piper Daniel Laidlaw of 7th Battalion KOSB, leading the fight for Hill 70 on the first day, the battle achieved little.[†]

---

† Piper Laidlaw won the VC on 25 September in the attack on Hill 70, where, with pipes playing, his inspirational march over the top into the teeth of enemy fire became the stuff of legend.

The strategic balance was unaffected. Field Marshal French's career was another casualty. His position had steadily crumbled throughout 1915 and Haig had unashamedly been jockeying for his job. He fully exploited his influence with the King to undermine his commanding officer. Their final meeting on 18 December, by which time French was all too painfully aware of how he had been intrigued against and betrayed, was far from cordial.

Hang On and Hope

We were now in the range of the enemy's guns,
Shells were dropping round us, I should say in tons.
At last the Hun's artillery had really found their mark,
And to be cut up by unseen foes, was to us no lark.
There was only one thing for it, each man to dig himself in,
And keep well under cover, if he valued his life or skin.
Men were going down like sheep, it's awful to relate,
We lay in mud and water, and could not retaliate;
We got the order to advance, under heavy fire,
But owing to murderous gas fumes we had to retire.
We did not mean to give in, even if it meant ruin,
We attacked and we held the village of Fortruin.
— Anon.[61]

Sergeant Robert Constantine served in 9th Battalion DLI. He was born in Newcastle in 1887 and enlisted at the age of twenty-three. He served at 2nd Ypres and wrote to his brother, Jim, from Potijze on 13 May:

After nine days nice rest we are back again in the trenches and it's hell all day long, shells of all sorts bursting about but the German shells are not very good because I've seen a lot of them not burst at all and others are full of marbles and some of our chaps were saying they had seen some burst that were full of nails, a nice thing to put in shells, eh? I put in an awful day in yesterday, it was the longest day I've ever had and I felt properly upset and could not get a bit nap at all.[62]

Already, those who had 'cushy' jobs back home were becoming objects of envy:

Tell Ben Hodgson he should be very thankful to be where he is, I would just like to change places with him now! We passed a large city on Tuesday night on our way to the trenches and the whole place from end to end was on fire, what a sight, it's just done for wilful destruction and nothing else. We all know about 'Lusitania' but have not seen the papers with any of the news yet … You shouldn't grumble about going to bed without a light, you should be lucky you have such a nice bed, I know I would just now.[63]

John Walcote Gamble, originally a native of Derbyshire, volunteered with the Public Schools Battalion at Ashtead in Surrey, transferring firstly to 16th Battalion DLI but actually serving with the 14th. He went to France in October 1914 and served till he was wounded on 8 January 1916.[†] He wrote to his family on 23 October, describing life in the trenches that autumn:

In our company mess (there are six of us) we do have some cakes, and also a few extras which we are able with difficulty to get from villages nearby, such as tinned fruit, salmon or sardines and vegetables … A three-days-old newspaper usually drags through but I shall always be glad to get papers or magazines of any description.[64]

Life in the trenches was uncongenial:

---

† He was wounded at the start of 1916, rejoined his unit early in February, wounded again on 22 May and died the day after. He was twenty-two.

We are in these alleged trenches for a week, and hope to get relieved on Sunday night. They are more breastworks than trenches, and are by no means sound. We spend all spare time strengthening and repairing them. At one point we are right up close to the Germans and can hear them quite plainly at times. It rained hard last night and the 'ditches' were in a frightful mess this morning, literally over the boot tops in mud everywhere. I think, considering that the British have held them for many months, that the regiments who have been in before ought to have seen to it, that they were well-drained, bomb-proof and comfortable long ago. I suppose the explanation is that one regiment only occupies this part of the line for a short period at a time and they don't like wasting time improving trenches for someone else's benefit. The last lot the 14th [DLI] were in were absolutely top notch, properly drained, boarded and concreted, and in every way comfortable and safe; but you see a Territorial Brigade had been there for two months and taken real pains to get their quarters jolly good.

On 20 November, 2nd Lieutenant Gamble acquainted his readers with a new parody of 'Little Grey Home in the West':

> There's a shallow wet trench near Houplines
> 'Tis the wettest there ever has been,
> There are bullets that fly,
> There are shells in the sky,
> And it smells like a German 'has been'.
>
> My dug-out's a haven of rest,
> Though it's only a tumble down nest,
> But with 'Johnsons' around,
> I must keep underground,
> Till the golden sun sinks in the west.

Humour masked a dank, exhausting and unendingly miserable existence with the added zest of constant danger:

It was intensely cold; the hail came across with such force that it seemed to be mixed with bullets and I'm sure many men must have thought they were shot by hail-stones. The harder we pumped, the deeper the water seemed to become. If we had left it undisturbed, we should have been frozen in and the Boche was rather active with his artillery. We discussed various ways of using or abusing the liquid devil. One bright idea was to cut a trench through from our line to theirs, make it fairly deep, run in the water and torpedo them! Boat and swimming races were dismissed as frivolous but the idea of skating about the support trenches was seriously considered!

Getting out proved as hazardous as staying in:

There were great rejoicings when we were relieved yesterday morning at dawn, although we had quite an exciting time getting out; you see we usually empty about half a dozen communication trenches along the line but on this occasion only one was really safe from drowning casualties. It was an extremely tedious business getting a battalion out by one route and we could not get started till after the appointed time, owing to the relieving people meeting with similar difficulties.

As winter deepened, the harsh weather continued, sliding into deep cold. Opportunities for relief were few, even shell-shattered Ypres proved a slight diversion. Gamble recorded in his letter of 23 December:

On Saturday then I took advantage of the temporary calm, and had another look round Ypres. It is really a wonderful sight – weird, grotesque, and desolate of course, but most interesting. I expect the place will be flooded with sightseers and tourists after the war, and they will be amazed by what they see. The ancient ruins of Pompeii and such places will be simply out of it.

This was a very early version of the battlefield tour:

> Willis (a topping officer who was attached to us and who was
> very badly wounded on Sunday) and I went round the ruins
> of the Cathedral. It must have been a magnificent building before
> the strafing and was reputed to have some wonderful stained
> glass windows. We found there was only a fragment of this glass
> remaining and that it was a very difficult place, but we clambered
> up through heaps of shattered stonework and debris, up a rickety
> and tottering belfry staircase, swarmed the remains of a window-
> frame, and obtained few splendid pieces of this glass. These will I
> guess, be valuable some day and are certainly already historic. I've
> got them safely stowed away in my kit ... also got some fragments
> of a 17-inch shell which had burst amongst the Cathedral ruins
> the previous day.

Next day, Sunday, was rather far from restful:

> About 05.30, I was aroused in my dug-out by a gas-helmeted and
> scared sentry, the sound of voluminous rifle fire and big guns,
> and above all a choking feeling. Our dug-out was already full of
> gas, and for a moment the terror of waking up to such a situation
> properly put the wind up both Eyre (who shared my dug-out)
> and myself. I could not at first find my gas helmet, and began to
> splutter and choke, but eventually I got it fixed on, and went out
> to get to business at once. And how terrible it was! The gas was
> rolling across towards us in thick whitish-yellow clouds; men were
> running about with their weird-looking gas-helmets on, and shells
> were bursting all around. It was, of course, quite dark and, as each
> shell burst, it caused a tremendous crash and a horrible flash of fire.
>
> As I emerged from my dug-out there seemed to be a hundred
> big shells bursting, lighting up everything. The noise of all these
> tons of high explosives bursting all round was almost unbearable,
> and then to put the tin hat on it, every British gun in the vicin-
> ity began to pound away at top speed. It took me some time to

realise what was happening but I soon got information and orders that there was a gas attack on in the front line and we were to man the reserve trenches at once. A number of men were already gassed, but we got into those trenches amid a huge bombardment and expected to see the Boche coming across at any moment. The men began to stifle and choke, and the shells were doing a great deal of damage amongst our troops but they stuck it wonderfully. The gas still came over in great clouds and the shelling continued unceasingly.

They evidently anticipated a big attack as they were peppering all the roads, rails and communications up which reinforcements might be brought, and were simply battering our reserve position to nothing, they seemed to be using every big gun they had, and were sending over every kind of shell from a 17-inch down to a small whizz-bang. The noise was appalling and nerve wracking, and there was no cessation for three hours. Then the gas began to thin and the shelling toned down, and the joyous news came through that our two companies in the front line had repulsed the first German attack.

Their ordeal was not yet over:

We stood to all that Sunday morning, strained and waiting after 3½ hours under gas and shell-fire and without food, and then came the order for us to go up to the front trench to relieve the companies who had had a shocking time. We'd already had a lot of casualties and Willis was horribly wounded early on, and Iveson knocked out by shell-shock. Iveson had recovered splendidly by the time we went up into action however, and we'd just got the company formed up and were starting up the road from our reserve trenches, when we got a 'Jack Johnson' right into us and laid out a lot of good fellows. We had a nasty job getting right up, but we manned that front line, and were ready for the Huns coming over. They did not attack again on Sunday but we were on the watch all night and early the next morning, they gassed again, but we did not allow them to get into our trench, and all day Monday we potted away hard, until by the evening the show seemed about over, and the Germans gave up the idea of getting through.

Though the fury of attacks ebbed, gas and shells continued to arrive:

They gave our line a furious strafing to finish up with though, and Eyre got two wounds in the hand and back, and another 16th officer, Hickson, had been gassed previously; well, we hung on until late that night, and then came out; of course getting shelled and machine-gunned coming out. We got back about 0200 hours on Tuesday. We had been without rest or food for nearly 48 hours; been under gas for over three hours at one time, and I just collapsed, but am alright again now, except for sickness and headache, owing to that devilish gas ... The effect of the whole show on one's nerves defies definition, but with all those millions of tons of high explosives flying about, it seems as if something must break in the head – but one just hangs on and hopes.

As ever in the maelstrom, odd anecdotal details stuck in the mind:

One thing I must tell you, before I stop and that is about a little bit of diversion during the gas attack. I had just been bandaging up a couple of wounded, when one of them called my attention to a couple of big rats which were staggering about on their hind legs as though drunk. It really was one of the funniest sights imaginable. One usually gets only glimpses of rats as they scuttle rapidly by during the day, but these two were right out in the open, and their antics were too quaint. They were half-gassed of course but strangely enough it was one of the things I remembered best after the show was over – one good thing the gas did was to kill a lot of the little beasts!

†

'The Things That Matter'

'Twas in the war, nineteen fifteen, at early dawn one day.
Our orders were to take the trench which opposite us lay.
The battle raged around us fierce, the air was thick with shell,
But no man flinched as we advanced to drive the Hun to hell.
Our object gained, we paused awhile to get our breath much needed
(And all this time, I'd have you know, the battle still proceeded)
The ground behind us now was swept by all the hostile guns,
To stop reserves from coming up – a habit of the Huns.
On glancing back, to my surprise I suddenly observed
From out the smoke a figure rush, a VC he deserved;
'Go back' I cried, 'Go back at once' – my words passed quite unheeded
(And all this time, as I've remarked, the battle still proceeded).
He reached our trench though wounded thrice and, as he fainted,
A message form into my hand, that gallant soldier planted. 'What's
this?' I gasped, as I read out the message written there,
'Report at once the method used by you to cut men's hair.'
'No time to lose' I shouted out; 'now who will volunteer
To take the answer back "at once", though 'twill be late I fear?'
'Let me go, sir' the cry went up from every lusty throat.
I picked a man, then sat me down, and this reply I wrote.
The method used by me to cut the hair of men who need it
Is sometimes just to burn it off, and other times to weed it
And often rasps are used instead; these latter cause some bleeding
(I'd like to add, to let you know, the battle's still proceeding).
With bated breath we watched him start, the gallant man selected
To take the message back to those by whom it was expected.
'Twas with relief we saw him gain a spot from whence we knew
He could proceed with safety with his message to HQ.
'The war is won', I told my men. 'No need to use our rifles
While those behind look after us, we need not think of trifles,
Such as the Hun in front of us or when it's time for feeding'
(But all the same, I'm loath to say, the battle's still proceeding!)
– Anon.[65]

FOUR

SOMME, 1916

'Puzzled'

With occasional eatin' and drinkin'
An' just forty winks now and then
An' work on the trenches
Along o' the Frenchies
We don't get much time for thinking,
We men!

An' what me an' my company ain't yet made out,
Is wot's this 'ere culture they're talkin' about?
Though we don't get no 'Specials' we've had a
Round dozen who tell the same tale
How Germans will pillage
A poor little village
And quiet the natives by murder
Wholesale.

An' what me an' my company ain't yet made out,
Is wot's this 'ere culture they're talkin' about?
They slash up the pictures with sabres,
Which seems a bit spiteful an' odd,
Wi' search lights they shows up,
The churches they blows up
An' [Kaiser] Bill when they've ended their labours,
Thanks God!

An' what me an' my company ain't yet made out,
Is wot's this 'ere culture they're talkin' about?
Then the brave kindly men will strip lasses
An' mothers and wives to their skin
And when they're a-cryin'
An' hopin' they're dyin'
Will jeer at each one as she passes
An' grin!

An' what me an' my company ain't yet made out,
Is wot's this 'ere culture they're talkin' about?
I'm reckoned an 'ot argumenter
An' fust-rate at waggin' me chin
But sharp as a bay'nit
I can't explain it
An' shan't till we've licked 'em an' enter Berlin

An' what me an' my company ain't yet made out,
Is wot's this 'ere culture they're talkin' about?[66]

Verdun

On 21 February 1916, German shells came screaming over innocuous country to herald the assault on Verdun. The city, situated in north-east France, guarded the route to Paris. At the heart of the city lay the Citadel, whose complex of underground tunnels provided accommodation for her troops. Ringed by a circle of eighteen large underground forts and twelve smaller redoubts, Verdun was formidable.

This great bastion, strategically remote but imbued with intense and lasting lustre for the French, could not be allowed to fall. Erich Falkenhayn, who had replaced the burned-out shell of von Moltke, did not particularly care if it fell. Rather his intention was to draw the French into a fiery cauldron that would consume their armies, grind them down in bloody unending attrition till France lay prostrate. Falkenhayn believed she very nearly was and that this huge blow might finish her off. Cannily, he had already deduced that Britain was fast becoming the major opponent and, by knocking France out of the ring, he would seriously weaken the English effort.

Verdun tortured the very heart of France and, in part, all that Falkenhayn had predicted occurred. What he had not foreseen were the depths of French resilience and the equally dreadful losses Germany would suffer. The Germans launched their last major attacks in the third week of June but the horror ground on until autumn mud forced a halt. Neither side could lay claim to anything resembling victory. Verdun heralded the dawn of a new age of suffering. None of the earlier battles, terrible as these had been, could compare with the bloodletting at Verdun. The very name became synonymous with a new kind of earthly hell.

At the Chantilly Conference in December 1915, Sir Douglas Haig and General Joffre had discussed ideas for joint offensives in 1916. Haig was by no means confident of his ally's capacity to do more and was increasingly (and correctly) of the view that Britain must shoulder the greater burden. A week before Verdun furiously erupted, the two commanders met again. The concept of a major joint offensive astride the River Somme was, at least in general terms, agreed with a proposed start date of 1 July. Haig was not a fan of the Somme area. Strategically it had little to offer. As ever, he preferred to look toward Flanders.

Verdun changed all this. Without Haig's full support it was feared the French would crumble. When, on 26 May, Haig informed his ally that his New Army divisions would not be ready till perhaps August, Joffre was appalled. The French, he expostulated, might very well not survive that long. Haig rather drily observed that a fine vintage brandy calmed Joffre's Gallic nerves most admirably. That the British would attack in the Somme was now a given. Haig's misgivings were secondary to his need to prop up Britain's ally before the weight of German blows proved too much.

> Beef steaks when you are hungry,
> Best beer when you are dry,

Fivers when you are hard up,
Heaven when you die!
– Private M. Gill, 8th Battalion Leicesters

The Plan

On 1st July 1916, the first day of the battle of the Somme, many
thousands of Englishmen, mostly young English men – were
killed. That was a day of terrible, heavy casualties and it was our
first experience on a great scale of the bloodiness of modern war.
Two thousand men were killed trying to cross a piece of ground
not as big as Orchard Field; trying, for they failed. It is no use
trying to describe the conditions during a great attack for, since
my own experience of them, I have always been convinced that
no one who had not been there could possibly even imagine the
effect on body and mind of all that is heard and seen and felt by
those who are taking part.
– Stanley Purvis MA, sermon, November 1943[67]

General Henry Rawlinson, leading the 4th Army, now held the right
of the British line and the brunt of the coming battle would be
borne by divisions under his command. The fight would be spread
over a front of some twenty miles, across the deceptively mild chalk
downs of Picardy, from Foncquevillers in the north to Mericourt in
the south where the British and French sectors would intersect on
the line of the River Somme. Much of the British sector lay on the
line of the Ancre and some felt the battle should have been named
accordingly but by then it was too late. The Somme featured too
prominently in the public consciousness. It still does.

In an age where history is often disregarded and dimly understood, those who have heard anything about the Great War will
probably have heard of the Somme. As with Verdun for the French,
it symbolises the loss of a generation, a frightful gobbling up of
blood and manhood for seemingly trifling gains. Some writers,
even those as rightfully revered as the late Sir John Keegan, have

asserted that after the Somme Britain declined irreversibly and was ruined as surely, if less evidently, than France.

Along the otherwise insignificant ridge running from Thiepval to Ginchy, the Germans had turned sleepy hamlets into bristling fortresses: Serre, Thiepval, La Boisselle and Fricourt. Their front line studded with strong redoubts, with successive belts riding the crests of ridges behind, like spume on breakers, were each a major tactical problem in itself. Chalk, firm and clear to Tommies after the mud and slop of Flanders, was ideal for carving deep dugouts; the enemy line was immensely strong and utterly formidable. Rawlinson himself was an advocate of 'bite and hold': a series of limited assaults, each quickly consolidated and then built up in readiness for the next. Haig needed rather more. He had to have breakthrough, a smashing of the enemy line and a clear run for his cavalry to Bapaume, up the dead straight Roman road from the town of Albert. This would signal victory and his political masters demanded no less.

Rawlinson diplomatically, if with reservations, bowed to his superior's wishes but insisted on massive, drenching bombardment as a necessary prelude. A continuous deluge of fire so utterly over-whelming it would crush the enemy front-line defences to dust and decimate the troops holding it. Kitchener's New Army men would be the main attacking force and it was feared their training was insufficient to instil complex 'fire and movement' tactics. Instead, they would move forward from their start lines in four orderly waves, rifles sloped, and walk towards the enemy front line which would simply be theirs for the taking.

Charles Moss, now Lance-Corporal and commanding a Lewis Gun section of the Durham Pals and who had first seen action during the defence of Hartlepool in December 1914, remained very much a product of the radical tradition. He was scathing about the direction of the war and the scant regard paid to the efforts of the PBI (poor bloody infantry):

Dispatches sent by war correspondents to the censored capitalist press never did justice, or give reasonable insight actions of the rankers … how we used to laugh and scoff at the War Office threadbare communiqué 'All Quiet on the Western Front'. We knew that during the period covered by the communiqué, there had been terrific bombardments, bombing raids, fighting patrols, wiring parties, trench digging, mine-tunnelling and many other dangerous activities, especially at night that meant hard work, constant courage, ceaseless vigilance, disciplined conduct, the loss of life and limb…

Our battalion was in reserve, with the exception of 'D' Company, part of 93rd Brigade, 31st Division commanded by General Sir Aylmer Hunter-Weston. The other battalions in the Brigade were the Leeds and Bradford Pals of West Yorkshire Regiment. The Leeds Pals with our own 'D' Company were to be the first wave over the top followed at half-hour intervals by the Bradfords and then our battalion with the object of hold-ing that part of the line captured by the West Yorks. It was to be our job to consolidate the position against German counter-attacks. Our 'D' Company had a special job in the first wave to link the Leeds Pals with the Seaforth Highlanders on our right,[†] 'D' Company had a special objective, to capture the fortified position called Pendant Copse. The sector of our attack was in front of the village of Collincamps and nearly opposite to Beaumont Hamel held by the Germans: our Division had done the trench duties and worked on this part of the front, digging telephone and assembly trenches since we arrived from Egypt in April 1916.[68]

Their training had at least been not been completely neglected:

We did not know that we were preparing for an attack until we had a sort of rehearsal of the plan and method of attack a few weeks before the time to 'go over'. A miniature copy of the

---

† The Brigade was part of VIII Corps tasked, on 1 July 1916, with the attacks on Serre and Beaumont Hamel; gains were negligible and losses extremely high.

German trenches had been prepared for this purpose on the open country a few miles behind our billets. A few brass hats explained the plan of attack, the timing of the attacking waves, the control of the artillery barrage and the formation of each battalion wave. Then each battalion practised their part in it. The Leeds Pals were to be first over and capture the German front line, each man a few paces apart with loaded rifle carried at port and with bayonet fixed. The Bradford Pals were to follow in the same manner and pass over the top of the Leeds Pals to capture the second and third lines of trenches. Our battalion was then to follow and make strongpoints to hold the front at all costs against enemy counter-attacks.

Charles Moss was no respecter of fools and maintained a healthy disdain for those above who knew not what they did:

I was shown exactly where my Lewis Gun post was to be but when I asked the officer what my field of fire would be like he couldn't tell me. I pointed out that the sort of country in front was the most vital thing for me to deal with enemy counter attacks, he resented my calling his attention to this, and all he could say was that I would find that out when we got there. I thought that was a poor lookout when so much depended upon this very necessary information and told him so.

There was to be two sets of distinguishing marks to be included in our equipment. All ranks of the West Yorks would have a triangle-shaped piece of tin, cut from empty biscuit tins, fastened to their backs, so that the airmen who were going to watch the progress of the attack from the air, would be able to recognise our men and report to HQ how the attack was going. Also each man had a few pieces of coloured tape fastened to his shoulder straps and hanging down his back so that the battalions would be able to recognise each other as no regimental badges or numerals were to be worn. Each colour represented the colour that had been given as a name to the trench they were to capture.

It was essential that the bombardment should not only crush the
Germans huddled in their deep dugouts but it should also cut those
dense belts of barbed wire. In many instances the shells failed to do
their work. Some were duds and inexperienced gunners were not
sufficiently adept at cutting their fuses just right to part the strands.
Intelligence and patrolling produced only garbled reports. By now
the offensive, this imperative for action had assumed a dreadful
momentum of its own. Any note of dissonance was heretical.

Those who had doubts, and there were many, including Rawlinson,
kept these to themselves and permitted no mutterings by others.
The deadly equation was defined as 'the race for the parapet'. If the
attackers could cross no man's land and occupy front-line enemy
trenches before those defenders who survived could bring their
weapons, particularly their machine guns, into action then they
would win the day. If not they would pay a heavy price.

The start of the attack had been fixed for June 28th but it rained
so heavily for about a week before that, despite the terrific
bombardment by our artillery, most of the German barbed wire
entanglements were still as strong as ever on the 28th. These barbed
wire defences were a great wonder to me; all the daring hard work
there had been put into them. They were a great, massive rusty
wire wall built along the whole of the Western Front. They were
about five or six feet high and three to four yards deep in most
places built up on strong wooden and iron stakes, the German
wire always looked a far better job than ours, the Jerries were out
working on their wire every night. Every break our artillery made
in their wire during the day, they repaired during the night, and
on June 28th their wire was still as strong, despite our terrific
and long bombardment that the attack was put off until July 1st
… It was impossible to get any sleep during the night because of
a heavy, long-distance battery and a great howitzer belching all
night long.

We were on fatigues during the day, carrying ammunition and
'plum-pudding' mortar shells to dumps near the front line. The

shells were brutes to carry. They were about the size of a football with a steel shank attached. Many of these never reached the drops because many of the carriers, to save themselves from struggling down the trench with them, just tipped them into the deep gullies that crossed the communication trenches, everybody remained in good spirits despite all the rain and mud and bad feeding arrangements and the filthy and verminous condition we were all in.

Charles Moss's platoon officer, Lieutenant Simpson, had asked the Lance-Corporal to volunteer for a night-time mission out into no man's land where he and the subaltern would attempt to report on the state of German wire. As he'd been on exhausting supply duty all day, Moss was excused, though pleased his officer reposed so much confidence in him, 'it would have been a miracle if we'd got back alive'. During Friday 30th, the battalion took up positions in the line south of Collincamps, finding rough and ready billets in 'the ruins of a badly strafed chateau'. In the evening their CO briefed the Durhams on their role in the forthcoming attack:

There was to be no turning back, every man must advance at a steady pace. All officers had authority to shoot anyone who stopped or tried to turn back. The wounded had to be left to be attended to by the stretcher bearers and RAMC [Royal Army Medical Corps]. The grimmest order to me was that no fighting soldier was to stop to help the wounded. The CO was very emphatic about this. It seemed such a heartless order to come from our CO who was a Brigadier-General of Church Lads Brigades and looked upon as a religious man (I thought bringing in the wounded was how Victoria Crosses were won). We spent the rest of the evening being issued with field dressings, extra ammunition, picks and shovels, camouflaging our tin hats with scraps of sandbag and sharpening bayonets.

There was a good deal of light-hearted talk amongst groups of us concerning what we should do when we got into the German dugouts. We had heard they were well supplied with cigars and sausages. I was very fond of some Medalcion Cigars which I had bought while on holiday in Hamburg so I arranged I would swap any cigarettes or sausages I found for any cigars that they found.

That evening, in the deepening dusk, the Durhams marched via a railway hollow to the communication trench, 'called Eczema all the time we had used it for front-line duties but it had been renamed Southern Avenue for the purposes of the attack'. German artillery was zeroed on the entrance and the Tommies had to dash between shell-bursts.

The Germans had intensified their bombardment of Collincamps and the village was soon enveloped in flames. As the fire reached the ammunition that was stored in the village, the explosions of the Stokes Shells Mortar which had a specifically shattering effect and the peculiar rattling effect of small-arms ammunition added to the shrieking, whining and crashing of both British and German artillery, made deafening pandemonium complete … the fitful glare of the fire broke the cover of darkness across the open plain on our left towards Hebuterne. We could see in a lurid glow sections of troops moving slowly forward towards the trenches. The whole awesome scene was lifted so much above reality to me that, although some of us were setting out to be killed, wounded, taken prisoner or to win glory none of those thoughts entered my head. I was too fascinated by the mightiness of the spectacle … I had no thoughts for anything else.

Merely reaching the front line was both hard and tiring for the overladen Tommies:

It was slow and hard work to get along that Railway Trench. We so often had to fling ourselves down in the trench to avoid the shrieking shells. When we reached the entrance to Southern Avenue, the area was so crowded with troops that it was some time before we got into it. It was marvellous how each section kept together in such a mix up. We were all carrying so much it was like a free-fight to move at all.

Over and above our ordinary equipment, rifle, ammunition and bayonet, I had a khaki bandolier full of .303 [calibre] six loaded Lewis Gun magazines carried in a horse's nose-bag because we hadn't enough proper containers available, two Mills Bombs and a pick with the shaft stuck down behind my haversack and we were called 'light' infantry! But most ironical of all was the dirty tricks our clumsy bad-fitting tin-hats played us; if the chin-strap wasn't trying to strangle us, the 'soup-basin' was falling over our eyes to blind us. Steel helmets always got more curses than blessings from us. After many stops and much struggling, falling down and getting caught in signallers' telephone wires we reached our assembly trench at about 4 a.m. on Saturday 1st July.

1 July 1916

'The Tyneside Scottish at the Battle of the Somme'

Now listen to my story
I won't keep you long
It's about the Tyneside Scottish
And the Battle of the Somme
It was on July the First
When the Scottish made to attack
The shells began to burst
But that didn't keep them back

Oh, it was a terrible day,
They fought with all their might
Poor fellows, they were falling
Both on the left and right
And when all was over
I am sorry to relate
All that we could number was

One hundred and twenty-eight
Now my friends, remember
What the local lads have done –
They fought and died for their country's sake,
At the Battle of the Somme
– Private M. Woodhouse, 1st Battalion Tyneside Scottish[69]

Charles Moss and the Durham Pals were very near the front of the front as dawn broke:

The trench was just a temporary assembly one, about four feet deep without any firestep or proper parapet. It was dug just to afford a bit of protection from machine-gun and rifle fire, while we waited to move to our jumping-off trench in readiness to go over. Most of us got into the assembly trench in pretty fair condition. Our artillery was blazing away, a terrific bombardment of the German lines. The Germans themselves were comparatively quiet until about 6 a.m. They must have waited till we were all in position, then they opened up on us with all they had and in every calibre. There was no need for them to do any range-finding, they were dead on our front at once. Along on my left, there was soon word being passed along for stretcher bearers [DLI].

We heard that several of our company had been hit by their first salvo; the trench was so shallow I was having to crouch low into the front of it but, regardless of the danger, Lieutenant Simpson kept moving up and down the trench with his head and shoulders in full view of the Germans. I told him he was 'asking for it' but he took no notice and kept on having a word here and there with the fellows while we waited. At 7.30 a.m. – Zero Hour time for the first wave to go over, we heard a great heavy rumbling thud which was the exploding of our great mine.[†] This mine is recorded

---

† The Hawthorne Ridge Mine, one of ten exploded by the BEF on 1 July, went up at 07.20 hours, ten minutes prior to the infantry attack. Despite the huge blast, that short gap allowed the Germans an opportunity to bring up machine guns to cover the enormous crater.

in the official account as being the greatest mine that had ever been blown.

This flank of the attack from Serre to Beaumont Hamel was to prove disastrous and costly, producing no tangible gains though some of the Durham Pals did penetrate as far as Pendant Copse. A few even struggled through as far as the ruins of Serre. Without support, they were inevitably picked off.

I wanted to see how our attack was going so I moved some of the chalk on the front of the trench in such a way that I could be protected from German sniper fire and took a good look at the German line in front of us. But all that I could see was fountains of chalk and smoke sent up by our artillery barrage. It was like watching heavy seas roaring onto Hendon Beach as I have seen during winter storms. Whilst I was watching I saw the barrage lift and storm further back over the third German line. As it got clear of one of the German trenches, out onto the top came scrambling a German machine-gun team. They set up their gun in front of their parapet and opened up a slow and deadly fire on our front. The gunners were without their tunics and worked the gun in their shirt sleeves in quite a different manner to their usual short, sharp bursts. Their fire was so slow that every shot seemed to have a definite aim. Except for that gun team there wasn't another solider either in British Khaki or German grey to be seen.

There was only one other visible occupant of this vast battlefield that morning: the 'Mad Major', an unknown Allied pilot who regularly swooped over the German trenches. Incidents in the trenches continued.

Just as I spotted the German machine-gunners come into action, we got the word to move to our 'jumping-off' trenches and to be ready to go over. We had to cross a communication trench to get there and as I got into this trench I nearly bumped into a soldier who seemed to be carrying a big piece of raw meat resting on his left arm, he was doing a sort of crying whimper and saying 'why have they done this to me? I never did them any harm.' Then I realised it was the remains of his right forearm he was carrying in such a way. Many more soldiers were making their way up the trench, they were walking wounded going to the advanced dressing stations of which there were several dug into the sides of the communication trenches.

When we got into our jumping-off trench I found it was in one of those deep hollows that were peculiar to this part of the front, and was called 'dead ground' because of the protection it afforded. Part of it was occupied by our battalion HQ. The CO & Adjutant were there. As soon as I got there I found out something had gone wrong with our procedure, because Lance-Corporal Fletcher had been called away with No. 1 gun. The arrangement had been that No. 1 gun was to stay with HQ but as it had gone I had to remain with HQ with my gun. A little further along the trench there were some scaling ladders up which some of our fellows were climbing. 'Big Lizzie' – the nickname we had given this officer – was brandishing a revolver, shouting and urging them up the ladders. I watched this for a minute or two when down into the hollow came Corporal Forshaw, one of the battalion runners. He was very excited and was shouting as he came, something to the effect 'the whole show is a b***s up!'

The CO spoke to him but I could not hear what he said for the infernal row of the shell fire but the CO came near and shouted to 'Big Lizzie', 'wait a moment, Mr ******* a minute or two will neither win nor lose this battle'. The officer at once stopped waving his revolver and stopped the fellows who were climbing the ladders, and then they all crouched down at the bottom of the trench. In that moment, along came an Army Corps runner and handed the CO an envelope. The CO opened it, read the message it contained and striking a dramatic attitude he turned to the Adjutant and said 'Ah, ah Mr Lowes, this is where we come in' and he read the message; 'Your attack has failed, 18ᵗʰ DLI take over the front line from Point to Point.'

Lance-Corporal Moss had cause to thank providence for delivery from near certain death, if not delivery at least postponement. Had there been no confusion over the placing of the Lewis Gun teams and had the runner not arrived, Charles Moss and his comrades would have gone over the top at that point and been shot to pieces as had so many of those who had gone before. The first of July 1916 was the bloodiest in the history of the British Army. A total of 57,470 casualties were sustained, some 19,240 of these were fatalities. German machine guns did fearful execution and, with the exception of the southern part of the line, hardly any gains were made. Names such as Serre and Beaumont Hamel would be synonymous with bloody failure, made worse by the extreme heroism of Kitchener's civilian soldiers. Some like the 36ᵗʰ (Ulster) Division, north of Thiepval, fought like tigers and hacked out illusory gains, all briskly eliminated by powerful, local counter attacks.

If Charles Moss had been temporarily spared, the Durham Pals still had a surfeit of woe ahead:

The CO & Adjutant had a brief consultation, and then the CO gave 'Big Lizzie' an order to muster as many men as he could and occupy that part of the front line which had been allotted to us. The artillery fire was much quieter by the time we reached what had once been the front-line trench but it was impossible to tell it from no man's land. Most of the revetting and fire-steps had been blown in. The whole of the front was an awful chaos of duck-boards, sandbags, and stakes, and wire netting, barbed wire and dud shells, tumbled and strewn about. It was impossible to recognise a revetment from a fire-bay. Amongst this awful wreck were the dead bodies of what appeared to be a Leeds Pals Lewis gun team, with their gun and drums of ammunition lying near them. One of my team picked up the Lewis gun and we took it with us making two guns for the rest of the time we were in the front line.

One of these dead soldiers was a horrible sight; a shell must have burst so near to him that it had ripped all the uniform and flesh from the front of his body. I was surprised to see a black retriever roaming about but it disappeared down the remains of a dugout when we got near it. This dog was the only living thing we saw as we struggled along the front line. Most of the West Yorks and our 'D' Company had been killed or wounded in their assembly trenches on our sector during the intense bombardment before Zero Hour, this was coupled with the tactical mistake on our High Command's part in having a fixed time for the lifting of our artillery barrage from one German trench to the next after Zero which meant that when the barrage was lifted off the German second line it allowed them to bring their machine guns out of their deep dugouts and fire them on top in comparative safety, while our barrage during that tragic half hour was concentrated for that fixed period on the German third line.

Moss and his comrades learned from the few survivors that the whole of the first three attacking waves had been savaged either prior to or immediately after zero hour. Many had not survived long enough even to get out of the British trenches. Scything MG fire and a hurricane of shells had winnowed those who did.

After seeing the dog disappear, my gun team and I kept on struggling along the trench past several bodies of West Yorks until we reached a position well to the left of the Lewis Gun post I knew so well. I had been in charge of this post when we did our ordinary front-line duties. It was at the corner of the road that led from Mailly-Mailly to Serre. This road was part of no man's land for some distance. It was about forty yards wide at this point and commanded by the famous German Quadrilateral Redoubt. The whole front had gone very quiet along here and, during the afternoon, I set up our Lewis Gun a bit north of Rob

Roy Communication trench not far from Fonquevillers [swiftly anglicised by Tommy as 'Funky-Villas'].

Despite the scale of carnage, no Tommy ever neglected an opportunity for productive scrounging:

A good deal of webbing equipment was lying about in this sector. It had been thrown off by the wounded when they got hit, so we stripped off our leather equipment and put on webbing in its place. We had been issued with leather equipment when the battalion was first formed but we found that leather shoulder straps cut into our shoulder when we were in full marching order. Webbing was much easier to wear and had a more fighting-soldier-like appearance, so we weren't long in dumping the leather, changing into webbing and feeling more like seasoned troops.

There was so few of us to hold this part of the line that I thought what a walkover the Jerries would have if they were to attack us. This was the only chance we had had to get anything to eat and I was especially thankful for a packet of Sunmaid raisons I had received in a parcel I had from my sister in Winnipeg. Most of the food and water we got had a filthy taste because of all the chlorination there was in it but those raisons went down well with some of the hard wheaten biscuits that I liked to crunch so much. We had a reasonable rest until it was dark then we moved into no man's land and set up the Lewis guns in a shell-hole. To get into no man's land we had to pass one of those deep hollows with a few bushes growing in them. This one may have been St John's or St Paul's Copse. As we passed the place, we could hear many awful moans and agonised cries for stretcher-bearers coming from the depth of the hollow. Many of the badly wounded had managed to struggle into this place for protection from shell and machine-gun fire...

So ended the first day of the Battle of the Somme. There were 140 days left to go.

High Summer

There are several sorts of peaches,
But I find in you alone
The one that's full of sweetness
And without a heart of stone.
– Private W. G. Glenn, 9th Battalion Royal Inniskilling Fusiliers
(wounded near Thiepval, 8 May 1916)[70]

Rawlinson's idea which, as Richard Holmes points out, was the novel one of reinforcing failure, involved more costly and fruitless attacks on those strong points where earlier costly and fruitless attacks had failed. In the south, opportunities beckoned. Attacks put in on 3 July did indeed gain ground though it took another nine bloody days to secure Mametz Wood. On 14 July, the 4th Army mounted a dazzling night attack with a full and effective bombardment. The infantry was preceded by a hurricane fire, brief but devastating. Significant gains were made for, by Somme standards, modest losses. This was 'bite and hold' in the best sense but it was not a breakthrough. Far from it; those key areas of Delville and High Wood remained in German hands and the taking of both would be long-drawn-out and terrible.

Manning their outpost in no man's land during the night of 1/2 July, Charles Moss and his comrades had no leisure for pondering on grand tactics:

The darkness of the night was often broken by brilliant light from arching Verey lights [flares launched from a gun] being fired across no man's land. As each light died out, we were blinded, the darkness being deeper than ever. The sudden change from blackness to such weird and ghostly light thrown onto the tragic shapes of the charred stumps of trees whose tops had been blasted off during previous bombardments made the place such a terrible eerie sight, that I felt as though I was no longer in the civilised world.

People have heard a lot about Hell, but no one has come back from there to tell us what it really is like. I know I was very near to it as the red light from the star shell and explosions fell on the hollow, whilst the cries of despair from the wounded mingled with the Devil's tattoo of rifle and machine-gun fire. We thought the Germans might send a bombing raid over so we'd had to struggle out into no man's land where we got into a big shell hole and set to with picks and shovels to make it into a Lewis gun post.

One of my gunners 'got the wind up' very badly. He would dash himself from one side of the hole to the other at each shell-burst. I was urging him to keep still in the bottom of the hole when he gave a great gasp and groaned 'Death, oh death! They've knocked a bloody hole right through us'. He scrambled out of the shell-hole before anyone could help him and I saw no more of him till I reached the 3rd Battalion at South Shields in 1917 where I found that the shrapnel had wounded him in the shoulder and given him a Blighty that got him to England.

Next morning the gun team had scrambled back to the wrecked front line and 'stood to' with the remainder of 'C' Company. Despite their fragile position, no attacks came. Charles Moss and his comrades retired along a communication trench,

this was one of the shelters that had been used as an advanced dressing station. The duckboards inside were covered with a horrible mixture of blood and chalk puddle, used field dressings and the remains of hurried operations. It looked so repulsive that we were hesitating about going inside when there was the crash of a 5.9 shell a bit further down the trench, the blast from it nearly blew us inside and as the strafe continued close by we went inside and thought it best to stay there. We shovelled out, as best we could, the shocking evidence of the suffering of the wounded and the harrowing work of the 'worst paid' [first aid] wallahs. Then we set about cleaning our rifles, Lewis Guns and ammunition drums.

The rest of the gun-team had finished their issue of cigarettes, and seeing as we hadn't got any of those German cigars that we had joked about, I still had my issue of 'Ruby Queens' so I shared them out. I seldom smoked my issue and often came to their rescue at a time like this. What strange brands we had dished out to us. What a rare luxury a Woodbine was to many of the fellows. The army cooks had found where we were and sent a container of bully beef stew down to us. This was the first meal we had since we left Collincamps on the Friday night.

While we were in the shelter the talk amongst the team became very morbid and downhearted. They would persist in talking about the cruel and gruesome sights they had seen, and how easily such things could happen to them. One of the youngest, a lad of about 17, was becoming very distressed as the despondent talk continued. I realised I would have to get their minds onto other and more cheerful things, so when one of them passed the remark that had become a favourite army saying when things were looking black, 'it's a bloody good job we've got a navy', I took this as my cue to turn the talk to ships and the sea. So I got them interested in some of my trips with the Merchant Navy, especially my trips to Europe on the Londonderry boats out of Seaham Harbour [his Lordship maintained a small squadron of armed coasters]. It was marvellous how they responded to the change of subject, the young gunner brightened up considerably and the rest of them stopped their depressing gossip.

At Agincourt in October 1415, particularly glutinous Somme mud had slowed down heavily harnessed French men-at-arms as they slogged forward into the arrow storm. It was wet, slithering, all-encompassing and everywhere. A wet summer churned chalk into mire, a dismal humid season dominated by the incessant roar of the guns. Artillery was fast becoming the regnant despot on the battlefield and though the British gunners had much to learn from their mistakes, they proved apt pupils. The Royal Flying Corps's local superiority gave them clear eyes.

This was not necessarily apparent to those mud-caked and weary survivors of the Durham Pals:

The position where we were was a sort of small salient. It over-looked a broad part of no man's land where there were many dead. These belonged mainly to the Hull Pals and KOYLI of 92nd Brigade. One of the dead soldiers was just about ten yards from us. At first sight you wouldn't think that he had been killed, because he had dropped onto one knee and steadied himself by putting the butt of his rifle on the ground, and there he stayed in an upright position balanced by the grip he had on the barrel of his rifle – a strange thing I noticed about him was that his moustache and beard had grown strong, stiff bristles since he was killed.

Prevailing German tactical doctrine, hammered home to local commanders by Falkenhayn, was that ground must firstly be held at all costs and, if lost, recovered at all costs. These grim summer battles of attrition cost both sides equally dear. In the course of this bitter, savage stalemate, the 4th Army sustained another 82,000 casualties, a butcher's bill undreamed of in previous, pre-industrial conflicts. Waterloo, a very great battle by the standards of the day, cost the British and their allies 17,000 dead and wounded. The Somme would cost at least twenty-seven times as many.

For the moment, as the July offensive was resumed south of the Durhams' positions, Charles Moss and his gunners remained largely out of harm's way:

At daylight on Tuesday morning we moved to the notorious Monk Trench. This trench was looked upon by our fellows as a suicide post because of the bad name it had for casualties while we were there on tours of duty. It was on a spur of high ground which overlooked the narrow part of no man's land. It was a favourite place for the Jerries to vent their hate in the shape of Minnies, coal-boxes and whizz-bangs. The weather had been close and overcast all that time from Zero Hour but, as we reached this trench, there came of a terrific thunderstorm and deluge of rain which poured into the trenches from the higher ground and the trench was soon filling up with water.

We had a setback right at the entrance to the trench, the man who was leading the gun-team backed away from a disembowelled body lying beside the firestep. I eventually led them into position where we found several of my platoon. One of my pals Corporal Charlie Cross had just found one of our 'D' Company officers wounded in a shell-hole and had him brought in, he'd lain there since Zero Hour. A year or two after I was demobbed I met this officer in Seaham harbour. He'd had both legs amputated but he was very bright about it and got out of his car to demonstrate how cleverly he could use the artificial legs with which he'd been fitted.

The storm had increased so much that we had to climb onto the parados to save ourselves from the danger of drowning. We had put the Lewis guns on the parapet in ground sheets, the chalk was bouncing up, driven by the force of the rain. I was having to shake the guns clear of chalk to prevent them getting buried in it. To have fired them would have been impossible. We were wondering what we could do to get the flood out of the trench when we saw two or three Jerries climb onto the parapet of their trench and start digging with those long handled shovels of theirs. They must have seen us because as the water came pouring out of their trench, one of them lifted the blade of his shovel into the air and waved a 'washout'. I at once gave them the same signal with the butt of my rifle. It seemed to me that this was an event that was apart from the ordeal and enmity of battle. The forces of nature had restored the sense of common humanity after all the carnage there had been since the battle started. Not a shot was fired on either side while we stood in danger of being drowned.

For the Durham Pals their current purgatory was nearly at an end; a company of the Gloucesters came up as their relief, 'splashing towards us, I was surprised to see that they were in khaki shorts'. Charles Moss and his gunners plodged back along Eczema trench, away from the front line.

> As we struggled along the trench I noticed a ground-sheet cover-
> ing a long body lying on the parapet. I wasn't surprised when I
> was told that it was the body of Lieutenant Simpson and that a
> sniper had got him in no man's land. His death meant very much
> to me. Apart from him being a very brave and pally officer, he was
> the only officer who had seen my previous exploits that he could
> have used to my credit when it came to the award of the Croix de
> Guerre which went to Sergeant Allison.
>
> It was nearly dark when we got out of the communication
> trench. Here we found a great dump where troops from other
> regiments who had been relieved were dumping fighting equip-
> ment they had salvaged from the battlefield. We had to leave on
> this dump the Lewis gun that we'd picked up. But when the gun
> we carried back to battalion was checked the next day, it was
> found, by its number, which we had not been able to check in
> the dark, that we had left our gun on the dump and brought
> back the one we'd found. This incident gave me further proof of
> the callousness and inflexibility of army routine and discipline.
> We had survived five days and nights of exhausting experiences
> but these stood for nothing in comparison to having brought the
> wrong gun back to Battalion!

Despite the suffering and horrors of their tour in the trenches, Charles Moss and his Pals had not quailed in their terrible ordeal. Their baptism on the Western Front had been both harrowing and relentless. Yet these were not regular soldiers; they were a citizen army:

> Our feelings had not been brutalised by our civilian occupations,
> we were not time-serving professional soldiers. Most of us had
> left soft jobs. We had in the ranks many with college and univer-
> sity educations, who had volunteered for the duration of the war.

When our battalion had been formed we had not been psychologically hardened for the hardship and mentality of the rank and
file regulars … I was deeply thankful to be able to answer the roll-
call that so many thousands would fail to do after the first phase
of the many phases of the criminal waste of men and material in
the Battle of the Somme.

It was part of the lore of the Western Front that German dugouts
were far better constructed and, by comparison, luxurious. The
Germans had, after all, chosen the line they intended to defend and
had dug in for the long term. One of those who certainly appreci-
ated the finer points of enemy dugout-construction was Captain
Stanley Moffat of 5th Battalion NF who got his first taste of the
Somme during the humid summer.

3 August: … went to advanced HQ, a beautiful dugout with
about thirty steps down to it, painted white; inside a splendid
kitchen, with mirror and electric lights, had been a Boche dugout
and we'd captured it from them!
    The following day I visited many of the trenches and in
one of the old Boche ones saw a half buried British soldier, an
awful sight for me having just come out … 5th August; Seventy
Germans, headed by a captain dashed over to us and surrendered;
the Germans fired on them but did not hit anyone. They said
they'd come over on account of our heavy bombardment, rations
could not be brought up and they had not had food for nine days.
Five hundred men surrendered to the Anzacs, when they rushed
over they [the Australians] thought they were counter-attacking
and opened fire, killing three hundred, the survivors were
taken prisoner.
    9th August: Visited front line, saw many dead enemy lying
about and much booty … saw two graves on the Boche parapet. One was a German with the inscription 'here lies so-and-so
in God'. The other was French with the inscription; 'here rots
a Frenchman!'[71]

Despite the rocketing casualty lists reported in British newspapers, the press kept an upbeat tone in their carefully tailored view of the fighting:

We are now in the fourth week of the great British–French offensive, and although we have not secured anything in the way of sensational successes, splendid work is being done. There are no doubt many who, owing to the absence of the spectacular, follow the proceedings with little interest, and thereby do a great injustice to the men who are fighting so strenuously out there in the trenches. To the Germans our troops and our guns are accomplishing the impossible. They have all along declared that their positions were impregnable. They did not speak without good reason. Their trenches are made on the most elaborate plan. When bombarded they can retire to dugouts 20 and 30 feet below ground level, taking machine guns with them, when the infantry attack begins they are back in their places…

Our enemies, though not fighting with any real hope of recovering lost ground, are straining every nerve to prevent a further expansion of the British offensive. They are using up masses of men in their counter-attacks, and are not deterred by the fact that time after time their advancing lines have been broken without reaching our trenches. The battle fluctuates from day to day. Sometimes there is a lull; sometimes the German troops fling themselves against our newly won positions; sometimes our gallant push forward and seize a fresh point, often at heavy cost.[72]

Those at 'the sharp end' like Private W. Roberts of the DLI had a rather less measured view:

We were the fourth battalion to go over, which we did about an hour later. The short but terrible rush through the fierce curtain fire with men falling on all sides, I shall never forget high-explosive shells fell all round us. The sights I saw are too terrible to write about and men blown to pieces were lying side by side.

Unable to proceed further, the order to retire was given and I thanked God I came through the terrible ordeal unhurt. I went out to work in our front line at night but had to come away as it was almost blown to pieces. There again I saw dead and wounded lying side by side. Some were moaning and others had so far lost their reason that they were laughing and singing…[73]

Private Roberts, a native of Boston, Lincolnshire, died of wounds on 15 June 1917 and is buried in Duisans British Cemetery.

Such reflections were usually confined to private diaries (the keeping of which was of itself a breach of military discipline). When writing home, soldiers attempted, as a rule, to strike a lighter tone. Writing to his mother on 6 August, Lieutenant Frederick ('Eric') Rees made light of the wound he'd received:

At last I have a chance to get a letter off. I expect you have been looking out for one. Well, little mother at last I really have got some news. I have been one of the lucky ones and have what we call a nice, cushy little wound in the leg, quite a nice one and I am now settling down to enjoy it.

Now you are not to worry because I am not hiding anything or just making the best of it to you. I really am quite alright and as comfortable as the proverbial parasite. We were up in the front line and had a fairly warm night of giving old Mr Boche a warmer one and about 2 p.m. Saturday, were just thinking of being relieved by another regiment when a few shells came over and a bit caught me in the left leg above the knee, a shrapnel bullet which are round so it made quite a clean little hole. I rang up the Adjutant on the phone (sounds quite civilised doesn't it) and told him I was caught and made my way back to the doctor further down the trench. He bound me up then sent me out to a village about a mile behind. From there in a motor ambulance about four miles to a dressing station where I had some tea and then again by motor ambulance for a two hour journey right back to a hospital where I am now. I arrived just about dark last night;

was re-bandaged and retired to bed and had the best night's rest I've had for some time.[74]

Lieutenant Rees was born in Ireland in 1891 and attended Durham University. He joined 13th Battalion DLI at the outbreak and was deployed in December 1915. His wound (rather more serious than his letter suggests) was sustained in Munster Alley. He'd led a bombing party, taking prisoners and inflicting losses, capturing some sixty yards of trench until halted by a strong barricade, well wired in and beefed up with two Maxims. This proved an insurmountable obstacle and the Durhams set up their own barrier to consolidate ground won which they continued to hold against vigorous counter-attacks. Rees was awarded the MC for his actions and latterly served in Italy where, in October 1918, he was again wounded. Having survived the war and recovered from his injuries, he spent the remainder of his long life as a clergyman.

Sergeant Robert Constantine, writing home to brother Jim on 4 September, expresses the cynicism and weariness which had replaced those earlier, more naive enthusiasms:

We have now been out of the line about three weeks but we are training heavy to take part in the push and I am only wishing the war was finished before we go up, but no such luck; never mind I'll just have to take my chance the same as all the other boys.[75]

Meanwhile, on an entirely pragmatic note, there were some inedible rations:

We are getting awful grub just now and I don't see how I am sticking it and the small place we are in at present you can hardly buy anything fancy, 1½ francs or 1s 3d [6p] for a loaf of bread and tin stuff is awful dear, sardines 10d [4p] a tin, same in England for 2½d [1p], each boxed at that. The sooner this is over and I'm back home the better. I am getting properly fed up and sick of the damn job but it's no use grumbling, I'll have to stick it.[76]

Constantine, like so many tens of thousands, was never coming home. He was killed in action on 15 September 1916 – he has no known grave and is commemorated on the Thiepval Memorial.

One of the major technical innovations of the Great War was to be the tank. Regarded by Rawlinson and others as oddities, these new weapons would soon become increasingly important so that armies for the rest of the century would judge strength by the weight of their armour. Haig was optimistic and, by late summer, badly needed a decisive success. Still, when on 15 September the new leviathans rumbled forward at Flers-Courcelette slow, ungainly, yet still impressive, they achieved an immediate impact. German defenders, who had never encountered these armoured monsters except perhaps in nightmares, found their worst nocturnal terrors made real, noisy, alien, ponderous and seemingly invulnerable.

One of those who saw the new wonder weapons in action was Lieutenant Catford of 6th Battalion DLI. On 25 September he wrote:

Having seen the famous tanks both before going into action, when I inspected them very minutely, I am very much amused at the illustrations of them in the Press. Of course since it has been so stated in the papers, there is no harm in my telling you that we were in the great attack on the 15th. Our division did exceptionally well and not only reached all objectives but even advanced beyond them in some places to a distance of 800 yards. The whole show is very ghastly. Our artillery simply blew the Germans to bits and naturally their artillery which is both powerful and very efficient was not at all pleasant. We were to have made a second attack but as the Hun kindly walked away and obligingly gave up what was to have been our objective we simply took possession of it without any fighting. Would that the Boche always did this! It comes to the same thing in the end and he may as well give up his ground to us as fight for it.[77]

On 28 September Lieutenant Catford wrote again:

We have been having a very rough time of it lately. The army has again advanced and our division is exceeding all expectations. Yesterday I must admit we had a very anxious few hours. I had 21 casualties in my company alone and was also wounded myself. A huge shell burst on the parados of the trench killing two men, wounding three others and slightly wounding me. I had a very lucky escape and was fortunate in not losing my right eye. As it was I was blown clean off my feet, have several small wounds on the right side of my face and have my eye swollen and the eyelid bruised. I shall be none the worse for this shaking but of course am not feeling too frisky. As the CO wished to retain my services and as I am the senior officer left in the battalion, I decided to remain with my men and not leave the trench. The bravery of the men exceeds anything anyone could possibly imagine…

In the afternoon there was another big attack. Our artillery which is indeed too terrible for words simply blew the Germans to smithereens. The whole of their ground for about a mile back was absolutely one mass of terrific explosions followed by clouds of earth, limbs of men and debris, (I am now writing this in a captured German trench). Two days ago, we were a mile from here. When our infantry attacked yesterday afternoon, I think I witnessed the finest sight I have ever seen. Under a hurricane of shell and machine-gun fire they advanced as if on parade. A huge shell would drop amongst them; you would see the gap made in the line, but they never wavered, never even lost their dressing. Of course the Germans put up no fight at all … they are the greatest cowards directly you get close to them.

You would be amused if you could see me now. I am dressed just like a private soldier except I carry a revolver instead of a rifle and have a couple of bars on each shoulder. I have neither shaved nor washed for several days and am plastered all over with mud. In addition I look a very desperate character about the right side of my face … It is about three weeks since I was in a civilised and inhabited town.[78]

He penned what was probably his final letter on 30 September:

> I have only one officer left in my company. One left last night
> with shell-shock. I do not wonder at it seeing what we have to
> put up with. I expect to be on leave in a month's time and am
> looking forward to seeing you all. Tomorrow, we go into our big
> final attack. Do not worry if you don't hear from me for a day
> or two.[79]

Whether his injuries were more serious than he'd thought, or if
infection set in, or indeed if he was again hit, Lieutenant Catford
died of wounds on 5 October 1916 and is buried in Dernancourt
Communal Cemetery Extension on the Somme.

Captain John Evelyn Carr, a native of North Northumberland,
who served with the 11th Battalion Sherwood Foresters, 70th Brigade,
had been a pre-war Territorial. In August 1914, he was appointed
as a remount officer and furnished with 'a branding iron and various books including a cheque book, given full instructions and
a cheque for £100.00 placed to my credit in the bank for out of
pocket expenses'.[80] By September 1916, however, he was employed
on rather more dangerous work in the line near Martinpuich:

> My servant and I had two rather interesting experiences during
> the day. The first happened when we went up towards the front
> line to get a working party to clear out our dugout. I saw what I
> took to be a German sneaking about looking for cover. We had
> been having a lot of men sniped just behind our front line, I told
> my servant to give me his rifle as I felt very bloodthirsty and I
> meant to put this brute out of the way. My servant said 'Don't fire
> sir – he's an RE' [Royal Engineers]. I said he may be a German
> RE and let go at him. I then had a terrible feeling in case I had
> made a mistake but I felt nearly sure he was a German. We ran
> up and examined our prey. He was a Boche sure enough and I
> was quite justified in shooting him as he was fully armed and his
> pockets full of egg bombs.[81]

More followed:

> Our second jollification was when we were searching for furniture in the afternoon and I must say we were both nearly knocked out. We happened to enter a German dugout which looked rather promising and when we got into the front section there was a heap of about six to eight dead German officers and, as we went in, we were stifled by about a million bluebottles who flew out. We were nearly suffocated and I must admit I didn't have the pluck to examine them.[82]

Last Gasps

On taking over a billet in October, Charles Moss and the Durham Pals found this helpful ode written on the wall:

> Harken all ye whom duty calls
> To spend some time within these friendly walls,
> Others will sojourn here when you have passed,
> You were not the first and will not be the last,
> Therefore take heed and do what ye may,
> For safety or comfort while ye stay!
> Just put a sandbag here, a picture there
> To make a room more safe, a wall less bare,
> Think as you tread the thorny path of duty,
> Of comfort, of security, and beauty,
> So your successors when they come shall say
> 'A fine battalion we relieved today'.[83]

Autumn and the echo of bells that had rung out to celebrate success at Flers, where the lines had been advanced by as much as 2,500 yards, soon sounded hollow as fierce seasonal rains lashed the eviscerated landscape. The deluge flooded mud-sculpted ditches that passed for trenches, drenching the wilderness of craters, washing clean the whitened bones of the legions that had died, whose rotting remains polluted the ruined ground. Captain Moffat did find time to witness the RFC in action, a dash of chivalry amid the unending squalor below.

> 25 October: Saw a splendid aeroplane fight, a Boche plane fought with one of ours and forced him to land about 1500 yards behind our line. The Boche flew in within fifteen feet of the ground firing, set our plane on fire, wounded the pilot and got clear away!
>
> 12th November: At a conference, received more aeroplane photographs all through the night, company took up positions in the line. Next day: A beautiful morning, infantry all out in no-mans-land. At 05.45 prompt the artillery opened up a five minute bombardment. The ground was so heavy the attack [Serre] failed; our own casualties were around fifty percent and we took a hundred prisoners. The Fifth [Battalion] got as far as the fourth [German] line but was forced back. The [2nd] Suffolks were stuck in the mud up to their waists and mown down by machine-gun fire.[84]

Though further fighting was not formally called off till 18 November, general exhaustion and vile conditions meant the final gasps were sporadic. For the DLI battalions comprising 151 Brigade, there was to be one final test, yet bitterer and bloodier than those which had gone before. This was to be an assault upon the Butte de Warlencourt:

> Gird trench ran east and west from the Albert-Bapaume road towards Gueudecourt. On the left lay the Butte de Warlencourt, a mound or tumulus some forty feet high, reported to be an ancient burial-place similar to those found on Salisbury Plain. This, in September, when the Battalion first entered the Somme fighting, stood out from the surrounding country a green, conical-shaped hill. Of little or no strategic importance, except that it provided observation of all ground toward High Wood, Martinpuich and east of that village: It had been so battered by the daily shelling that all signs of vegetation had now disappeared and it stood a

shapeless, pockmarked mass of chalk. Beyond the Gird Trench lay a stretch of undulating country with Bapaume clearly visible in the distance, and midway almost hidden in a small valley, Le Barque. The remainder of the attack frontage held no special feature except a considerable amount of dead ground to the rear of the objective.[85]

The Butte, a squat carbuncle, lay like a gauntlet in the path of any further British advance. The Durhams of 151 Brigade (6th, 8th and 9th Battalions DLI) were to attack at 09.10 on 5 November. Their brigadier was Roland Bradford, who had won his VC in desperate fighting around Le Sars during the previous month. Roland, at twenty-five the youngest ever Brigadier-General in the British Army, and his brother George were to be the only siblings who both won the supreme accolade. Neither survived the war. Roland would die at Cambrai in November 1917, his brother in the course of the great Zeebrugge Raid on St George's Day, 1918.

At this late phase in the Somme Battle, conditions were dreadful; sodden, heaving ground churned into a noxious, cloying soup, raked and scarred by endless shelling; a featureless, mud garnished oblivion. Yet, despite Roland Bradford's deep misgivings, expressed in his letters to his family, the attack was to proceed. The brigade would advance each battalion with three companies up; four waves, thirty paces between each and in columns of platoons.[86] Their combined task was to secure the Butte itself, the quarry in front of it, sections of Gird and Gird Support trenches. Conditions were worse than ever, pounding rain matched the familiar, seemingly endless tattoo of guns. Wild wind buffeted the struggling Tommies, wading through deep muck, weighed by heavy pack and wet wool.

Lance-Corporal Harry Cruddace, 1/6th Battalion DLI was amongst those waiting for the order as dank, unfriendly dawn crept near. Every soldier was looking to his gear as zero hour crept near, a mean wet, bitter morning. Pals shook hands and wished each other well, stiff and soaked in the pre-dawn chill. The enemy, his antennae alert, kept up a ceaseless bombardment of the British trenches.

As ill luck would have it, the Durhams were to assault the German trenches at a point when the garrison was being relieved so the defenders would be far more numerous than anticipated. Harry Croudace and his comrades stumbled forward as the officers' whistles sounded the advance. The first wave was winnowed by a merciless and accurate fire, the second fared little better. Casualties were mounting and the Durhams were still lurching over no man's land. Dragged down by the sinking slime, the numbed Tommies inched forward into enemy fire:

Out of my two sections of fourteen men there were two of us left – a No. 1 on the gun by the name of Private Allen and myself. I pushed on with one gun and a quantity of ammunition to about 30 yards from the German trench and took up a position in a shell hole. We opened fire on the opposing troops who formed an excellent target. In taking up my position in the excitement I placed myself on the right side of the gun instead of on the left, which was fortunate for me. After firing one or two magazines, the enemy found us with a machine gun and succeeded in wounding my No.1 in four places down his left side.[87]

The hurricane of enemy fire cut swathes through 6th Battalion and the 8th were similarly winnowed, together with the Australians on their flank. Only 9th Battalion clawed out a precarious foothold in the German lines, a series of posts or mini-strongholds being carved from Gird Trench, the Butte and Quarry areas.

Bradford's men found their precious gains very hard to hold. Despite the skill of his deployment, the Germans were intent on ejecting the surviving Durhams. Artillery rounds and the angry buzz of snipers blew and snapped overhead:

The Germans in the dugout on the northeast edge of the Butte brought a machine gun into position and were worrying us from behind. Many gallant efforts were made throughout the day to capture this dugout without success. All our parties who tried to rush it were destroyed by the German machine-gun fire and the large numbers of snipers in Warlencourt.[88]

As morning dragged towards noon, sporadic counter-attacks began to nibble at the margins. These were seen off. During the early afternoon more determined efforts with bombing parties were also beaten back.

Though the Durhams held the Butte, that surviving enemy dugout was a constant menace. Successive attacks caused mounting casualties and the dense curtain of artillery shells ploughing the wastes of no man's land prevented any attempt to bring over reinforcements. Mid-afternoon and the pressure was relentless: 'We have been driven out of Gird Front Line and I believe my posts there are captured. I have tried to get back but the enemy is in considerable force and is still counter-attacking. It is taking me all my time to hold Butte Alley.'[89]

All through that long, wet autumn afternoon the Durhams clung with bitter tenacity to their shrinking enclaves:

> About 6 p.m. the Germans made a determined counter-attack preceded by a terrific bombardment and we were able to get to close quarters. A tough struggle ensued but our men who had now been reinforced by the Reserve Company and who showed the traditional superiority of the British in hand-to-hand fighting, succeeded in driving out the enemy.[90]

There was to be no respite. Darkness brought no relief from an increasing tempo of German assaults, outflanking the Durhams rapidly shrinking salient. As 5 November drew to a close, the bloodied and exhausted survivors were being forced back towards their own lines:

> The Germans still holding out in the Butte dugout came out and advanced over the Butte. The enemy advanced throwing bombs. A party of about twenty Germans worked round our left flank and

attacked the Quarry in the rear. The enemy was in great strength. This attack was perfectly organised and was pushed in with great energy and determination. The enemy advanced beyond Butte Alley and evidently had intended to capture Maxwell Trench. Our men resisted heroically but after a desperate stand were driven back to Maxwell trench so that by 1 a.m. on the 6th we were in the same position as on the morning of the 5th prior to the assault.[91]

Mud now wholly engulfed the battlefield. Captain Moffat on 13 December:

Made a reconnaissance of the whole brigade front, including the new sector. I was with the company sergeant-major and had a most exciting time. The mud in places was armpit deep and the CSM [Company Sergeant Major] got stuck – he lost his stick and gloves and had to cut his gum-boots to get free. The trenches were so bad [we] ran over the top, then moved again as that spot was known to be unhealthy and we cowered under a piece of tin. We saw the spot where we had been standing badly shelled.[92]

One of those serving at the front was Private Harold Shuttleworth, 'A' Battery, 154 Brigade. Harold had joined under age, but his mother wrote to his battery commander on 22 November 1915, not so much to recover her child but simply to signal her acquiescence: 'However I am glad to know he is in a fit state to do his duty and I should be the last one to bring any disgrace on any one of my children.'[93] Prior to deployment Harold wrote, 'awfully sorry I shan't be home Xmas but will do my level best next year. Troops are going over [to France] today in thousands so the war will soon be over and when your humble son will get out.' By December 1916, the war was anything but glamorous:

I have been doing a bit of navvying – different to what I've been used to, but a devil of a lot better than front-line work. Alarmingly, I've caught a dose of the 'Hansom Cabs' [rhyming slang for 'crabs' – pubic lice] and would ask you to send me a tin of blue ointment … I reckon I must have caught them from some latrine seat.[94]

The year 1916 drew to a close with both the Allies and Germans pretty much where they'd been at the start. Two great battles, dwarfing in scale those which had gone earlier, had demanded a vast blood sacrifice. Neither side was seemingly any nearer to breaking the deadlock.

> From one who knows
> There's many a private soldier,
> Who walks his humble way
> With no sounding name or title
> Unknown to the world today,
> In the eyes of God is a hero
> As worthy of the days
> As any mighty general,
> To whom the world gives praise.
> – Private C. Wiles, 20th Battalion, Middlesex Regiment

FIVE

MUD, 1917

'Heroes of Home'

The boy has gone with his heart aglow
In an alien land to fight,
The mother who bore him watched him go,
And her trembling lips were white,
Yet she had bidden him strike his blow,
For his King and the cause of Right!

The boy in the midst of toil and fight
Small time can spare for thought,
The mother who sent him dreams all night
Of battles he never fought,
And seems him wounded, in desperate plight
Or by brutal captors caught!

He takes his hardship as so much sport
Being far too busy to whine,
But anxious fears at home distort
Each peril into time
The crowded hour is always short;
'Tis waiting hearts that pine!

He fell at last with thousands more –
Just one of thousands slain –

On a day when the land was drenched with gore,
From Dixmuide to the Aisne,
And he lay in peace in a world at war
And knew not toil nor pain.

The mother who sent him bowed her head
And wept for the lad she bore
Yet never she grudged her sacred dead
For her country's need was sore
'He died for his King and the Right', she said
'And no man could do more'.

But the dead, proud heart of her inly bled,
Though she showed her grief to none;
She was just one woman who mourned her dead
Out of many thousands – one!
But it's better to die when the blood runs red
Than to live when hope is done
– Eric Fitzwalter Wilkinson[95]

For Sir Douglas Haig, 1917 would not prove to be a vintage year. Russia would collapse and French armies, as though infected by the same discordant virus, in many cases refused to fight, at least on the offensive. Italy would be hammered at Caporetto and attempts in the Middle East to break the deadlock against Johnny Turk in Gaza met with scant success. Haig's offensive at Arras and Vimy achieved wonders at the outset, though the former swiftly degenerated into costly attrition. General Plumer and the 2nd Army performed tremendous feats at Messines. But then Haig's great summer offensive, the 3rd Battle of Ypres, popularly better known by the name of one of its objectives, Passchendaele, became the very symbol of fruitless slaughter in a hellish sea of mud.

The commander-in-chief's woes multiplied when the more compliant Asquith was replaced by fiery Lloyd George as Prime Minister. Both general and politician detested each other. The Welshman was understandably appalled by the losses incurred on the Somme and described Haig as 'a military Moloch' (ancient Canaanite God). Nor could Lloyd George work with Sir William Robertson, the Chief of the Imperial General Staff, and a Haig supporter. At the Calais conference in February 1917, the Prime Minister proposed that the British Expeditionary Forces should come under the orders of General Nivelle, Joffre's replacement. Haig offered to resign. Ludendorff (effectively Joint German Chief of General Staff and the man responsible for much of his country's tactical approach to the war) had meanwhile decided to shorten the German front and withdraw to the Hindenburg Line. 'Operation Alberich' (the malignant dwarf of the *Nibelungen Saga*) was a masterpiece of scorched earth, of vindictive, wanton destruction, inspired as far as the British could determine by deep seated malice. Anyone who had previously been sceptical about German atrocities was now converted.

On 16 April General Nivelle's great offensive, desperately flawed and pressed home with the frenzy of self-delusion, commenced. For their general's folly, the *Poilus* paid a fearful blood-price. Undeterred, Nivelle pushed on, casting blame on every head but his own. These failed attacks cost another 100,000 casualties. For many in the line this was simply too much. On 29 April the murmurs of discontent hardened into outright refusal.

Arras

On 9 April, Haig attacked at Arras. This was essentially a large-scale diversion intended to keep German reserves pinned in that sector while Nivelle's master plan unfolded. On the first day the Canadian Corps, fighting as a single cohesive force for the first time, performed magnificently and took Vimy Ridge. This seemingly impregnable bastion had bloodily defied all Allied attempts for the preceding three years. Allenby's 3rd Army made astonishing progress on the first day at Arras. Despite the vastly improved bombardment and deep penetrations, the British could not capitalise on this initial success. The Germans, resilient as ever, recovered their breath and stood their ground. The battle went grinding on, the same weary and bloody toll of attrition; Allenby lost over 4,000 men a day till further attacks were finally called off on 17 May.

Lieutenant Arthur Terry, destined to see hard service at Arras, served as quartermaster to the 4th Battalion Tyneside Scottish (23rd NF). He was a constant and detailed correspondent to his wife Dora to whom he wrote on 2 January 1917:

> Don't faint! I'm enclosing my promised poem; I'll bet you 8d [4p] you can't beat it. It isn't quite up to the highest standard but then it's wartime you know!

> Oh, thou who art the mainspring of my life
> My dearest love, my very dearest wife
> (That sounds as though of wives I had a few
> But truly I have none excepting you)
> Pray read between the lines of my poor lay
> All that my feeble pen can never say
> (By rhyming all these lines, I think there's six
> I've mastered one at least of poet's tricks)
> I long once more, oh how I long my Dora
> To feel the spell of thy benign aura
> (I rather pride myself on these two rhymes
> The poet in me comes out strong at times)
> I long to see they face – to hear thy voice
> I'd fly to there at once had I the choice
> (You'll notice that in couplets I must write
> I fear that otherwise I would take all night)
> I think of those at home while here I stay
> And sadly muse the long, long hours away
> (That's the Dickensian, sentimental touch;
> I hope it will be regarded as such)
> The night is cold and damp – it rains and rains
> Indoors I woo my muse until my brains
> Racked and tormented, swear they'll go no farther
> So I'll conclude, your loving husband, Arthur.[96]

That same week, Lieutenant Terry extended his creative repertoire by taking to the boards (4 January); 'I've made my first appearance in panto and as I didn't get hissed off the stage or have rotten eggs thrown at me, I suppose I didn't hurt the show!' The life of a quartermaster, while demanding, was frequently less imminently perilous than that of his fellow officers in the line (4 February):

> I did tell you I had got a decent billet didn't I? It is a long, low room with a bed in one corner which I bagged. A round table, an anthracite stove, mirrored wardrobe, a decent washstand and a wash basin of English proportions. My bed is covered with a rug with an enormous tiger, fierce and horrible … The padre sleeps in a little room opening out of the mess room, the interpreter upstairs and orderlies in the kitchen. We have to come through a tailor's shop to reach our room but that is much better than going through the family living room as we sometimes had to do.

The next week and a night's R & R in the local fleshpots:

> Tonight I rode into the nearest town (Caestre) and bought chocolate biscuits and cigarettes then went a buster on dinner. I had quite a nice time as I found some fellows I know and had them to talk to and a man was at the piano who played ragtime brilliantly and loudly with all the airs and mannerisms of a virtuoso and Madame, the proprietress, sang three songs, one a delicious Provencal tune and the man accompanied really awfully well. I had a good feed and wine and coffee and got safely home without falling off my horse!

Whatever diversions might, from time to time, arise, the war was never far away. On 13 February, Terry wrote to Dora confirming details of recent action:

> I came back today. I suppose, now that it is over, there's no harm in telling you that a strong raiding party of our battalion has

been out at the old billets training and that accounts for my long rides. The raid came off on Sunday night and was, on the whole, successful. Tom Heron has got back with a bullet mark right across his cheek but Percy was luckier – he has got a nice 'Blighty'; not dangerous at all I believe. Common has had a leg broken, as well as his head and the CO has a black eye and scratched cheek and another officer was slightly wounded. The tragedy of the affair was the loss of Freeman who died of wounds yesterday and Captain Daggett and a lot of men are missing. The battalion has got great kudos over the affair but it will always be doubtful to me whether these raids are worth the candle.[†]

By April the battalion was at Arras in preparation for the offensive. The 23rd was in reserve with the 21st and 22nd Battalions ready to go over supported by the 20th at Roclincourt. On 9 April, Easter Monday:

We attacked at dawn this morning and the affair has been a great success. The division has reached all the points allocated to it and our casualties on the whole have been very light, a welcome change from last July [the Tyneside Scottish had suffered terrible losses on the Somme]. Up to 5 p.m. four thousand German prisoners have passed through the cage. We seem to be doing just as well all along the line.

Three days later and more details have emerged:

Our battalion was acting as divisional reserve and came back to the huts for two days to fit out and rest. On Easter Eve [7 April] they moved up to billets in the forward area and we got orders to be clear of the camp by 5 p.m. next day. There wasn't much of an Easter Sunday feel about on that day, I can tell you!
    There was no lack of excitement though, because while we were

---

† The Battalion War Diary states the raid was undertaken with twelve officers and 257 ORs; casualties were around sixty.

waiting the Boche started to shell the camp with heavy artillery. He managed to hit one cook house just across the road from my stores and killed one man and wounded two others.

The divisional objectives were three lines of German trenches known as (1) the Black Line (2) the Blue Line and (3) the Brown Line and the first definite news we had was from brigade to the effect that the attack had been most successful and that the Black Line had been taken with very few casualties. No news of the 4th but as we had been detailed to follow up the other battalions to the Blue Line this wasn't surprising and we had to content ourselves with going to see the Boche prisoners and watch our Tommies throwing tins of bully beef over the barbed wire, receiving in exchange all kinds of souvenirs from tunic buttons to wrist watches.

By now, the Blue Line had been designated as the divisional resupply point and convoys of rations and ammunition had to be sent up, initially by wagon but then onwards by mule.

Well, to go on – I left camp at 8 p.m. on Tuesday night to catch up the ration convoy, with instructions to call and see the OC divisional pack mules about getting them on to the dump. I reached the rendezvous about 9 p.m. and joined Hunter [transport officer], only to find that all our mules had been out that day and we had to wait until the men and animals had been fed and rested before we could go on. We finally got away about midnight and had to go about two or three miles to the dump. We hadn't gone far before we found the road blocked with traffic and after that we moved at the rate of about half a mile per hour. Ration wagons, mules, artillery limbers and guns simply choked the road. We got nearly up to out late front line and then the block was so bad that Hunter decided to unload the wagons and load the mules on the roadside.

While we were doing this a message came down the road to say that a rations party was waiting for us so I left Hunter, and taking with my RQMS and another sergeant, went on to assure the party that they wouldn't have long to wait. We soon got past our front line trenches and then the road began to get very bad. Pioneers had been busy all Monday night and Tuesday trying to repair it but they couldn't do much in the time and, as a consequence bits of barbed wire, logs of wood displaced by previous traffic and so on were sticking about all over. In the first instance our barrage must have pounded the road to pieces. Luckily, there was a bit of a moon and we had some idea of where to walk – otherwise I think we couldn't have got on.

As it was I tripped and fell about four times. No man's land was a sight – shell-hole after shell-hole in regular succession with the earth heaped up on the edges until it looked like a field with huge, nightmare molehills all over. From the road of course, one couldn't see the holes – only the huge mounds in rows. We finally reached the place where the Boche front line had been but there was no sign of a trench as our guns had blown it up so badly. The traffic eased off hereabouts as most of the field guns had been rushed into positions and now busily engaged in firing at targets which we could only conjecture were probable places of concentration for counter attacks. There were still some guns with teams of eight horses struggling through the mud up to advanced positions.

At last I found the ration party, desperately tired and hungry but still cheerful and very pleased at the success of their efforts. When I tell you that some of these men only joined us the day before the attack, you will realise that their cheerfulness under the circumstances had something fine about it. Taylor, the officer in charge of the party, was wide eyed with lack of sleep and looked very weary but was otherwise quite all right. The mules arrived about 4 a.m. and we got them unloaded and then Hunter went back so see to the comfort of his men and animals who had had a gruelling day, while I went with Taylor and the ration party to find out what we could do for the comfort of the men in the line. We set out but after crossing two fields Taylor confessed he had lost his way so we trudged back to the road to wait for daylight.

Happily a savvy sergeant found them a guide and they made their way into a snaking communication trench which wound for two miles across the blasted ground.

> The first man we saw (except for the dead, still lying in the trench) was Metcalfe, at present CO of 'D' Company, lying sound asleep on the snow covered side of the trench. There was absolutely no cover up there and the trenches in places were only breast high. The Boche evidently spotted the ration party at one rather open place, because in a moment or two, bang came two shells which fell short of the parapet although one could hear the burst quite too near to be pleasant, and feel the earth spraying over the top in showers. As soon as possible the ration party dispersed to the various company positions, and then we three of the store staff went along to battalion HQ. When we reached a certain point we had to get out of the trench and cross the open for about 200 yards and then we dropped into another trench.

Terry found the battalion CO in 'an old Boche dugout' utterly exhausted, 'shivering with fatigue' buoyed by a deep pride in his Saturday-night soldiers:

> He described with evident pride, how the battalion went over alone (those battalions detailed to move forward on either flank had not come up in time), and marched up under our barrage and took the Brown Line. What he did not tell me was that he led the battalion over and was nearly the first man in the Brown Line trenches instead of waiting till the line was taken before he moved from the Blue Line which was what brigade expected all CO's to do.

Their mission over, the logistics team began the tortuous journey back to their start line:

> By daylight the scene was much more desolate looking than at night – not a tree on the road but had been struck and I was impressed with the similarity between this road and that to the Vimy trenches

I told you of last year. Further down we saw parties of men, evidently clearing the battlefield, stretcher parties with both our and German wounded, pioneers hard at work road making and, most welcome sight of all, motor lorries which had brought up the material for the pioneers. Brigadiers with their staffs were hurrying up the road on foot and, as usual, lots of men who seemed to have no aim or object in life although probably every man was detailed for some job and was just waiting for material to begin.

Exhausted, the crew were happy to hitch a ride with motor transport:

The night before we'd been on the road with transport mules, and were cursing the motor lorries for taking up all the road and blocking traffic. This morning, after we got on the lorry, we cursed all horse transport for being so slow and stopping us on our run down! I'm not quite sure about it but I think that all the guns of the British Army were concentrated within 200 yards of this point and were all firing at once. To make matters worse a Boche plane was sighted and two 'Archies' [anti-aircraft guns] started barking at it and they weren't fifty yards from me. What with tiredness I went sound asleep as I sat there in spite of the noise which, by the way, gave me a bit of a headache and didn't waken until the driver poked me and shouted at me!

Having gained their weary rest, the Fusiliers had barely time to turn around before the drums began to beat once again:

Tonight, since I started this orders have come for a move in the morning, so I'm going to have a bath and turn in early. Goodness only knows when I'll get another. I trust that this is the beginning of the end of the war and that I'll be home sooner than we thought possible.

Millions of men on both sides of no man's land were no doubt wishing for the same thing. All would be equally disappointed.

Many an exhausting march and trek to the battered front line awaited Lieutenant Terry and his comrades who, if they were at the tail rather than the teeth, were the sinew and muscle of every battalion. By early May, dismal snows and biting winds had given way to the full promise of spring and even these hardened Northumbrians could feel its warmth:

11 May: Really, you know there are worse things than trekking about the back areas of France in the springtime. The other day we stayed for about twenty hours in a delightful village and the transport lines were down one of the prettiest lanes I've ever seen. Symmetrical hedges, somewhat thin but very fresh looking, lined each side of the lane, which being practically only a bridle path, had a thin carpet of grass and orchards stretched out beyond the hedge on either side – small but very beautiful.

Sir Douglas Haig had plans for that approaching summer.

Messines

'Private Tommy Atkins'

On army forms 'Tommy's' the name he bears
But in the ranks this Monica's no good
If he's a Murphy, whatever he cares
He'll get no other name than 'Spud'.

And if he's one of the family Clark
And was baptised Fred, or Jack, or Bobby
Or uses his number to keep it dark,
He will always loudly be called 'Nobby'.

And if his true surname should be Miller
Let him be a fraud, or good and trusty,
A man or a mouse or a ladykiller,
You'll find he will always be called 'Dusty'!

Soldiers must ever be ready to die
When they get their baptism of fire,
And be forgotten, wherever they lie,
But their nicknames will never expire.
– Charles Moss[97]

Haig was always of the belief that Flanders was the crucial sector and that it was here the war would be lost and won. His plan for 1917 was an ambitious one. He proposed that a major thrust would secure the higher ground which was crowned by the small town of Passchendaele while a strong left hook would punch a path clear towards the Channel ports which could be seized in a coordinated amphibious operation. This was bold indeed and flew in the face of more conservative, purely military concepts of 'bite and hold'. Haig's task was an unenviable one for whatever he proposed had to pass a hostile War Cabinet and thus he had to dangle the carrot of great gains – in reality, these were almost certainly unattainable.

Before this great offensive could be launched, vital high ground around Messines and Wytschaete, ceded in 1914, had to be won back, a mission entrusted to 'Daddy' Plumer. This was indeed a Herculean task but the commander of the 2nd Army was ready. His 30,000 tunnellers had been digging beneath German lines since 1915. Mining was an area where the British had built up vast expertise and a clear superiority. Those who have read Sebastian Faulks's evocative fiction *Birdsong* will be acquainted with the Tunnellers, of whom rather more later. Plumer's preparations were meticulous. Logistics and intensive training were undertaken methodically and efficiently. Artillery preparation was far more sophisticated and effective than in the previous year. At 03.10 on the morning of 7 June, nineteen great mines exploded beneath Messines Ridge,† eruptions of biblical and apocalyptic proportions, which jellified

---

† One impressive crater remains at Spanbroekmolen – 'the Pool of Peace'.

stunned survivors. By Great War standards the battle was a resounding success with moderate losses, an impressive bag of enemy dead and some 7,000 prisoners.

Captain John Evelyn Carr, destined for a role in this offensive and still serving with 11th Battalion Sherwood Foresters, spent the early part of 1917 in Flanders:

> On Easter Monday which was somewhere near the end of March the Germans made a very determined attack on that portion of the line, held by 11th Sherwood Foresters. They came over very suddenly in large numbers, in the early morning just before daylight; they got through our front line and there were heavy casualties on both sides. Some of the Boche got right down to our Battalion HQ. Amongst others who was killed was our adjutant Lieutenant Cavell who was a cousin of Nurse Cavell who was murdered in Brussels. He met the Boche face to face and was shot at arm's length, a good many of the HQ personnel were also killed with another officer named Thorn. The Germans all carried dozens of egg bombs and had picks and shovels with them, so they'd evidently intended to stay. They were all driven out; either killed or wounded but the operation cost us between 40–50 men and three officers.[98]

By late April, even though an offensive was imminent, there was still some time for R & R:

> Spent an hour or two in a lace shop owned by four sisters in the Rue d'Ypres (Poperinghe) and we had tea in the 'Cave' below the shop. Some shells burst very close near to us and the second youngest girl was in a rather nervous state, the other three were very brave.

He was assigned in a training role, based at Toronto camp:

> The rifle range was in great request and we had an excellent bombing ground and bayonet fighting course. We started a garden

and, amongst other things, I planted a thousand cabbages which I don't suppose we will ever get the benefit of but it gives those men who are keen gardeners something to do.

By the early part of May, the drums could clearly be heard, their tempo building: 'We have come to this area so the brigade can practise for the attack we are to make at the beginning of June. Trenches have all been prepared as near as possible to the German lines we shall have to take which are on Wytschaete Ridge, near Messines.' Carr was, by this time, attached to Battalion HQ:

We were kept very busy and had to do most of our work between six and ten in the morning so the ground would be fully ready. In this village [Boeschepe] cock fighting is carried on and we got to two or three fights while we were here. The cocks somewhat resemble our Black Red Game Cocks but are heavier and clumsier and I think a real good English bird could have knocked any of them out. In many cases here, either one or both of the competitors is killed.

He returned to the line 22/23 May, now as CO of 'Halifax' training camp.

It is not very far from Vlamertinghe, the camp was a little distant from my billet and my mess was inside the camp in a hut. On 24th May, Goldman (gas officer) and I went up to Poperinghe for dinner at Skindles. In the middle of dinner the town was bombarded and there was a great panic. One shell hit the building we were in, glass and brick were hurled onto our plates. The waiters quite simply flew down to the cellar and left us all to help ourselves and we did so, especially with the wine! There was a great amount of damage done in Poperinghe and on our way home we noticed one house, the front of which had been ripped clean off and the house opened up from top to bottom with everything, furniture, bedding etc intact. In the dusk and walking along dusty roads we passed long, long lines of transport; a most wonderful sight, miles and miles of men, mules, lorries and carts.

By 26 May, the drums were sounding louder still:

Our camps were rather badly shelled this afternoon so we dug some trenches for the men to get into when we are bombarded and thereby saved a good many lives. A band from one of the Welsh regiments was playing in our camp during the afternoon. What an extraordinary contrast when a band plays 'Come to my garden of Roses' accompanied by the thundering of the guns! Both camps and dumps were badly hit, 7th Division's beautiful theatre was absolutely blown away and they lost everything, together with the canteen, YMCA hut and other timber buildings.

As May faded into June, none could doubt something major was brewing and tensions mounted:

I had a nasty case today to deal with just as we were having dinner in the evening; I heard a shot go off close by in our camp. I said some silly bugger must have buzzed off his rifle when a corporal came rushing in saying one of the men had shot himself. We went to the place which was a shell hole with some bushes around and in it two men. One had shot himself through his foot and the other was just going to do so when we got there in time to stop him. These were both old soldiers and they wanted to get out of the scrap.

On 5 June the brigade went up into the line:

The huge mine at Hill 60 at which miners have been working for the last year or two is to be blown up at 3 a.m. on the 7th. I shall not forget that march. It is a sad sort of feeling for all. The band played 'Tipperary' and many other well known tunes, the men were joking all the way along and I felt quite out of it having to come back. Now and then we had a shell near us as we went up.

Darkness fell and the voices faded away, the men seemed to have been swallowed up!

The night of 6/7 June was electric. Everyone knew the offensive was due to unfold and that the mines would explode first.

Captain Payne came along to our bivouac and we sat with our watches on the table. The time for Hill 60 to go was 3.30 a.m. ten minutes before; we filled up our glasses and waited. The time came and, almost to the second, there was a rumbling noise and the whole world seemed to shake. I could see the whisky and water in our glasses quivering for some time but there was no huge report. Mr Lloyd George at Walton Heath who said he heard the report must have had his nerves worked up to some pitch as it was a dead sort of noise and how we knew it had gone was by the shaking ground but the noise from the guns after that moment was fearsome and deafening.

On 7 June the assaults drove forward, British gains were impressive and optimism prevailed.

We had a very large haul of prisoners during the day. I cannot remember how many, a curious crowd including many officers who were very surly and resented being examined. The men were very dirty, haggard, hungry and thirsty looking creatures. Some were terrible looking creatures, Russians who the Germans had made fight for them. As soon as they got out of sight of their officers, they became different men and appeared to be very glad to be caught and their spirits rise the further away from the shelling of their own guns they get. Generally, the news was very good and things had gone almost better than we had expected, we'd got well onto Messines Ridge.

Despite the success at Messines, there was no immediate follow-up and Crown Prince Rupprecht of Bavaria, commanding German forces in Flanders, was given time to take in the lessons of Messines and strengthen his line accordingly. He was advised by Colonel Fritz von Lossberg, the Vauban of trench warfare. He now created a series of grid fortifications studded with redoubts and fronted by a deep but thinly held outpost line, manned primarily by machine-gunners sheltering in blockhouses or ruined farms. These, the elite of the German army, promised to exact a high toll of any attacker before the main line was ever reached.

The 3rd Battle of Ypres – First Attacks

'1914'

One hundred years have passed,
Still the blame goes on,
No black, no white,
No good, no bad,
There stood glory,
There fell fate,
Where was sense,
Where was shame,
We must never forget,
Those who gave,
Their todays,
For our tomorrows, nor those who lived
And bore the scars for life.
– Arthur Roberts[99]

Haig was partly hamstrung by political doubts. The War Cabinet was insisting on adequate French support for his main offensive. In the circumstances, this appeared highly improbable. It was not until 25 July that he was given the green light. The intervening weeks had given Rupprecht the breathing space he needed and Flanders weather was clearly with him. Flanders ('Flooded Land') was low lying and clay based. Generations of patient farmers had corralled the waters by ingenious irrigation and drainage but three years of neglect and endless churning of shells had destroyed their clever systems. The summer of 1917 was exceptionally wet. Mud was the prevailing characteristic of Flanders that year. A mud so omnipresent, so cloying, so lethal, waiting to suck the heavily laden down into its black heart, that it has come to define our memory of the forthcoming battle.

Arthur William David Roberts was born in Bristol in 1897 of mixed-race parents. His father, David, was a ship's steward. At some point in the early twentieth century the family moved to Glasgow, where the young Arthur was educated at Kent Road School. He remained in full-time education till he was eighteen and it is clear from the quality of his prose he was a highly intelligent and articulate young man, something of a 'dandy' in his style.

For most of his adult, working life, Arthur was employed as a marine engineer but he volunteered for military service in 1917, firstly with the 2nd Battalion, King's Own Scottish Borderers and latterly 2nd Battalion Royal Scottish Fusiliers:

> For so short an army career, I think I may safely say, my life during that period was as varied, and eventful, as most private soldiers of a similar length of service. A soldier during war time if capable is pushed into many breaches whether fit for the front line or base. I have been fit for both; consequently I have filled many breaches. The last sentence will perhaps lead the reader to think I am possessed of great capabilities, and this belief may be strengthened when I say that I have been company-runner, batman, guide, dining-hall attendant, bugler, dispatch clerk, aircraft-gunner, hut-builder, stretcher-bearer, and one or two other things. Now it has been unintentional, if I have seemingly blown my own horn about my military accomplishments, but I think this book, written as frankly as I could write it will exonerate me from any imputation of self-aggrandizement.[100]

His first experience of the trenches was in the spring of 1917, as the BEF was gearing up for the 3rd Battle of Ypres:

On the night of the 8th June we left Poperinghe by rail. The train travelled at a walking pace in order to make as little smoke as possible. It stopped at Vlamertinge and the battalion got out and formed up on the line. When all was in order we marched off. After going a little way, we formed into single file, each man at six paces interval. A steady jog trot was started, and in this manner we went through the city. The night was very hot and our steel helmets were slipping all ways and, what with our heavy packs and rifles, we were in a very warm state when we reached the Ypres Railway. The embankment was climbed and we proceeded between the shell-torn rails. The streets had been bad but, oh the railway was a thousand times worse. The metals were twisted into every imaginable shape, the sleepers were where one never imagined them to be and often we were balancing ourselves along a stretch of rail extending across big shell holes…

I first actually entered the trenches on the dawn of 9th June, 1917. I can tell you, after our gruelling march (described in the diary), I was a physical wreck. That night as I plumped down in a dugout, I was so tired that without taking off my equipment, I almost immediately fell into a trance. All the Kaiser's horses and all the Kaiser's men could not have put the wind up me that night. No, I was too far beyond the stage of self-preservation. Sleep and welcome oblivion was wanted. I believe I should not have cared if I had been told I should never wake up again.

Even sentry duty was, in the first undreamed of instance, a novelty:

Of course it was novel to me so the time did not seem so long as it did later on. When the novelty wears off it is a dreary, monotonous watch and at this time of the year in France, the early mornings are very cold and usually wet. At times like these, a chap often imagines he sees things such as men crawling about in front and when the wind blows stray whispers of barbed wire against the metal poles it confirms the idea. Often a chap with this belief will open fire and consequently the parapet is manned at once and everybody has a go at something imaginary. Naturally, Gerry gets the wind up and he starts rifles, machine guns, and bombs, grenades and the racket might last about an hour then fizzle out. Next day's news; a strong attack on our trenches was successfully beaten off, many casualties to enemy.

Prior to the opening attacks which would be directed at recovering ground at Pilckem Ridge, Gheluvelt and Langemarck, gunners of Plumer's 2nd Army and Anglo-Irish Commander Gough's 5th pumped over 4,500 shells into von Lossberg's improved defences. The toll of German defenders was terrible and damage, not just to defences but to the quaking ground, considerable. On 31 July, British infantry went over the top in Flanders.

For Arthur Roberts, like so many tens of thousands of other Tommies, the opening of Haig's great summer offensive and the battles which followed were to be their baptism and Calvary combined:

It was the 29th July 1917 and we were lying on the outskirts of Dickebusch waiting to move up to go over the top … The ground, being low lying, soon became a mass of mud and slime, the small bivouac tents were poor shelters from the drenching downpour. Under such conditions no fires could possibly be lit no fires could possibly be lit. All that day we squatted under our low tents, wet and miserable, so that when orders came to prepare to move we were glad to have something to do.

Their march was purgatory.

At the appointed time we 'fell in' and muddy and weary as we were, we started forward, with the slow, ponderous movement so common to the BEF. The roads were calf deep with mud, while the rest of the country was half-lake, half quagmire. Frequently, enemy shells would land in the near vicinity with sudden slaps and mud showers, so that we had a mud bath every now and then. Dead animals and disabled wagons lay scattered in profusion. In many cases, these objects were almost buried in the boggy terrain. At last we came to a corduroy road that is a roadway of tree trunks which was also plentifully dotted with deceased mules and timber wagons. This road was the stopping point for the transport evidently and some of them had stopped for good. We turned along this road and slipping and stumbling over the wet logs, we made our way cursing and grousing until we came upon our own transport wagons, waiting to be unloaded.

Finally, they plodged into the shallow communication trench:

The sides of the trench were of such shifting nature that frames of wire netting were required to hold them up. The least touch caused slime to ooze through. The bottom was on average covered by a foot of water; plainly speaking what was being misnamed as a trench, was only a common ditch. In the dry season I should say it would be about six feet deep, at this time it was anything from seven feet.

Arthur selected the driest funk hole he could find but, barely had he laid aside his rifle than he and several others found themselves selected for fatigues. In this case it was the laborious business of unloading transport wagons. An old hand by now:

Ah well, I thought now I'm here I'll make the best of it and I selected a sack of jam. These needed less careful handling and all true soldiers always keep an eye for the main chance. Before I regained the ditch, one of the pots of jam was mine!

That night, they stood or huddled in their sludge-garnished ditch, damp creeping through muscle and bone, no bright explosion of summer dawn, just a dank, cloying mist. All day they remained in uncomfortable waiting, 'like kittens in a box we became restless as the day advanced'. Their trumpet to glory did not sound that day, however and darkness again closed down upon us, bringing fresh supplies of rain and we longed for the attack if only to relieve our monotony. The water in our ditch had risen considerably, but we thought it better to stand in it than out on top getting the icy wind that was blowing.

At 9 p.m. the rum ration arrived with orders for movement at midnight. Arthur was not a drinking man, with little taste for grog

but this night I would have supped with the devil himself if I could have bettered my case by doing so. Rum rations at the best were never of generous proportions … but as we were all fairly well knocked up, the ration on this occasion was passable. Mine, I know, did wonders for me.

They marched under the wet blanket of darkness, 'moving along the intricate trenches like a giant reptile wriggling through an enormous crooked tube'. Each by now had acquired an outer casing of Flanders mud, 'but I have to admit even if it is dirty it certainly keeps the heat in and the cold out'. Their laborious, slime-drenched marches were drawing them closer to the front:

German artillery kept up a desultory action but he was registering too close for our comfort. As we proceeded, the effect of the gunfire [was] becoming more apparent to us. The trenches were taking on a more battered look and the dead men lying in them were getting more numerous as we went forward. The trenches soon had been so badly shelled that in some places we were walking in the open, where big shell holes had taken the place of that bit of trench. In the surviving lengths, dead men were so numerous it was impossible [to] proceed without walking on them. This section of trenches was awful. One moment we were wading up to our middles in water, the next we were wobbling and balancing over the bodies of our unfortunate comrades.

Hell's ante-chamber,

that journey was like a nightmare, even yet as I write this I can fancy I can see the gruesome forms lying in the flooded craters by the green relief of Verey lights which reflected on the ink-black water, casting an opalescent glow on the ghastly faces. There was no time, nor was this the place to be sentimental and we were hurried forward to be in our positions by 2 a.m. appointed time for the kick-off.

Soon it would be their turn.

As we knelt there, waiting the command of our officer who constantly gazed at his wrist watch with the sheet of blackness before us, and the German curtain-fire behind us, roaring in its seeming impatience; my thoughts were strangely far distant from the battlefield.

Arthur was swept with a wave of pure pride,

here I was among men sharing the risks and uncertainties of being in the very front ranks of the empire against its enemies ... patri-otism was strong in my breast then. Reality, the tiny grim imp swiftly re-asserted itself; waiting is worse than a hundred deaths – Heavens, will the order never come. Whizz! Shhh! Crash! Bang! Boom! 'Forward men', calmly said our officer.

His fears of fear forgot in the rush of action, Arthur with his comrades struggled ahead into no man's land.

The barrage of our guns fell about fifty yards ahead, exactly at 2 a.m., for a few minutes it shattered and battered the German front line, and then it roared forward. It was as if the earth had opened in half and vomited forth flames and sparks of gorgeous rich colours.

The ground was in an awful miry state, but we had not squelched forward very far before three or four prisoners came up to us unarmed and with hands held high. Our officer obtained what information he could but the corporal treated them guardedly as if they had been bristling with guns. We had no time to lose, so we hurried on as best we could but with the boggy ground and detours we had to make round small lakes, our barrage soon thundered away into the distance, leaving us hopelessly behind. The section about thirty yards on our right, received a heavy German shell right in their midst. Shortly afterwards, I saw one of the tanks in front of us catch fire. I think by the blaze it must have been a supply tank.

Enemy fire began to take effect:

The enemy pestered us with a slow but annoying fire of 5.9 shells and an assortment of smaller rounds. As we plunged on, one of our section who was walking at my left shoulder, suddenly collapsed with a sigh, a splinter had pierced his abdomen. Some stretcher bearers were following our party but, before they came up, the poor chap had expired. Afterwards, it was remarked that, during the previous day, the unfortunate man had been very reticent in his speech and actions. Strict orders had been issued before the battle, that nobody but stretcher bearers were to stop for wounded and that water bottles and bandages were to be for personal use only.

Dawn had overtaken night and the black, mud-slicked plain was deepening in yet more rain, waterlogged shell-holes coalescing into wider lakes of sulphurous filth, 'through which rising pieces of mud appeared like tiny islands'.

Their attack had been carefully rehearsed but the neat topography of a model battlefield and the surgical view of aerial observers did not coincide with the shot-torn morass through which Arthur and his comrades struggled.

The HQ staff seemed to think the plan would work so, as a consequence, we started off in one direction, then we suddenly swung sharply to the right, then some yards further on, we turned half-left and I'm sure we covered a mile before we even saw a trench. At last we dropped into one and the first thing I saw was an officer lying dead with a handkerchief over his face, and his servant collecting his books and papers.

Now we were in the enemy trenches, our work commenced. We had carried our sacks of bombs a long way, and they were heavy, so we thought the sooner we delivered them, the sooner we would lighten our load. The dead officer made us more merciless than we would otherwise have been, so we went along that trench and every dugout we came to, we flung in a bomb or two then called on the occupants to come out. The Mills Bomb goes off five seconds after the pin strikes the cap, we held it for three seconds while by the time we had shouted, four seconds had elapsed so that the Jerry down below usually stayed there.

Once again the Tommies were entering a 'race for the parapet'. Their painful and exhausting trek through water and mud meant the creeping barrage sailed off with majestic élan and,

we were now exposed to the German machine-gunners. Under their withering fire our section was soon dispersed. We would be ploughing forward when suddenly the stutter of a machine gun and the vicious swish of bullets would send us rolling into the nearest shellhole, invariably full of water. In a short time officers were without men and men without officers. Bombers and grenadiers and Lewis Gunners and riflemen were all mixed up. Some parties consisted of nearly all NCO's whilst other groups didn't have one. Nevertheless, forwards was the order of the day and mixed up as we were, in parties of threes and fours and in some cases a dozen, we moved on, always being broken up by the gunners. Sometimes, I was alone when a sudden dive for safety would land me among a party.

Despite the weight of enemy fire and dreadful ground, the attackers slogged forwards:

Due credit must come in and will be given by me to the German rearguard that held us up that day. It was certain death for them because our waves of infantry had got between them and their main body in most cases. To expose themselves was to draw fire. Like the heroes they were, they fought like tigers, withdrawing from crater to crater and we steadily but very slowly pushed on.

Though the assault progressed, all cohesion had been lost.

At length I found myself going forward with a lance-corporal and two privates of my own battalion, and a couple of chaps from a Manchester Battalion. We could see none of our own troops near us now and, as we happened on a German trench that was wicker-lined and had at least a semblance of dryness, we dropped in and prepared to hold on till such time as we could reconnect ourselves with another body of our comrades.

Gunmetal skies continued to spill torrents of rain while tendrils of mist still clung to the fire-gouged field,

but the stutter of Lewis and machine guns came to our ears. Occasional bursts of rifle fire now plain, now faint reached us also. The artillery of both sides seemed to have given up the contest. As I peeped over the enemy's parados, all I could see were big sheets of water reflecting sullen skies, all lashed by heavy rain while here and there lay a body soaked and sodden and muddy.

During the long day, Arthur and his new comrades held on in their improvised defences. The battlefield now seemed deserted, as though dragged down by the weight of mud and rain. As dusk began to gather, they were relieved, stumbling back to the rally point and a shivering night in dripping woods.

Another wet dawn brought fresh tribulation:

Parties were told off to act as stretcher-bearers. The party I was with was to carry wounded from a subterranean post to some ruins called Dormie House. The post was a fair distance from the house and it was no joke wading knee deep in mud with one corner of a stretcher on your shoulder. Some German guns were playing on our quarter, and the job was made perfectly nerve-breaking.

For the Scots, already exhausted, begrimed and hungry, the German bombardment proved a particular trial:

One of our guns had been put out of action near the house and I think Gerry was firing at it, not knowing of its plight. There was mud on nearly every square inch of me. The last issue of rations I had received had been three days before at Zillebeke Lake, since then my iron rations and that purloined pot of jam, had been my only subsistence.

Separated from his fellow stretcher-bearers, Arthur became lost in a fug of exhaustion till, mainly by good luck, he stumbled back into the Regimental Aid Post at Dormie House: 'The RAMC men manning this post and who had been smelling the rum jar oftener than was wise for them, informed me that all the working parties had departed for the night.' Wearily, he departed towards a distant rest:

Along the masses of communication trenches I plodded, a lonely soul in a lonely landscape. It was still raining. At length I left the trenches, but arriving at our own camp found it deserted. Judge the depths of misery into which I was again cast, I was tired, footsore, weary, hungry and mucky. It was darkening and nobody was in sight.

Despite his numbing tiredness, Arthur spent a fruitless night stumbling through the ravaged land, seeking his battalion.

Morning, another rain-swept dawn, brought solace:

I remember walking towards a cluster of tents and limber wagons. The next thing I recall, I was half-lying against a wagon with rain beating on my face and my own section-officer giving me a good drink of rum. Everybody was pleased to see me but I took most to the post-corporal for he had a parcel and letter for me. I demolished the parcel, the letter had to wait for, like a pig that has been fed, I rolled over and my thick coating of mud helped to keep me warm while I slept.

Arthur survived the fighting – recurrent foot problems kept him out of any further active service. He returned to Glasgow when he was demobbed in 1919 and completed his apprenticeship in the shipyards of the Clyde, where he would help to design the Queen Mary.

In the early fighting, gains were made though these were modest when measured against losses. Over such dreadful ground, tanks were of little value, constantly getting bogged and offering target practice for German gunners. Attacks continued through August though the ghastly weather continued. Von Lossberg's defences proved a very tough nut indeed and by the end of August, the 5th Army had lost some 60,000 men.

The Dogfight: Menin Road, Polygon Wood and Broodseinde

When the burden was shifted from the 5th to the 2nd Army, Plumer was to focus on the Gheluvelt Plateau. As at Messines, 'Daddy' Plumer had thought long and hard about the tactical problem. His artillery would be both sledgehammer and scalpel while still providing a shield to the infantry. Their main assault would be preceded by trained skirmishers, the basis of infiltration tactics. Attacks would proceed on a local 'bite and hold' basis, a pause between each bound for consolidation and allowing fresh units to pass through. Reserves would always be on hand to reinforce success.

Norman Gladden had left school in 1913 intending to join the civil service. He had no notions of going to war, 'fit enough but not robust'. When his call-up papers arrived in May 1916, he was three months short of his nineteenth birthday. That wash of patriotic fervour that had guided Kitchener's volunteers had receded in the face of a mounting, seemingly never-ending recital of casualties. By now there was no glory, only stalemate. Norman was initially assigned to the 2nd (Home Service) Battalion of the Hertfordshire regiment. He was transferred to 11th Battalion Northumberland Fusiliers. Those who'd gone out for the fighting around Le Sars in the dying throes of the Somme had been greeted by war-weary Tommies as 'more for the slaughter-house'.[101] Dying for your country was no longer 'sweet and right'. The new conscripts marched off from Catterick on 1 May 1917 to the strains of the song 'Cock of the North'.

On 31 July, the great offensive in Flanders opened. Private Gladden, while on the march, witnessed a unit of the new Chinese Labour Corps, unloading trucks. The use of 'coolie' labour had been controversial and he wondered what these men from so very far away and from such a different cultural background made of the whole thing.

Billeted in the pleasant village of Quelves, the Northumbrians initially endured no greater discomforts than sharing their barn accommodation with resident livestock and slopping through omnipresent mud. They trained nearby and with the comforts of the YMCA on tap.

Few doubted that this was anything other than the calm before the storm. Rumour, the solider's bush telegraph, began to circulate. As always there was one who professed to be 'in the know' brimming with 'confidential information'. As they had been training so hard, the prospect of early action did not demand any particular powers of divination.

As wet August passed into dank September the Northumbrians made ready, but no orders came. They were billeted now in the hamlet of La Clytte where they could still see vestiges of the trench system of 1915 which had linked up with Locre and Kemmel. A small cemetery near the shell-marked church contained the graves of those who had fallen in the earlier fighting.

By degrees the battalion moved nearer the front, first to Brewery Camp by Dickebusch, dwelling in sandbagged bell tents: 'Most of [the camp's] recent occupants had been shelled out of the place, a report that was supported by the existence in the vicinity of a number of large shell craters.' Gladden was part of a Lewis Gun team and improvised timber mounts for anti-aircraft fire had been rigged up.

They didn't have long to wait. Across the skies, sailing obliquely towards the camp, a regular enemy armada of planes was approaching, bomber machines shielded by a swarm of fighters or scouts as they were called. As they sailed unhurriedly above, he counted at least fifteen large aircraft. Men huddled in shallow drainage gutters which criss-crossed between the lines or dived down behind low sandbag barriers by the tents.

The three of them remaining near the gun with spare ammunition ready felt horribly exposed, like perfect targets for the approaching enemy. Goffee (the Lewis-gunner) fired up towards the advance line which was likely flying far too high while Norman and his number one crouched nearby. Shrapnel and bullets sprayed around. The raiders were now directly overhead still sailing forward with majestic unconcern. The moment of crisis passed as the gun-team held their breath. Other camps nearby were not spared.

As the vortex of battle inexorably sucked fresh blood into its maw the Northumbrians moved up to the support line. Bouts of offensive were interspersed with preparation, livened by raids. Norman, like so many soldiers, admired the raiders, their courage, dash and elan. One of the company runners, a dangerous enough posting, was prominent in these vicious trench raids. Unremarkable, unmilitary in appearance and small of stature, always undemonstrative under stress; he neither won any awards nor accepted any rank.

The Fusiliers moved through the tortured skeleton of Ypres, past Shrapnel Corner, moving over the shell-scarred waste along an elevated timber causeway:

Eventually we approached the ridge where the scene of desolation challenged description. All around us stretched a morass in shades of grey and black, looking like some petrified inferno from Dante. Waterlogged shell-holes almost touched one another, rendering the ground pretty near impassable except where the duckboards ran. Gaunt, leafless trees stood out aimlessly here and there to break the monotony. Perched along the ridge itself one of our field batteries was firing furiously over the barrier while heavy German shells were searching along the crest in reply. In the hollow lay the derelict corpses of a couple of tanks, hopelessly bogged and badly shattered.

Zero hour on 20 September was set for 5.40 a.m. and the battalions were to be ready in their jumping-off trenches by 3.30 a.m. Once the barrage lifted, 11th NF would attack and take the Red Line, allowing their comrades in 10th Battalion to pass through and assault the further Blue Line.

A company officer, coming forward from the groups behind, snapped his watch into his pocket and signalled them forward. A few moments of surreal silence – then the barrage burst out from behind them and they were pelting forward in the reflected light of the artillery. Norman felt he could feel and see crowds of men moving on all sides, spreading waves of infantry, pitting puny flesh and blood against the inferno. The earth heaved with the discharge. The air above seemed to be filled with shrieking shells. In front of them, a curtain of flame and smoke completely blotted out the landscape.

Norman experienced a peculiar and almost dreamlike condition. Though his feet were moving with all the energy needed to carry him with his burden of rifle and pack across the ground, he felt that they were in fact rooted to the earth and that it was all his surroundings that were moving of their own accord. The barrage, a wave of inconceivable confusion, began to creep away from the edge of the wood, whose trees stood out ever more clearly as the fumes gradually cleared. Now, the whole situation changed as if by magic, diabolical for the Fusiliers! Zipping snipers' bullets began their deadly work. Machine guns opening out ahead began to traverse methodically across their front, crossing and re-crossing as they sprayed the advancing lines. He felt the tearing stream of lead streaking across as muzzles were elevated. He could not believe he had come through unscathed.

A man a few yards ahead slipped to the ground and lay in a heap. Redoubtable Sergeant Rhodes was still in front, urging the men forward. Machine guns cut across again and single rifle shots echoed their steadier rattle. The defenders were resisting with fierce resolve. He heard screams around him. Agony and death seemed to be cutting a swathe through the advancing lines. From the edge of the wood, now much closer, flashes from rifles and machine guns filled the air like angry hornets.

He could distinguish the Tommies' front wave clearly for daylight had broken, lifting such protection as the pre-dawn dark-ness afforded. Men in front were dropping to earth, whether from wounds or for cover he couldn't tell, likely a mixture of both.

By now 'B' Company coming up behind were bunching with the survivors of 'A'. Norman Gladden took advantage of a scrape in the ravaged earth to seek sanctuary from a merciless fire. Attempts to dig in were futile. One comrade who whipped out his entrenching tool immediately had the handle shattered by a random shot; 'a sniper clearly had the spot marked'. Dead and wounded crumpled in and around, 'in my imagination, the pincers of death were clos-ing in upon this spot for my insignificant benefit'.

This hiatus was short-lived. There had been a halt in the forward flow which now resumed with increasing momentum. Inaction seemed intolerable. Gathering himself, he rose and dashed forward, hoping the sniper had been dislodged or had better marks for his rifle. The covering barrage was now well forward, no longer followed by masses of troops. The attackers were moving all over the place in scattered groups, taking advantage of any cover they could find. Wicked 5.9 bursts were churning up the ground behind. Straight ahead there was a gradual slope to the low horizon, like a vision of ground before the madness, practically free of moving men.

Like a parting of the waves the impetus of attack slewed away from the open rise, either towards the woods to the left or towards an enemy parapet on the right. For Norman Gladden, as the trench seemed nearer, it offered the less risky alternative.

As he breasted the parapet, he viewed a litter of devastation. A splutter of bullets forced him down amid the horror. The trench, which was little more than a wide gash in the ground, was strewn with dead and dying, British and Germans in grim equality. The place was garnished with blood and entrails, a regular slaughter-house. Other fusiliers were dropping into the shelter of this very lightly protected pit of hell. For a moment the red curtain fell before his eyes and he saw, emerging through the awful mist, the fixed ghastly look of a sorely wounded German who someone had propped against the earth wall of the trench. Those eyes looked right through Norman to the eternity which, for the wounded man, was clearly so close at hand.

Objective reports might consider the situation fluid. In fact it was a shambles of confusion. The plan was that 10th NF and 13th DLI would pass through to assault both the Blue and Green lines. Norman Gladden, crouched in the temporary, blood-washed haven of the German trench could not see any of his comrades from 11th NF. To regain the survivors of the unit he would have to attempt the perilous dash over open ground to the fringe of the woods. 'Running across from shell-hole to shell-hole, I eventually struck the woods diagonally some way in advance and was pleased to join a party of troops who had collected near an enemy strongpoint.'

All of the company officers were down, dead or wounded. Formidable Sergeant Rhodes now commanded the remnant. Captain West, commanding 'B' Company, lay in the wood mortally wounded where he had fallen at the head of his men, continuing to press forward despite an earlier wound. Second Lieutenant Edwards, Norman's platoon CO, had been shot dead by a German who had already given himself up at the strongpoint. His gratuitous murder was immediately avenged by the sergeant leading the group. The other Germans had been sent back to brave the dangers of their own barrage. On the roof of the concrete pillbox a sniper lay sprawled in death on the very spot to which he had climbed when the British barrage had lifted.

Within the shifting carapace of trees, groups filtered blindly. All order and cohesion had gone. For a while Norman Gladden was put in charge of a small group of British wounded, a task he hardly relished. Despite his own terrors, he was aware he still packed the spare drums for the Lewis Gun. These would be needed. He had to press on, beyond the wood where Tower Hamlets Ridge swelled just ahead. In this flat, sodden polder even the suggestion of higher ground counted.

He had found the survivors of his own platoon, still led by Sergeant Rhodes and was re-united with his comrades from the Lewis Gun team. Casualties had been heavy but the tide of battle had moved forwards over Tower Hamlets Ridge.

Nonetheless, German snipers were still a regular menace. The Northumbrians both admired and hated these admittedly brave men. Admired them for their persistence and bravery, hated them, illogically to some extent, for what the Tommies considered was unsportsmanlike action. Possibly they were more desperate than brave, having been taught that they would get no quarter in any case. Of course, their persistence meant that it often worked out this way, for the moppers up didn't take any chances

It wasn't until midnight on 21 September that survivors of 'A' Company, having seen off several enemy counter-attacks, were withdrawn. In Staff College terms, the attacks on 20 September were successful. Attacking formations, moving behind the barrage, attained their objectives. Swift consolidation meant ruin for the three German divisions sent into counter-attack. 'Daddy' Plumer's careful and considered preparations had again paid dividends. On 26 September, Plumer once more attacked and the Australians took Polygon Wood. His third bound on 3 October came up against modified German response tactics and the Anzacs had to use their bayonets in taking Windmill Hill.

Ernest William Greenwood was a native of South Shields or

possibly Sunderland. He was a printer by trade and later a council-lor, and probably served in the Lancashire Fusiliers.

> On 4th October, 1917 we boarded London buses at a place called
> Coxcyle Bains to set forth for Ypres. One feature of these buses
> which amused the Tommies was a notice – 'id all the way' – which
> of course was a relic of their heyday in London. Whilst we halted
> in Ypres it was found that the company runner was missing, a
> very tall lad whose nerves were all gone … I afterwards learnt that
> this last, whose name I will not mention, was caught at Boulogne,
> and shot for desertion, which fact grieved me very much, as he
> had more than done his bit and had been wounded three times.[102]

Greenwood and his mates were in the reserve line astride the Menin Road.

> There were no breastworks or trenches, simply tens of thousands
> of water-logged shell holes … There were a large number of dead
> Germans and men of 1/6th Battalion Lancashire Fusiliers lying
> about. Our hunger made us search dead men's clothes for food
> but without success but we were successful in finding two gallons
> of water in a German petrol tin. That night it started to rain and
> rained on and off for the next three days until our shell hole had
> about nine inches of water. I somehow managed to get a shave
> each day and some of my pals who did not want to shave were
> annoyed with me for shaving, as they thought the captain might
> make all the lads shave!
>   On the morning of the 8th [October], we were assembled for a
> lecture and told that we had to take no prisoners alive and leave
> none dying who was dying. One of the boys who had just come
> out from England (being just eighteen years old), very nearly lost
> his life in one of these [shell] holes. It took us two hours to get
> him out; it was a question as to whether he would have to be
> shot so that the Battalion could get ahead. Well we got over the
> top eventually, having a go through Fritz's barrage … we had not

gone far until we were held up by heavy machine gun fire and while lying on the ground the bullets were passing over our heads in great quantity. A boy next to me got a bullet through his hand but I could do nothing for him. A military policeman tried to move us on but as our officers were lying on the ground in front of us, we laid till the machine gun fire had ceased. This military policeman must have had a charmed life as the bullets were flying around like hailstones and he never seemed to flinch.

By now impetus was lost and the attack had become disorganised:

Lieutenant Dyer and myself were sitting [in a shell hole] facing each other and without any apparent reason this officer, who was a brave man, turned as white as a sheet, and very suddenly, as though he felt it was his duty to get ahead, jumped up and said 'Come on Greenwood, let us get ahead!' We had not travelled far when eight Germans approached and, remembering our order of the previous evening, I got my rifle ready, but my officer turned to me and, laying his hand on my left shoulder said 'let them go, they are some poor mother's sons'. These Germans gave me my first impressions of what it must have been like on their side of the line. If I ever saw the face of death in anyone, it was on these men; it must have been hell on their side. It was very shortly after this that Lieutenant Dyer was killed at my side, and being company runner, I got permission from a Scottish officer to go back and report his death to the captain.

On 26 October the Canadians began their assault on the pulverised ruins of Passchendaele. On 6 November, they took the place. Fighting stuttered on for another couple of weeks till late autumn finally closed in on the battlefield. British casualties were stated as 244,897 dead, wounded and missing, German losses were estimated as considerably higher. Not everyone accepted this and the political consensus appears to have been that losses were about equal at nearly 400,000 each. There had been no breakthrough.

Cambrai

'Pat at the Front'

An English, Scotch and Irishman
Had once been called upon to plan
A fair division through the three,
Of four fresh eggs laid down for tea.

The Saxon failed and could not show,
Nor did the clever Scotchman know;
'Those two' said Pat, 'are for you two'
And these there two are for me too.
– B. G. Roughead, 12 October 1917[103]

On 20 November 1917, the church bells rang out across England. There was a victory to celebrate. Some jubilation was needed for the summer had brought nothing but continually mounting casualty lists and fresh rivers of broken and damaged men, all for little or no gain. Russia was gone, Italy defeated, France precarious and the Germans more or less where they had been in the spring.

Brigadier General Tudor, commanding 9th Division's artillery, was a pioneer of new and vastly improved ranging techniques. He had suggested that a section of the mighty Hindenburg Line between the St Quentin Canal and Canal du Nord, west of Cambrai, might be suitable ground for a large-scale raid. The aim was to fracture the line. He further suggested that tanks might be used to hack through the dense belts of wire rather than guns and provide cover for the attacking infantry. Haig, after 3rd Ypres, needed a quick win, and breaking in at Cambrai could have a seriously disruptive effect. The raid grew very swiftly into an offensive. Brigadier-General Elles, commanding the Tank Corps, encouraged by Lieutenant-Colonel J. F. C. Fuller, brilliant and acerbic, was keen to show what his monsters, deployed in large numbers over suitable ground, could achieve.

The BEF's youngest brigadier, Roland Boys Bradford (who we last encountered at the Butte de Warlencourt on the Somme) assumed command of 186th Brigade of the 62nd (West Riding) Division a mere ten days before the start of the battle. The men were left in no doubt as to their new commander's zeal:

> By the help of God I will try to lead you to the best of my ability, and remember your interests are my interests. As you know, a few days from now we are going to attack. Your powers are going to be tested. They must not fail you. Above all, pray! More things are wrought by prayer than this world dreams of! It is God alone who can give us victory and bring us through this battle safely.[104]

One of the most testing elements of the attack, as the brigade trained some four miles south-east of Arras, was the need for tank/infantry cooperation. Tanks, as impressive as they seem, cannot advance effectively without infantry support. Well-trained gunners can take them on and sections of enemy infantry, armed with grenades, can stalk the armoured leviathans like mammoth-hunters. Roland Bradford was an enthusiastic advocate of tank warfare: 'They [tanks] should go with the infantry. This gives confidence to our men and helps to demoralise the enemy. If they came on later the enemy is more prepared and will be able to devote more attention of his artillery to dealing with them.'

If Roland's divisional commander, Major-General Braithwaite, was an equally enthusiastic convert, Major-General Harper, leading 51st (Highland) Division to their right, was not. He mistrusted the new weapons and his reticence would lead to many difficulties on the first day. For the 62nd Division, their objectives lay in the fortified villages of the Hindenburg line; Havrincourt, Craincourt and Anneux. Brigadier Bradford's brigade would be in reserve with orders to pass through the leading elements, take and hold a line from Craincourt to the Bapaume–Cambrai road. They were also to secure the Hindenburg support system, take Anneux and finally link with cavalry on their left, occupying high ground just to the west of Bourlon Wood – an area whose notoriety would swell as the battle unfolded. Roland Bradford's previous experience had taught him the folly of keeping reserves too far back. These needed to be as close up as possible to exploit success before the enemy could recover his breath.

His senior officer was impressed:

I felt that there was a great deal in what Bradford said, and therefore I decided to 'chance my arm' and so I gave him instructions to keep moving forward, and directly the leading brigades had gained their initial success (which we hoped for and anticipated with a certain amount of confidence) that the 186th Brigade should push through. It was taking a bit of a risk but if it came off it was well worth it. As a matter of fact, it did come off and had a tremendous effect on the fortunes of the day alone because Bradford was a born leader and led his brigade with conspicuous success.

Dawn of 20 November witnessed some astonishing feats. The tanks, mighty in numbers, came rumbling forward out of the mist, grinding inexorably through the grand, seemingly impenetrable defences of the Hindenburg Line. Both leading brigades of 62nd Division secured their objectives by mid-morning. A vast haul of stunned defenders was netted. As Roland Bradford's battalions surged through, their brigadier was everywhere, exhorting, directing and leading. All was not going as well as it seemed. Harper's highlanders were stalled before Flesquières. General Braithwaite ordered a halt so that his surviving tanks could be redeployed and assault the village from the west.

As the attack faltered and lost momentum, Bradford's battalions were bombing their way up the German trenches, grenades and bayonets busy in a fury of action. Resistance was stiffening and fighting raged deep into the autumn darkness. Roland had his subterranean HQ in the ancient vaults of Craincourt church. Men under his command had surged forward over four miles on 20 November, arguably the deepest advance by any equivalent formation since the end of mobile warfare in the autumn of 1914.

Here, in the catacombs, he briefed those tankers who would be fighting alongside his brigade next day. Then they would be moving against the high ground of Bourlon Wood and village, a very tough nut indeed.

[T]here was a brigadier of Braithwaite's who stood head and shoulders above the rest. Boys Bradford, 25 years old, commander of an infantry brigade and holder of the Victoria Cross, was not of the common run of men. His brigade was ordered up from Craincourt to the assault on Bourlon: his battalions could not have been better chosen. Bradford was the ideal general for work of this kind.

Next day witnessed fierce fighting. Infantry and tanks worked their way doggedly forwards. Lewis-gunners of 2/4th Battalion Duke of Wellington's fired bursts from the hip, Chicago-gangster style, spraying windows and embrasures where enemy snipers lurked. The ridge of Bourlon Wood remained out of reach. The Germans had rushed reinforcements into the area. Both sides knew this to be the key. Exhausted, the 62nd Division was briefly withdrawn before being thrown back into the assault on 26 November. Roland Bradford's brigade was to attack the very centre of the ridge, going over at 6.20 a.m. on the 27th. This time there would be no miraculous advances. The dogfight would be vicious and at extremely close quarters in the tangle of trees and undergrowth. All day they scrapped and by dusk had forced a way onto the ridge. Ground so hard won could not be held and the survivors were forced to withdraw.

That night, the division was relieved and the weary Tommies plodded back to billets east of the Canal du Nord. As was his custom, Roland Bradford went out during the evening to tour outposts. Next afternoon, after a search, his body was found. He'd been killed by a single shard of shrapnel. General Braithwaite later wrote to the CO of 151st Brigade, the Durhams, with whom Roland had served:

Bradford was only with me, as I daresay you know, for about a
month, but during that time I and everybody else in the division
conceived a great admiration and affection for him and we all
felt his loss very keenly. He did simply splendidly … Personally I
think he is the most remarkable character that I have met during
this war. He had an absolute genius for war and a fine tactical
instinct, and I think men would have gone anywhere for him.
His loss is not only to the division but to the whole army, for he
would certainly have gone far.

Roland Bradford's death at the moment the battle turned into
stalemate is perhaps a metaphor for Cambrai: a bloody end for
little gain. Very soon, the exhausted British were holding a narrow
salient and, on 30 November, inevitable counter-attacks crashed
home. In classic manner, the Germans sought to pinch out the
bulge by attacking at the shoulders. In the south their success was
alarming. Desperate assaults barely stabilised the situation and by
5 December both sides ground to a halt. The British, while they
still held elements of the Hindenburg Line, had lost ground in
the south.

Cambrai had cost the British some 40,000 casualties but important lessons had been learned. These lessons would bear valuable
fruit during the break-in battles of 1918. The Germans, though they
might have missed the significance of the first-day tank successes,
were also developing new tactics. In the east, General Oscar von
Hutier was perfecting his concepts of infiltration. German victory
would release battle-hardened divisions for service in the west. The
BEF's hardest test was yet to come.

SIX

KAISERSCHLACT AND THE HUNDRED DAYS, 1918

'Never Mind'

If your sleeping place is damp,
Never mind!
If you wake up with a cramp,
Never mind!
If your trench should fall in some
Fill your ears and make you dumb
While the sergeant drinks your rum,
Never mind!

If you have to rise at four,
Never mind!
If the morning's dark and raw,
Never mind!
If a duck-board should elope
And your container has no rope,
And you have to wade and grope,
Never mind!

If the cook's a trifle new
Never mind!
If you get your tea and stew
All combined,

And you find your pint of rice
Has a coat of muddy ice
Try to think it blanky nice,
Never mind!
– Anon.[105]

The Kaiser's Battle

Who was the wag, who during a weary march in file from the ramparts to the trenches, passed back the message; 'Last man shut the Menin Gate?'[106]

George Harbottle was, at the war's outset, apprenticed to Tyneside shipbrokers Cairns Noble, based on the bustling Quayside. His wages were 7s 6d (37½p) per week. A three-course meal at the YMCA could be had for 2s (10p) or more modest fare at Carrick's could be enjoyed for sixpence (2½p) less. One of the firm's directors served as a major in the Territorial gunners. With the great rush to volunteer, apprentice clerks were assured their jobs would be kept for them should they feel the tug of service to King and country irresistible.

George and his best pal Laurie Benson joined the flood, enlisting in 6th Battalion Northumberland Fusiliers. Having reported to 'A' Company at Tilley's he was depressed to find that the beautiful dance floor which was the scene of so many happy memories now resembled a much encumbered parade ground.[107]

George spent two years in the infantry, seeing much action. In 1916 he retrained with the newly formed Machine Gun Corps, commissioned into the 15th Battalion. The Corps had been formed in 1915 to boost infantry firepower, deficiencies in automatic weapons being a prime lesson of the battles of that year. An MGC battalion comprised 'four companies commanded by a major with a captain as 2 I/C. each company had sixteen guns arranged in four sections of four guns'. In the divisional structure, each MG company worked with a brigade. This was not a popular arrangement as the MG officers ruled their own fiefs and were not directly answerable to the infantry. In March 1917 George found himself at Arras: 'the front was a strong one, because we had gained the best strategic positions in our successful offensive in Easter 1917'.

For George Harbottle, his comrades in 15th Battalion MGC and for the whole of the BEF, an immense trial now lay ahead. It was not only the British who had been working on improved artillery and infantry infiltration tactics. Colonel Georg Bruchmüller, 'Breakthrough Müller', was re-defining the use of German guns. A new or re-invented breed of infantry soldier, the storm-trooper, was emerging. The idea of elite infantry, hardened and motivated to bludgeon through the crust of enemy defences, was not new. Grenadier companies were a feature of eighteenth-century warfare, distinguished by their unmistakable mitre caps. By early 1918, fully fledged storm battalions, their firepower beefed up with more machine guns, flamethrowers and an infantry gun battery, were being groomed to break the deadlock. Their role was to punch a hole through the defenders' lines, attacking at the weakest spot, then pushing on, leaving the business of mopping up to infantry moving in behind.

General Ludendorff, despite sweeping victories and Russia's near collapse in the east, knew that time was a luxury he did not possess. Russia might be prostrate but America was now entering the war. Though her troops were initially few, the trickle would soon swell into flood. To break the front meant breaking the British, now senior partners in the original alliance. If Germany could successfully breakthrough in the north and turn the Allied flank as had been attempted in autumn 1914, the long delayed victor's laurels might still rest with Kaiser Wilhelm.

It only remained to decide where the blow, or blows, should fall. Flanders was unattractive for all the reasons the British themselves had incurred such huge losses to demonstrate. Arras/Vimy sector was too strongly held. Further south, however, where the Hindenburg Line offered a perfect jumping-off point, opportunity beckoned. Three great hammer blows, code-named 'Michael; I, II

& III' would strike General Gough's 5th Army, their thinly held
lines stretched taut, desolation of the old Somme battlefield at
their backs.

For Haig, his opponent's timing could not have been worse.
The BEF was ground down by cruel losses in the preceding year.
Conscripts dragged unwillingly into the terrible attrition were not
the men their bright-eyed predecessors of 1914 or 1915 had been.
As the French stumbled, the BEF had to accept responsibility
for yet more ground. As German tactics shifted, new responses
were needed. Lloyd George and his 'easterners' had little time for
their commander-in-chief. His pleas for more men went largely
unanswered. Besides, there was none more to be had. Britain
and Germany were like two punch-drunk fighters clinging to the
canvas, both very nearly played out but not willing to quit the ring.

British military intelligence was aware the blow must fall. The
question was where. To cope with these new threats and reflecting the transitions in positional warfare through 1917, the British
line was now a layer cake of three connected levels. A lightly held
forward zone relied upon wired in redoubts, supported by machine
guns and a thin artillery line. Perhaps a mile or more behind was the
fighting line with most of the infantry and more guns; behind this
the rear or support zone. Like most innovations, this revised system
had its critics and some local commanders retained a tendency to
stuff too many soldiers into the forward zone. Gough had fourteen
under strength divisions to hold over forty miles of the line. His
defences were patchy, often incomplete. An invitation to disaster
and not one Ludendorff could afford to refuse.

George Harbottle was one who witnessed the breaking storm.

On the morning of Thursday, 21st March, I came out of my
dugout with my runner to stand to at dawn with my guns. We
were walking along the top of the trench when suddenly there
came the biggest bang I have ever heard or ever wish to. The
German 1918 offensive had started and at Zero-hour everything
had opened up simultaneously. The green, yellow and white

SOS lights were shooting up into the air and all our artillery was busy immediately plastering the enemy lines, as were our own machine guns.[108]

George's machine-gunners were in the second line around the village of Monchy-le-Preux, mostly occupying old German positions captured in the previous year's savage fighting where the British cavalry and their horses had lost heavily. An unmistakable reek of decaying horseflesh cloyed the air.

In George's sector the front line, despite a massive bombardment, appeared to be holding. 'What we did not know was that south of us our lines had been completely broken and the enemy was pouring through the gaps he had made on a wide front.' Indeed he was. Fog blanketed the initial German attacks, conferring some respite from British MG fire and parties of storm-troopers infiltrated behind the forward redoubts. Despite heroic stands such as that of the 16th Manchester Battalion, ground was swiftly lost and in some cases the defence at best half-hearted. By the end of that first day, Britain had lost 38,000 men, over half of them taken prisoner and the old trench line system, held before the July 1916 Somme offensive, was soon penetrated.

Amiens and Arras, key bastions, were threatened. It was a very black time for the BEF. George Harbottle and his machine-gunners had withdrawn to an old German redoubt in the valley which lay between Tilloy and Monchy-le-Preux. The place was strong but isolated. George was sent back to the top of the ridge to seek further guidance from the infantry. A further withdrawal into the main Tilloy line was urgently recommended.

'Where the hell are you going?' an engineer officer demanded as George returned down the valley with uncomfortable news that the position had been overrun. There was nothing for it but to pelt back uphill, fearful of what might have become of his company. In fact the machine-gunners had wisely withdrawn beforehand. George noted, 'I found them in a strong position in our front line on the ridge with a beautiful field of fire over the whole valley'. For the Germans Tilloy Ridge would be a very formidable obstacle. George's guns would have inflicted grievous loss but the swell of attacks ebbed like a receding tide. On one flank, George's division was thrown forward to keep contact northwards. On the other, the line was bent to the right as forces southward were still being pushed back. As Richard Holmes notes, one of the key ideas developed by the military thinker Clausewitz is the diminishing power of the offensive. Ludendorff's push had bitten deep. Although the line had been dramatically pushed back, it had not fractured. There was no breakthrough.

French and British commanders met at Doullens on 26 March 1918 to co-ordinate their operations on the Western Front. Allied fears resounded like the clap of doom. Haig was under pressure from Lord Milner and from the newly appointed CIGS Sir Henry Wilson. Robertson, who'd fallen foul of Lloyd George once too often, had gone and the slippery Wilson finally got his job. It was the fiery General Foch, one of the most dynamic French commanders, who maintained a staunch defiance. Pétain, the hero of Verdun, was more morose. The upshot was that Foch assumed de facto overall command of all Allied forces. This was important news. For the first time the Allies would come under a unified command structure. Haig had previously agreed to be subordinate to the bombastic General Nivelle, if not with good grace. Here was something different, the makings of a real partnership. Despite those disasters which had befallen the BEF, the British were still very much in the ring.

For George Harbottle and his gunners, there was little fresh employment. German attacks at Arras had largely petered out. The earlier system of linear trenches with dense belts of wire and clearly defined tracts of no man's land had given way to a more flexible and frequently fluid defence.

Between the old front line running from Fampoux to Monchy and the present position at Tilloy and Feuchy, the situation had become far more fluid. One of the most dangerous sectors was up the Scarpe River Valley, which ran from Feuchy through to

Lieutenant Stanley Purvis, who served with 5th Green Howards. In his letters he used familiar East Yorkshire scenes as similes for trench warfare in an attempt to make the experience more relevant to those at home. © Green Howards Museum

BELOW LEFT Captain George Purvis, 5th Green Howards, Stanley's elder brother, one of those 'temporary gentlemen' and one who failed to return. © Green Howards Museum

BELOW RIGHT Private O'Donnell, DLI. Formerly a shipyard worker and yet another who did not return and whose wife received a typically terse War Office report of his death in action. His comrades, however, wrote more kindly. © Durham County Record Office

Sergeant Robert Constantine, DLI. A Gateshead man who volunteered before the outbreak in 1914, he fell on the Somme and is remembered on the Thiepval Memorial.
© Durham County Record Office

Armorer Patterson, who served with the Northumberland Hussars and was captured in France, pockets bulging with letters from his sweetheart.
© Tyne and Wear Archives & Museums

Sergeant George Thompson MM (back row, third from left), who served with his beloved horses, seen here with his DLI comrades. © Durham County Record Office

Reverend James A. G. Birch, DLI (front row, second from left), ordained before 1914, served as chaplain to 5th Battalion before being invalided home with trench fever in 1915.
© Durham County Record Office

Lieutenant Frederick L. F. Rees MC, DLI, joined 13th Battalion in 1914, seeing much action. After the war he became a clergyman and died at the age of ninety-two.
© Durham County Record Office

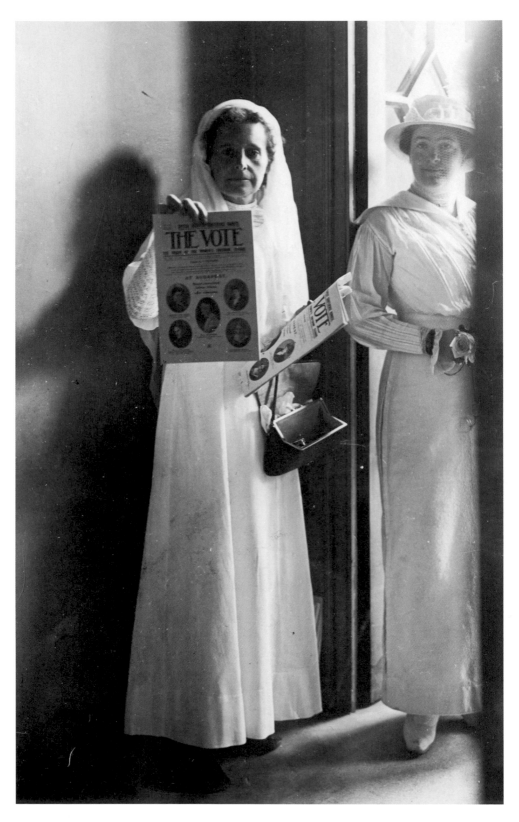

Katherine Harley at the 1913 International Women's Conference. © New York Public Library

Evelyn Luard, seen here nursing in South Africa during the Boer War. © Essex Records Office

Pat Beauchamp at her wedding – both bride and groom had lost limbs in France. © Celia Washington

LEFT Examples of Tommy humour: 'Recollections of my pleasant time at N.W. Hospital.' This is typical of Tommy art and doggerel preserved in survivors' scrap books © Author's collection

RIGHT 'Has the orderly taken your temperature?' © Author's collection

'The last post!' © Author's collection

'Britannia' © Author's collection

'Tommy' © Author's collection

'Visions of Blighty' © Author's collection

Peter the cat with his victory ribbons, though still looking very grumpy. © Tyne and Wear Archives & Museums

Butte de Warlencourt, near Le Sars, Somme, memorial to the 151st Brigade's heroic but costly attack, November 1916. © Durham County Record Office

Fampoux and despite the constant fire, was still heavily wooded. A brace of wily Gordon Highlanders, cut off in the initial German onslaught on 21 March, made it back to British lines having survived a vagabond existence in the maze of old trenches and abandoned dugouts.

One of the machine-gunners' outposts was both remote and exposed. It could only be relieved at night. 'Rather a difficult place to locate in the darkness because it had to be approached alongside the little Scarpe River ... this narrow little valley was littered with half broken trees, branches, undergrowth and rocks and could lead us onto the German lines unless due care was exercised.' When George's section attempted a midnight relief, their guide got hopelessly lost, quailing before the NCO's invective. After some coaxing, he found the way. This position was at the front of the front, hopelessly exposed in daylight to shellfire. So, the machine-gunners spent their days crouched in a rather makeshift and unsound dugout. They lived like creatures of the night, only surfacing in darkness or, should it come, in the moments before an attack. None did come.

Their next, equally improvised, lodgings were further back, in a warren of passages burrowed into a railway embankment. Here, their existence was little more comfortable. The only reading George could find in his dugout was a month-old continental *Daily Mail* and the Horsforth Chapel magazine, left behind by a previous occupier. Curiously enough he had often attended that chapel as a boy when visiting an aunt who lived there just outside Leeds.

Ludendorff's offensive was slackening into fresh attrition, the more ground taken, the greater the burden of tenure. On 28 March, he unleashed 'Operation Mars' – an attempt to seize ports held by the Allies. This was a fresh blow but like breakers beating on the shore, the hurricane force was fading. On 11 April Haig issued his famous 'backs to the wall' order but the crisis had already passed.

Next, Ludendorff would try further north; the 'Georgette' offensive represented a weakened thrust. A more ambitious previous operation – 'George' – had earlier been discarded in favour of the onslaught against Gough's 5th Army. On 8 April the Germans launched a new attack in the Lys River in the Armentières sector. Part of this front was being held by the Portuguese contingent (known to British troops as the 'Pork & Beans') and the weight of the onslaught broke them completely.

The Portuguese were in the line by Neuve Chapelle and Georgette inflicted another smashing blow into the British sector. All the gains of 1917, the terrible, bloody mud-coated slog up Passchendaele Ridge were lost, and Tommies fought from the ancient Vauban walls of Ypres itself. Those ravaged and ruined remains, the tattered ghost of a city, were held.

Like their enemies, the Germans were scraping the barrel. Their surviving elite was groomed for the storm-trooper battalions but paid a heavy price. The rank and file coming on behind often failed to exhibit the iron discipline so expected of the German war machine. These German troops were not the equal of their predecessors, the lure of loot often proved irresistible. Places they now reached, such as Estaires and Merville, hitherto untouched by war and with shops fully stocked, were thoroughly despoiled.

George's previous division, the 50th Northumbrian, was amongst those relieved when Foch sent up reinforcements. Re-deployed in a nominally quiet sector between Soissons and Rheims on the line of the Aisne and Aisne Canal, they found their welcome rest very short. This area along the Chemin des Dames, so frequently fought over, was now considered 'the sanatorium of the Western Front'. It was over this unsuspecting ground that Ludendorff unleashed 'Blucher', his next attempt. Again, initial gains were made and the Allied defenders, assailed by Breakthrough Müller's brilliantly directed guns, were pushed back savagely. Then this fresh offensive, like its predecessors, ran out of steam. By this time the Northumbrians had lost heavily. George Harbottle, whose MG Company formed part of 15th Scottish Division, found himself being redeployed further south towards the new cauldron north of Amiens.

'Tout le monde a la bataille'

'The Lone Pine Charge'

The boys of the First Brigade stood to their arms;
From the lines of the foeman rang out the alarms.
We crouched as we waited the shrill whistle blast,
Each knew that his effort might well be his last.
The signal rang out and we sprang to the work,
With bayonets in line and each face to the Turk;
And we thought every gun in the universe talked,
As the reaper, grim death, took his toll as he stalked.
The wounded fell prone, ne'er again would they rise,
For the shrapnel sowed death as it rained from the skies
But the remnant pushed on and came up with the Turk,
Great gaps in their ranks but in stern mood for work,
Some Turks stood their ground – there were some who had fled.
But we harried them well and the trenches ran red,
They plied us with shot and the dread hand grenade.
Yet slowly, but surely our progress we made.
For six days and nights raged the battle apace,
And each showed the other the dash of his race.
But a silence crept over the trenches one night,
And we knew when it deepened, that we owned the fight.
Not a hand grenade thrown – not a shot from a gun
We breathed for a space – Lone Pine had been won.
– Anon.[109]

On 3 June the Americans fought their first action at Château-Thierry. Their next and savage baptism occurred in the bloody fight for Belleau Wood where they took all their objectives though at very high cost. It was not until 18 July that General Foch launched the first major Allied counter-attack, led by General Mangin's 10th Army. By the start of August, the initiative had passed fully to the Allies. The Americans would fight on the left flank in Lorraine while the British struck eastwards through Cambrai. The swelling US forces fought hard and well, their numbers growing daily. Battering through the Kriemhilde Line to reach Sedan, heavy with history, cost them dear but it was taken nonetheless.

George Harbottle had originally volunteered as a private but was later promoted to NCO. By 1918, having re-trained with the MGC, he was made 2nd lieutenant. In June, with his precious guns, he found himself being moved south. Re-shuffling of officers does not equate to further promotion, however, battalions are most often re-organised after sustaining heavy casualties. Like most of his fellow officers, he was by now in possession of a horse, the officer's perk; the PBI made do with their feet as they had done since the days of Marius' Mules.

His new comrades in 'C' Company were known as the 'gramophone' unit; this on account of the fact the CO and 2 I/C were both 'to put it mildly besotted about music'. 'C' Company could boast 'a very good instrument with a large horn'. This prized possession was carefully transported neatly packed into one of the gun limbers (more usually reserved for ammunition) along with a fine classical selection: 'every officer who went on leave to England had to come back with a suitable record of equal calibre. The Misha [sic] Elman string quartet was very much to the fore in America at this period and we had many of their recordings'.

George got on well with his seniors, Major Hamilton, a Yorkshire-man, and the Canadian Captain Rosher. Amiable and imperturbable, the captain was a thoroughly decent type though rather eccentric in his time-keeping. 'His morning rounds of the guns, as often as not were in the afternoon, and as he would go into great detail about any gun position and talk to everyone, he would often be having dinner in the mess at some hour nearing midnight…' George's previous experience with billeting arrangements and his relative mastery of French meant he was selected for this role as the company concentrated south of Doullens prior to the big move. His new mount, charmingly named 'Jessica', proved more than lively attempting several times to relive herself of her officer burden. 'I … gave her a smack between the ears with my riding crop. She tried it again and got the same treatment, that terminated her antics and we lived very happily together until the day I was en route for England and demobilization.'

Billeting was a tedious and frequently difficult chore. 'We had to find accommodation for seven officers, the officers' mess, 50 other ranks and 40 horses and mules.' The Company had to spend a week or so in these billets while the division made ready. Getting the men onto trains, regulation two score per cattle truck, usually proved quite easy. Mules were a different matter … 'mules are the devil'. The rail journey took 15th Scottish some twenty-five miles south of Compiègne to the village of Creil on the Oise. George's Company was to be billeted in Pont-Saint-Maxence, an idyllic location, untouched by war, with a broad sweep of the Oise running through.

It was time for cricket. The CO of 'D' Company, a Major Forester, had, in peacetime, been a fast bowler in the Derbyshire County XI. He had the kit and had managed to locate a suitable pitch. Volunteers for an inter-company game were urgently sought. George, a keen cricketer, and half a dozen soldiers formed the nucleus of one team. Batting was opened by another county-level player, the aptly named Sergeant Bowley. Forester's bowling was deadly … 'Bowley being out, caught off his bat handle, when trying to protect his face, commented to me as he took off his pads that it wasn't pads I needed but a steel helmet!' Before George entered the fast-bowler's sights, the war trumpets sounded loud and clear and cricketing gear went back into a gun limber.

Such was the urgency, they moved up by motor vehicle, rather than with more sedate horse-drawn limbers. This was the time of Foch's first counter-stroke with the Germans now falling back towards the line of the Aisne, where they'd begun digging in during autumn 1914. As the Allied blow was itself running out of steam, the 15th Scottish would relieve the American 1st Division. The chase wound rapidly through a succession of townships, to the Château de Vierzy where officers slept in the superb library. Here they were surrounded by shelves laden with ancient, leather bound volumes and fine *Ancien Régime* furnishings. Miraculously, it seemed the random hand of fate had spared this treasure. Next morning they moved up towards the line where another château at Buzancy had not escaped the war. The Germans had invested and fortified the place: it was now a seemingly immovable bastion anchoring their improvised lines.

At midday, the machine-gunners grabbed rations just beyond a small river. Across from them, French infantry were about to consume cooked food which smelled infinitely more appetising and ate their meal to the accompaniment of their own singing. While the machine-gunners could not quite get the words, the lascivious gist was easily apparent.

George and his section moved forward, the guns sounding ever louder. The British were unprepared for the relative informality of their new American comrades and the rather casual handover. Their guide was fairly nonchalant but did point out a slight rise which was much visited by enemy artillery. With that helpful advice it was 'that's it chum, guess I beat it now – bye'. He disappeared, swift as a hare and the newcomers were on their own.

But they were not by any means alone. Their own infantry were ahead and the overall situation was extremely fluid – to the extent nobody was exactly sure of anything. A diminutive copse some 200 yards in front was thought to be an enemy nest and about to be swept by a fighting patrol. The guns would give covering fire and deal with any targets flushed out. In the event there were none. The trees proved innocent of any foe. The Germans did not intend to stand. What 'C' Company was facing was a determined rearguard, well dug in and supported. A very determined rearguard, as it proved, for a fortnight's siege. Seven attempts at break in did not budge them.

The machine-gunners found those French maps upon which George was obliged to rely inadequate, compared to British OS equivalents … 'pretty hopeless … small scale and without contours'. Next target was the formidable German bastion of Buzancy. For the current British escalade, the guns would support the right flank of the assault. Happily, there were some aerial photos of the château to hand. 'C' Company was not to advance with the first wave but to remain in support till the place was cleared, then move up and consolidate. At noon the signal came and George came forward with his two leading gun teams.

As ever in the fog of war, matters were not as clear cut as the optimistic message might suggest. Only part of the position had fallen. Enemy defence on the right was still holding up vigorously; 'the gap between our copse and the wall of the chateau was being swept by MG fire from a strongpoint on the right flank'. This was tricky and the gunners couldn't simply make a dash for it. If any of the team was hit then they'd be without a vital component or bereft of ammunition. A slight fold in the ground offered possibilities. The gunners now crawled forward, dragging their cumbersome charges. Only one man was injured. In front of them now the solid park wall of the château, a dozen feet high. Getting over with guns and gear was no mean feat. The men used each other as a human ladder, still under fire. Each climber straddled the rampart so kit could be passed up and over. At last, without loss, they were in.

A fresh challenge arose as they crept forward to find their infantry comrades. There was none to be found. In fact the British attackers had been dislodged and were falling back over open ground. 'I could see no officer anywhere and knew that a movement like that could develop into anything.' Spotting a tree line and hedge some 100 yards past the field, George sent two NCOs with a brace of Vickers to take firing positions there. Next, he found a sergeant from those Gordons who had put in the attack and instructed him to rally on the guns. This worked. Very soon the machine-gunners and infantry had formed a workable defensive line, backed by additional Lewis Guns and an abandoned German Maxim which was soon got into action.

His rally party swiftly attracted new members. At length several officers from the Gordons turned up and took charge of the thin khaki line. George's instructions were, the action over, to report to Company HQ. Here, his greeting was rapturous. The sergeant

leading the section behind, seeing George's team vanish over the
wall with the foot in full retreat, had assumed they were by now all
dead or captured. George was already posted as missing in action.
That night, the Germans withdrew leaving the battered château to
the British. The place was empty, only the dead remaining: 'These
attacks on Buzancy had been costly in casualties and while I was
crossing the field when taking my guns into the chateau grounds, I
noticed the dead of five nations: French, American, Scots, German
and English.'

George won an MC for his role in the attack on Buzancy and
came home safe, married and resumed his civilian occupation. He
published his memoir privately in 1981, though he wrote several
other volumes on sport. He died at the age of 103. After the fight
for Buzancy the 17th French Division erected a memorial to the 15th
Scottish. It reads:

'*Ici fleurira toujours le glorieux*
Chardon d'Ecosse parmi les roses de France.'
(Here the glorious thistle of Scotland will
Flourish for ever amid the roses of France.)

That pretty much says it all.

Black Day for the German Army

War requires an ingenious mind, always alert, and one day the
reward of victory comes. Don't talk to me about glory, beauty,
enthusiasm. They are verbal manifestations. Nothing exists
except facts and facts alone are of any use. A useful fact, and one
that satisfied me, was the signing of the armistice … Without
trying to drag in miracles just because clear vision is vouchsafed
to a man, because afterwards it turns out this clear vision has
determined movements fraught with enormous consequences in
a formidable war, I still hold that this clear vision comes from a
Providential force, in the hands of which one is an instrument,

and that the victorious decision emanates from above, by the
higher and Divine will.
– Marshal Ferdinand Foch[110]

One of the early casualties of 'Michael' was General Gough. The
failures of the 5th Army were laid at his door and his head provided
the requisite sacrifice. He was replaced by Rawlinson, a general
who, as Richard Holmes observes, had learned a great deal about
fighting the Germans since the Somme. Besides, the German
Army, like the British and French, was not what it had been two
years or even a year before. Ludendorff's gains had been won at
huge cost. The best and the bravest, as ever, paid the fullest price.
What remained, in qualitative terms, was simply not the same.

Having seen to his defences, Rawlinson came to the view that
the time was perhaps ripe for thinking in more offensive terms.
He could not conjure up more men but he could replace flesh and
blood which had failed against the terrible killing power of modern
weapons with automatic fire and steel plate; more machine guns,
more tanks. British artillery performance had improved already in
leaps and bounds. Tanks, those great lumbering juggernauts which
had rumbled onto the scene in 1916 and had begun to demonstrate their enormous potential a year later, were, with the new
Mark V substantially improved, faster or at least less slow and
more reliable.

Heavy bombers had made their appearance and the beginnings
of strategic air power which would loom large in the post-war
debate were stirring:

London Wednesday [1 August 1918] an official report from
the RAF independent force in France states that on Monday
night our machines attacked the railway stations at Offenburg,
Rastaff and Baden. Stuttgart and Solingen were also attacked.
Three hostile aerodromes and numerous ground targets were
bombed and subjected to machine-gun fire. All our machines
returned.[111]

In a war marked by filth, squalor, constant attrition and a vast, unceasing haemorrhage of broken and maimed, 'the knights of the air' seemed outwardly to represent something more chivalrous, nobler and more Homeric than mass slaughter on the ground. This was a fiction of course, encouraged by both sides' propaganda; war in the air was every bit as deadly.

The 'boy airman' is the most wonderful of all the wonderful combatants in this war. Those in authority like to catch him young, for his 'nerve' is better and he comes into training as an absolute stranger to fear. Shortly before the war an angry parent called in on his boy's schoolmaster, 'I don't know what to do with my boy', he said despairingly. 'All I can get out of him is that he wishes he were a bird and could fly'.

'Well', replied the schoolmaster, 'if the war comes we shall want all the human birds we can get hold of. Let him fly'. So the angry parent reluctantly 'let him fly'.

Three months after his training was finished, the boy came to see me. He had turned into a man, as the old lady put in 'an eye like a hawk'. He was in truth a human bird and told me of the dangers he had passed as coolly as if he were narrating the incidents of a football match. The second time he came, his face was disfigured by two of the most awful black eyes I have ever seen on any human countenance. 'How did it happen?' I asked. 'Oh', he said, in a matter of fact tone, 'I was making a turn and didn't put enough back into it, it's just like a side slip on a bicycle'.

'And you came down?'

'Of course I came down!'

'And did the machine come down too?'

'There wasn't any of it left in workable shape. A week in hospital put me alright'.

– G. B. Burgin, 'All the boys want to be airmen'[112]

In fact, the average life expectancy of a rookie flyer in the war was six weeks; in combat this could easily be measured in minutes.

A series of generally successful large scale raids led Rawlinson to believe the time ripe for a wider offensive. The Allied blow would fall along a front from north of the Somme to just south of the Amiens–Villers–Bretonneux road. Rawlinson had long been a believer in 'bite and hold'. Haig, as ever, wanted more and deeper. He would have a significant superiority in terms of tanks, guns and aircraft. The burgeoning role of the latter would be significant. Security was paramount throughout. When the blow fell at dawn on 8 August, the Germans were caught out and seriously savaged. Rawlinson was to say 'we have given the Germans a pretty good bump this time'. Both the official German history and Ludendorff gloomily concurred. This was indeed 'the black day' of a German army which had fought so very hard indeed throughout four years of titanic industrial war.

The 'black day' led to the Hundred Days which led inexorably to Germany's defeat. Victory was bought at enormous cost. British casualties in August 1918 amounted to 80,000. The Hundred Days in all cost 220,000 more. These came from a diminishing stock. Britain was bled dry, as was France and as was Germany. That summer was one of Allied advances and German withdrawals. The latter were never in danger of becoming a rout. Stubborn rearguards, as seen at Buzancy, shielded every backwards step.

Sergeant McGuffie Wins the Victoria Cross

'La Belle France'

The Boy stood in the ... (pardon) trench
As he was paid to do;
The life was ensanglante (French) [bloody]
The pay was one and two
And even that (if he might mention it) was overdue.

The mud was thick as you could find;
Its quality was such

As shops would call 'a special kind,
Most yielding to the touch'
He tried, but could not call to mind
Things he disliked as much.

He did not pat his diaphragm
Nor wave his handkerchief,
At sight of food. He gave no damn
(This passes all belief)
For Yuletide plum and apple jam,
For Christmas bully beef.

Explosive shells were overhead,
Do, mines were underneath,
'My Goodness,' more than once he said,
'This is a blasted heath'
He meant thereby that he was fed
Up to his backmost teeth.
– Anon.[113]

R. A. Urquhart was conscripted and posted to the 5th Battalion King's Own Scottish Borderers in January 1918.

> Our training during this period was mainly drill, physical train-
> ing and sport, the objective being to smarten us up and make
> us fit. One item I remember well was jogging around the public
> park most mornings before breakfast. When May [1918] arrived
> we were sent to Kelling camp in Norfolk where we joined up with
> other recruits for another KOSB Battalion. Here, we received our
> complete training for overseas and met up with the Sandhurst
> trained platoon officers who brought us to France.[114]

Arriving in Boulogne at the end of July and billeted in St Martin's camp, Urquhart read in the *Daily Mail* of a debate in the House of Commons:

One of the Edinburgh MPs, Mr J. Hogg had stood up in Parliament and accused the PM Lloyd George, of sending boys under 19 years of age into the front line. This was denied by the PM who also said that any boys under 19 years who were up in the line would be sent down.

Urquhart was only eighteen but on his way up into the line!

Like countless thousands of Tommies before them, the Borderers entrained on the unimaginably slow French railways in the familiar cattle trucks and chugged slowly and in near total darkness north-wards. Compared to the footslogging ahead, this would almost, and in hindsight, appear luxurious: 'From that day, I have no recol-lection of reaching any destination whilst up in the line other than by foot.' They now marched from Kemmel to Steenvoorde and then to Hillebroucq. Early August and the new recruits found their battalion at Wormhout. Here they were introduced to Sergeant Major (acting) Louis McGuffie. At the venerable age of twenty-five, he seemed to them an aged Olympian; 'he brought with him our first supply of cigarettes and tobacco'. They moved up closer to the front via Poperinghe and Plotijze. They were assured their first tour 'would be very quiet'. Perhaps they wondered how many other fresh recruits had received the same bland assurance and how many had in fact been hurled straight into the inferno?

On arrival I was surprised to see that the trench ran along the boundary of the communal cemetery – situated not far from the Menin Gate. There we were accommodated in dugouts placed between the graves. Since joining the 5th Battalion, the young lads were usually billeted along with an older member of the battal-ion. On this occasion, I had one by the name of McGregor whose perky sense of humour banished the morbid surroundings of our sleeping accommodation. At dusk we had stand to in the trench where I placed my Lewis Gun on the rampart beside a white wooden cross where Prince Maurice of Battenberg lay buried. He had been a Lieutenant in the KRRC, killed in October 1914.

At night the skies were brightened and illuminated by German flares and, by day, they had a view of the skeletal carcass of the once splendid Cloth Hall, a medieval building which was once home to the City's textile industry.

> A few days before we left the cemetery, we were informed that a supply of wines had been brought up from the cellars of Ypres and we were invited to bring our canteens to obtain our share. The connoisseurs amongst us were disappointed when we received our allocation which was Vichy water!

From the hollow shell of Ypres, the KOSBs moved towards Kemmel:

> As we marched, or should I say trekked, down a road towards the foot of the hill [Mt Kemmel] it became clearer, and we were able to see what was around us. We found ourselves walking on what we thought were discarded greatcoats and tunics. Eventually, we became aware of the situation and realized we were walking over the bodies of French and Germans who had been killed during the fighting earlier in the year. The surface of the road had been flattened by vehicles and in several places only the buttons of the uniforms along with scraps of cloth were visible as if they had been hurriedly buried or just run over and pressed down. Near the end of the road, an arm with a gloved, clenched hand was raised up from the elbow as if giving a signal to halt. It was a ghastly sight.

Strung out in a skirmish line, on attaining the summit Urquhart was sent on ahead with a small group of officers, over the crest and down the reverse slope 'like a group of hikers on a morning stroll'. Their stroll was soon halted by sniper fire as they moved towards the position known as Donegal Farm (and a particularly 'hot' sector):

> We saw a hedge on the left and ran towards it. It gave us some protection until we reached a cornfield through which we crawled

until we arrived at the path through the wood to Donegal Farm. There we found many shell holes. No sooner had we jumped into them when shells began to arrive behind me. On looking back, I saw stretcher-bearers carrying a lad away from a shell hole I had just left.

No further movement was worth even contemplating till night. Then, cautiously forward again. One member of Urquhart's section, blundering about behind searching for lost ammunition, called out his name. This earned both a swift rebuke and a German flare, arcing brilliant in the night sky; 'so I told him not to move. Fortunately, we were not spotted but I saw we were very close to the German positions.' They crawled forward into a shell-hole occupied by one of their own officers and an NCO. Plainly, they could hear German voices. The NCO volunteered to seek reinforcements but returned empty handed. Another, English battalion was behind but would not come up without orders from an officer.

They were at length relieved and moved back into the line. Though there was no large scale fighting to begin with, Urquhart remembered

… the three raids I took part in. The first was uneventful as far as though my section was involved, we did not see anything of the enemy. The second raid was similar, without sight of the Germans but eventful in the sense that an incident took place that I've never been able to understand. Before leaving, we were told that a rum ration would be sent to us. An unusual thing to happen and the only time such an arrangement was ever made before I took part in any action. The rum never arrived, so when I got back, I made enquiries and the explanation was that the two lads carrying the rum were challenged by a German, dropped it and ran off!

The third raid was the important one and, on this occasion, it was a 'sacrifice' patrol to enable the battalion to take up new positions for the big day. It seemed that the whole platoon was taking part. I had another Lewis-gunner with me and shelled the trench which was divided in two sections. The sergeant told me to remain with him and sent the others to the far section. As soon as they arrived there firing began and our Lewis-gunners went into action. When the German machine-gunners fired we were able to see them and noted their positions at the foot of the ridge.

As the initial exchange died down the NCO advised Urquhart he was expecting a runner with orders for them to withdraw. This forward position was too exposed and the Germans ahead would very likely soon be reinforced.

It was to be hoped the runner would arrive ahead of the enemy reserves.

This, however did not happen, 2.00 a.m. arrived but no messenger. Sometime after this the Lewis-gunner in the far section resumed firing until his gun jammed. I had to take my gun along. To reach the other section I had to jump a wide gap between the two and, when doing so, I landed among a collection of tin cans. When I jumped back [having swapped the jammed weapon for his own] I managed to avoid the MG rounds that struck as I got across. The firing continued and soon, stick bombs began to fall which made it impossible to remain. The sergeant decided we should get back. When we reached base we were told we would be mentioned in dispatches and that the cooks were preparing for us a very special meal. When it arrived we were unable to enjoy it as it had been sent up in petrol cans! The meal was cold rice pudding, flavoured with petrol.

On 29 September the Borderers went over the top at Wytschaete, sweeping forwards till halted by a German bunker whose occupants remained in residence. Despite this, a platoon of the Argylls pitched up beside and disputed their right. Sergeant McGuffie cut across the argument by winkling the remaining defenders out with grenades '… it was enough; out they came, "*Kamerad*"'. Their next halt was in a deep shell-hole, where they were 'pinned down by MG fire coming from farm ruins a few hundred yards to the left. Fortunately, the shell-hole was a very deep one which gave us good protection.' Sergeant McGuffie had acquired a good pair of German officer's binoculars as booty.

> There's some Boche coming down the road, let them have it! I got the gun into position and asked for a look through the glasses. I saw a single file of figures at the top of the road, just coming out of the wood. In front was a German but I noticed that the one behind him was British.

These were now seen to be British POWs with German escorts.

> We both got out of the shell-hole and McGuffie set off towards the gap in the wire. I presumed the prisoners were some of the A&SH – I was hoping they'd break away from their escort. They were about to do so when the Boche at the rear, who had a stick in his hand, touched the Argyll in front of him, indicating he should keep moving.
>   I then asked someone to pass me up his rifle. At the same time I said I could do with a bit of company so another lad came up beside me. The German in front took fright and went to his companion when we both raised our rifles. The Argyll's then threw themselves on the ground and the Germans ran off towards the road. We fired and they jumped into a small shell hole where they remained until McGuffie reached them.

It was the Germans' turn to become prisoners and McGuffie re-distributed the loot from their pockets, much of which was the property of the newly liberated highlanders. As the sergeant was doling out his gains, the platoon officer found them and advised that, as the company commander was down, he would have to take over, leaving the platoon in Sergeant McGuffie's capable hands.

> McGuffie took charge at 2.00 p.m. and came back to the

shell-hole 'come on lads, we have to join the rest of the company
up the road'. For ¾ of the way up we had cover from a high
embankment on our left which offered us protection from the
MG we knew was waiting for us. As soon as we lost that cover
and crossed to the other side of the road, the bullets arrived at my
feet. After the second burst, McGuffie and the lad in front of me
reached the wood and jumped into a trench.

It was at this point that Urquhart's luck ran out.

I was about to follow them when I was hit jumping into the
trench. McGuffie came back to me and, handing me some field
dressings, told me to dump the Lewis Gun and my equipment
and get back to the MO. As I was doing so a Lewis-gunner
shouted over to me that it would be safe to do so as he'd finished
off the German who'd shot me.

For his attack on the blockhouse, rescue of the prisoners and
assaulting several enemy dugouts, Sergeant Louis McGuffie was
awarded the Victoria Cross.

McGuffie deserved the VC. It is difficult to get to know officers and NCOs due to the high rate of change. At Wormhout
he welcomed me into the battalion and at Quarante Bois he
arranged for my departure. I shall always remember his coolness
and disregard for the German machine guns when he stood on
the edge of the shell-hole.

Private Urquhart had his wounds dressed at the ADS and was
transported on a stretcher to a base hospital at St Omer where,
after an operation, he was sent on to Boulogne. His wound was
a 'Blighty' one and he convalesced at Harrogate. He was finally
demobbed at Duddington camp near Edinburgh early in 1919.
Sergeant McGuffie was killed by a shell on 4 October.

Armistice

Thou shalt not covet thy neighbour's wife,
His ass though shalt not slaughter
But thank the Lord it is no crime
To covet another man's daughter!
– R. L. Morley, Royal Naval Air Service[115]

By the time McGuffie won his Victoria Cross, the Ypres Salient had almost been relegated to history, that ghastly charnel house of inestimable suffering which had bled both sides like a raging ulcer. It was also towards the end of September that 4th Army crashed through the Hindenburg Line, the seemingly inexpugnable bastion of German hopes. There were no more storm-troopers left. Ludendorff's offensives had cost his nation another million men. This was warfare on a scale never before attempted, nor even imagined. The ruin of the Hindenburg Line convinced the ever more pessimistic Ludendorff, of whose resilience the impossible burdens of high command had taken a fearful toll, that this was the end for Germany.

He was quite right. October brought nothing but endless fresh defeats and costly withdrawals. The Allies, scent of victory now in their nostrils, bore on relentlessly, though at a continuing dreadful cost to both sides. By the start of November the British were back at Mons where, for the BEF, it had all begun over four years previously. In that time the world had shifted. All the old certainties had gone and, of those great empires which had confidently raised their banners in 1914, most lay in the dust. Neither the French nor British would fully recover within a generation. Those who marched wearily to war in 1939 presented a very different image to their fathers.

At 10.58 on the morning of 11 November one Private Price, a Canadian, became the last Allied soldier to die in battle, a mere two minutes before it was all over, one of history's unenviable footnotes.

And then, finally, it was over. Officially, the Allies had won but their victory was entirely pyrrhic. Germany would be bludgeoned into taking the blame and the very harshness of the peace would ensure it could not endure. A fresh generation of Germans, raised in anger, shame and humiliation then forged in the ideology of intolerance, would seek to set the record straight. There was no 'war to end all wars' nor was there any 'land fit for heroes' to be found. From the wreckage of the old empires, new and darker titans would emerge.

War correspondent Philip Gibbs reported in his bulletin to the *North Mail* on 12 November:

> Our troops knew early this morning that the armistice had been signed. I stopped on my way to Mons outside a Brigade HQ, and an officer said "hostilities will cease at eleven o'clock." Then he added as all men add in their hearts, "thank God for that". All the way to Mons there were columns of troops on the march and their bands played ahead of them and almost every man had a flag on his rifle. There were flowers in their caps and in their tunics, red and white chrysanthemums given by crowds of people who cheered them on their way, people who, in many of these villages had been only one day liberated from the German yoke. Our men marched singing with a smiling light in their eyes. They had done their job and it was finished – with the greatest victory in the world.[116]

SEVEN

GENTLEMEN, TEMPORARY GENTLEMEN AND COMMONERS

'My Little Dry Home in the West'

I've a little wet home in a trench
And the rainstorms continually drench
There's the sky overhead, clay or mud for a bed
And stone we use as a bench
Bully beef and hard biscuits we chew
It seems years since we tasted a stew
Shells crackle and scare, yet no place can compare
With my little wet home in the trench
– Anon.[117]

For a long time there was a semi-enduring perception that the British Tommy was 'a lion led by donkeys'. This was allegedly a throw-away line uttered by Ludendorff and picked up by revisionist historians in the post-Second World War era, noticeably by Alan Clarke. Nobody could accuse Clarke of leftist sentiment yet he echoes the view being circulated amongst more radical writers. The view, as views are wont to do, has swung very much back towards a more romantic perspective of 'Henty-esque' derring-do and stiff upper lips. Contemporary authors such as John Lewis-Stempel have reverted to a more eulogistic, idealised perspective; equally flawed in its different way.

Inevitably, the objective truth insofar as this can be determined, lies somewhere between the two. Every army, especially one as large and all-encompassing as the British Expeditionary Force became, had a plethora of very good officers, some very bad and many who just did the job. Likewise with the PBI (poor bloody infantry) – the volunteer of 1914 was a different character from his less-than-willing conscript successor. Those hardcore professionals, the 'Old Contemptibles', who marched in their slender legions along the baked *pavé* in August 1914, were older than the volunteers, and soldiers by choice rather than by conscience or enthusiasm.

It would be true to argue that, in the first instance, most officers were public school products, imbued with everything that was good and bad in a society where class divisions were so marked. There was much good; a willingness to serve and, if necessary, to die, placing the welfare of your men above all personal considerations and a notion of 'playing the game'. Most of these characteristics would subsequently be derided by the revisionists, occasionally blinded by a different sort of prejudice. It remains a lesson of history that we must avoid judging those from the past by our own, biased and jaundiced perspectives. Many young British officers embodied the very finest notions of service and sacrifice, of deep patriotism and sublime piety. Their seeming flippancy was only skin deep and their integrity, however naive, gave nobility to their cause. They paid a very high price indeed.

As the war progressed, many officers emerged who came from less exalted backgrounds, mercantile bourgeois and professionals from the Territorials or Kitchener's battalions. If these were classed as 'gentlemen' by virtue of their commissions they were 'temporary gentlemen'. Their status would swiftly revert after the Armistice. Many in the ranks came from the same background, were 'temporary Tommies' and would return to their professions after the war. Those who joined from the lawyer's office, banker's counting house, academia or the arts served with the sons of toil, drawn from plough or lathe.

War is the ultimate leveller. Soldiers respected, even revered good officers, regardless of class and caste distinctions and despised those who failed to show good leadership. Even those educated rankers from a radical or socialist background wrote tellingly and poignantly of their sorrow at the death of a beloved officer who, whatever his background, had willingly laid down his life before theirs.

George Purvis was the son of Major J. B. Purvis of Bridlington.[118] Both father and son practised as pharmacists and opticians. George was educated at the Grammar School where he was active in the OTC (Officer Training Corp), mentoring the shooting team. From OTC colour-sergeant, he progressed to 2nd lieutenant in the Territorials (5th Battalion Green Howards). He went to France in April 1915 and first saw action at 2nd Ypres. Latterly, he was promoted to command a machine-gun company and was mentioned in Despatches on 9 April 1916. Both his father and younger brother Stanley also served. The boys' mother wrote of her husband and sons: 'These are all my men, and I am proud to feel they all held commissions before the outbreak of the war.'

Officer's diaries reflect the endless stream of routine chores and the considerable burden of responsibility that they carried. Junior officers from subaltern to lieutenant carried a heavier load as they remained responsible for the daily needs of their platoon and day-to-day maintenance and digging of trenches. As battalions were routinely moved from sector to sector, the grind was continuous. The higher up the command chain an officer mounted, the further he was distanced from daily routine and the greater his power to delegate. Generally, his prospects for survival increased. Attrition was worst at junior level, six weeks being the average life expectancy of an infantry subaltern. The odds were rather more stacked against him than the NCOs and men under his command.

George Purvis's diary for summer 1915 is typical of those of relatively junior officers. He chronicles the movements of his company and its deployments. The style is concise, a soldier's shorthand. He does not reflect on his personal experience or thoughts. An officer's prime duty is to provide for his men and play his part in the wider action. He would know more than the PBI as to the greater schemes afoot but perhaps not a great deal more:

28/4/15: Sergeant Warriner & I went right up to trench 4th Yorks & 4th E Yorks relieved our Battalion and the 5th DLI. We had a long tramp back to our rest camp where we arrived at 3am on the 29th.

17/6/15: We remained on the road side all day. The Battalion moved from their trenches to some dug outs there were prepared, where the N. Lancs had been. We moved in the evening up to Sanctuary Wood. We went by railway line past Ypres in daylight, a wonderful sight; arrived Maple Copse. No transport. Gill brought word that our guns had been dumped at H. corner as a tree had fallen across the road. Had to go back + fetch everything about 1½ miles.

18/6/15: We got into the trenches and relieved 7th DLI about 1.30 am. Stood to arms till 3 then slept till about 11 am. Very quiet day, nice & cool Sergeant Warriner came back last night but is very washed out and nervous: Went round with Charlton and found a sniper's post for Gun. Commenced digging at night but found by daylight it was wrong place.

24/7/15: I received a new gun this afternoon (Maxim). Met guides at level crossing and went into no 79 and 80 trenches. Guide lost Warriner's team.

5/8/15: We go up to trenches tonight; shooting on range after thorough inspection of kit: went up to trench 76 – 78 arriving about 10 p.m. A quiet night; had usual bother about dug-out. My gun is in a concrete Emplacement. Warriner not in position I expected.

6/8/15: I found Warriner all right in daylight. A very quiet day had Warriner's gun firing at night; on G. Transport.

12/8/15: No physical drill this morning went for ride with Lorry & Vause through inspection of kit and guns Left Port de Nieppe at

7pm. Arrived at Dyno 9.30. We relieved guns about 10.30 as they were trapped by outgoing Battalion, (7thN.F); Warriner's guide got lost as usual: poor positions fairly good dugout and trenches 69 & 70 two red light passes out.

23/9/15: As gun of 4th E. Yorks was out of action Sgt Warriner's gun from 67 was moved up to front line.

25/9/15: A wet windy day. Great attack started Heavy bombardment all along front, smoke bombs and straw burning to make a show Germans retaliated on our front and support lines. Sergeant Warriner & Private Wharton both killed by same whizz bang in 67 Right. I went to their funerals. Both buried at La Chapelle d' Armentieres. I cannot replace Sergeant Warriner. Private Jude replaces Wharton.

On 17 May 1915, George wrote to his brother:

My Dear Kid

Many thanks for your letter received about ten days ago. I hardly know where to begin and what to tell you, I have seen and done as many different things. Of course you being an officer can have things told you which could not be sent to the ordinary civilian, a sort of private notes from the Front. If I do this it puts you in rather an awkward position as then you become the censor of your own letters and must decide what shall be passed on for general information. I will try and take a between course. As you will see by the appearance of this letter it is raining and I am writing this in a very leaky hut in 'Rest' (pleasant) Camp.

I may say that the gales are produced by holes in the roof and walls. These holes were made by shrapnel bullets and fragments of shell on one of the periodic bombardments the camp is subjected to, within about a foot of my head as I sleep is a fair sized hole where a shell has exploded having come through the wall first.

Last night as I was out with a fatigue party we had the pleasure of seeing our happy little home shelled and found that the
Battalion had had to take to their dug outs for about an hour.
Also early this morning when we were first getting up they gave
us quite a nice little firework display, plumping between 30 – 40
Jack Johnsons into the camp in salvoes of 3 at a time. No one was
hit, although many of the men got quite useful mementoes which
fell near them!

Since writing to you we have been tramping about France and
Belgium moving almost every night. Sleeping in all sorts of weird
places, resting during the day mostly as it is too hot to march
then except in cases of great necessity and then we are rushed up
by Motor Buses. Practically everything has to be done at night as
the German aeroplanes are so active during the day. It is quite a
common thing to see 8 or 9 aeroplanes of various nationalities up
at once 50 per cent of which are being fired at either by our anti
aircraft guns or those of the Germans.

I will give you just a few of the places I have slept in since
leaving England. First of all one night in a ship's bunk, next night
in a tent on a very cold night in H – next night in a French First
Class Carriage, the next were in cattle trucks 40–45 in each then
for seven nights in a nice clean cowshed full of straw. After this
we went into the trenches … We returned to wooden huts which
were shelled while we were in them and had to occupy our dug
outs which we had made during the day. Next night we trekked
further back about 7 miles and bivouacked in a grass field with
only the stars above. Moved again next night I had spent the day
riding back to the huts to bring up some stores which had been
left behind. It rained slightly most of this day. The second night
we billeted in a little village of A-My rest in a sort of jack of all
trades establishment composted of 1, a shop, 2, Gendarmerie, 3,
a Grocers shop, 4, a tobacco factory and cigarette store, 5, a farm
and mill on a small scale.

I myself found a lodging in a second rate estaminet in a very
small, short continental bed. It is their shortness which I dislike most

in these continental beds. Move again that night. I spent most of the day sleeping in beautiful grass fields, move again that evening arriving in good billets about 9 am. We stayed in this place for about five days. The first day we were here Gen French spoke very complimentary and encouraging words to us making us very proud to be Territorials and practically saying that we had saved the situation.

Certainly, all seemed very touch and go at the time but the situation has improved immensely in the last three weeks. We ought to be very proud as it is no doubt a distinction us being sent straight into the thickest of the heavy fighting round there when there are Territorial battalions who have been in France since November of last year and have got nowhere near the firing line and only just got within hearing of the guns about 10 days after we had come from the trenches. After our five days in S – we were once more taken up towards the A line in buses. We however, only occupied some trenches and dug outs well in rear but still well within the danger zone from their artillery. Those two nights I slept under a wagon, a very warm place for a 'bivvy' too I can tell you. The third night we moved still nearer the 7 line and occupied more dug outs but the men had to dig themselves in as there were not sufficient room for them.

I might as well tell you now that we dig ourselves in every time we halt for more than few minutes and then I need not tell you that 'every night we dug ourselves in'. It is a standing order so I will not repeat it every time. These nights we sent out digging parties who went to various parts of the line and helped R.E to build new trenches, carry for them and generally make themselves useful. The rule is generally that the party works till 1 am and then gets back to its billet where they generally arrive between 2.30 or 3.30 am according to the distance.

It is rather risky work because you are generally working only about 1000^x from the front trenches and the Germans send up their star shells all night and desultory rifle and artillery fire just to keep things lively. We stayed in our dug outs 2 days and then some artillery came in and mounted their guns near us and made things too likely to be uncomfortable and dangerous so we moved still nearer the firing line and came to our old rest camp where the Germans have been giving us presents and souvenirs in the shape of shot and shells at intervals when they think we shall be 'at home'.

An extract from a Tommy's letter: 'I think we have them whacked, what I said that time, they have as much chance as a snowball in Hell!' A very good simile I think. Censoring letters is an awful business and wastes an awful lot of time if you do it properly. I must say the men are mostly very good and keep off prohibited subjects very well. It is the men who get home sick and wounded who talk about things which they should not and of course they cannot be stopped. They spin some awful yarns which get into the papers. For instance, one of my men who'd had colic and was sent to hospital wrote home to tell them he had been 'gassed'.

As a matter of fact, he was left behind in our farm No 77 when the section went forward to the Battalion as he had been sent up in daylight and had been sniped and it had got on his nerves. On the way back we were shelled with these beastly gas shells and there is no doubt it is beastly stuff. I got quite enough for my liking. It makes your eyes smart so that you cannot see and breathing also is made very difficult but the shells are nothing half so bad as those they send out of tubes from cylinders under pressure. Fortunately, our Battalion never got dosed with that but I believe the 4th Battalion did, much to their discomfort.

I will now tell you a little about one of the most interesting Sundays I have ever spent. I think we had a very good church Parade in the morning, spent the rest of the day in writing and censoring letters, watching the aeroplanes skimming about the sky and being shelled if they got too far over each other's lines. Then at 5.30 pm we paraded 200 men for digging. We marched 2 miles back to draw tools and then advanced about 5 miles forward to our 'digging'.

I had often wanted to go to the same town as Earp, got the stained glass from the Cathedral, in daylight but could never get permission. However, my journey this time caused me to cross right through the centre of it. It was an object lesson in the power of the modern explosive. The Germans have been shelling this place since October with every kind of gun and shell that they have got from 17" Howitzers to 4th grade firers. The whole place is a desolation, streets gutted by fire others simply heaps of broken bricks. The famous buildings simply a few isolated features such as a wall with two pinnacles on top connected by a very tumble-down wall to a tower and the other end that was the Cathedral. The other famous place was in a little better repair and it retained a glorious grandeur even in its desolation.

To come to more mundane things, the streets were littered with stinking carcases of dead horses, broken wagons and carts of furniture, shell holes of all sizes, but always circular and a general air of desolation and putrescence. I saw one shell hole where it was 42' across and over 20 feet deep. At the bottom was a dead horse! One small grass field outside the town would not be an acre in area, had at least a dozen large shell holes in it. It looked more like the holey end of a bagatelle board. We saw a high class hotel which had simply been left as it stood in ordinary everyday life, windows and doors were smashed but clean glasses and bottles full of various wines stood on the shelves. Tables and chairs were set out and even though except for the effects of the bombardment, it was as before.

When we got to our trench which we had to improvise and strengthen the parapet a lively night attack was taking place and the bullets were whistling and thudding down unnecessarily close. We also got presents of shells, 50 per cent of which did not explode. The battlefield on a nice starlight night attack is most picturesque with star-lights going up all around and flashes from the guns and bursting shells and the general din. It was all very fierce.

Must close; with much love your affectionate brother George.[119]

George Purvis was killed on 8 June 1917. At the time of his death, George was under orders for England to work as an instructor in a machine-gun training school. Nonetheless, he delayed his departure from the line because his company was, at that time, very short of trained and experienced officers. He showed exceptional courage and daring, captured a number of enemy prisoners and was recce-ing a new MG position when killed by a sniper. One brother officer, wounded in the same action, wrote to George's mother:

> I know it will be a relief to you how highly we esteemed and admired your son. His high moral character and strength of will made me admire and respect him as a man and his absolute fearlessness and thoughtfulness for the well-being of his officers and men made him a soldier to be looked up to, respected and loved. I personally would have followed him anywhere.[120]

George's younger brother Stanley, whose vocation led him, after the war, into the ranks of the clergy, wrote regularly to his mother from the Front and his letters were expanded into a regular press column 'The Life of our Soldiers' under the pseudonym of 'Orion'. These features were a bridge between those at home and those in the line. Stanley's particular talent was to make sense of the whole situation by using recognisable and homely images, guiding his East Riding readers around the intricacies of trench systems:

> Trench Systems
>
>   Probably all the trenches that you have seen yourselves are those dug along the cliffs for practice. They will give you many wrong ideas. In the first place these trenches have never been under fire and perhaps out here we should have little use for trenches dug that way. What you cannot realise from seeing trenches at home is that the trenches in France are part of an enormous system. Let me attempt a familiar illustration;
>
>   We will forget for a moment that Yorkshire has a sea coast. You and I, dear reader, are going to our front line. We pass along

St John's Street which unfortunately has suffered much from the enemy's heavy shelling. We avoid High Street because it is shelled regularly all the way along up to the ruins of the Bayle Gate and the Priory, so we turn instead along South Back lane. Here we find a shallow trench running along one edge of the road and out into the fields beyond and as the enemy can observe this spot from balloons we enter the trench and proceed along it.

A battery of our guns is firing below the shelter of the bank in Well Lane; the gunners have their dugout under the ruins of the rectory. A few yards further on the trench crosses the road which is pitted with shell-holes and then runs along parallel to the way to Boynton. The motor signs at the cross roads are still standing but perforated and scarred by shell splinters. The trench passes the mound of bricks which used to be Rose Cottage, (flowers in the garden continue to flourish in the midst of ruin) and then strikes off a little up the hill to the right.

Now and again you catch glimpses of similar long trenches cutting the slope on the other side of the valley, one above and one below the much battered Wandale Farm; a trench which comes out from the wood on the hilltop on that side cuts right across the valley and joins our trench … At every junction the trenches are carefully labelled; Oxford Street, High Street, Beck Alley, North Trench, Boynton Abbey, and they are all much used.

The woods have been greatly thinned by bombardments. At least half the trees are down and the remainder slashed and splintered by shells. The timber is utilised for building dugouts, repairing the trenches or for firewood. The trenches now become an absolute maze … they branch and cross in all directions in the most confusing way. Some of them are in good repair and regular use; some abandoned and falling in.

I have omitted the thousands of guns, machine guns and trench mortars, all in their emplacements, of dugouts and shelters, strongpoints, observation posts and numberless other features of trench life.[121]

†

'Kitchener's Army Soldiers' Christmas Day in the Workhouse'

'Tis Christmas day in the workhouse,
The paupers are called up in their groups,
The only men left here to grouse
Are the broken or lead-swinging troops

You ask me why the troops grouse sir,
When they've still got three limbs and an eye,
It's not that they're broken in body sir,
They're broken in pocket that's why

Don't think they're fed up with the workhouse,
'Cause they're fed the best of them all,
Far better than most of the mob sir,
Who've not answered their country's call

Of all the war billets they've had sir,
Like shell-fired farms out in France,
To sleep on a clean wooden floor sir
This Christmas, they're glad of the chance

You ask if there's any complaints sir
It's not just the rations you mean?
A soldier should never complain sir
But I'll tell you what I have seen

Our sergeant's a sarcastic time server,
Done his soldiering on the barrack square
And a bit on that big fatigue sir,
They call the South African War

He's never been 'up the line' sir
Or ever been 'over the lid'
Nor seen the square-headed swine sir
Behind a bombing-post hid

He don't understand Kitchener's Mob sir
Thinks soldiering is just dressing up,
Saluting and drawing your bob [n] sir,
And getting plenty of beer to sup

He sang, 'Oh, What a Lovely War' sir
While we 'stood-to' in the trenches,
He went 'square-pushing' all trim sir
The in the sex-war with the wenches

These BEF boys in the workhouse
Don't need 'spit and polish' parades
They're more used to going at night sir
On patrols and Mills-bombing raids!
– Charles Moss[122]

Families of dead Tommies got their sad news by an official letter, terse and universal:

9th March, 1916: Madam, It is my painful duty to inform you that a report has this day been received from the War Office notifying the death of (No) 14118 (Rank) Private (Name) Martin O'Donnell (Regiment) 14th Battalion Durham Light Infantry which occurred at a place in France on the 26th day of February 1916 and I am to express to you the sympathy and regret of the Army Council at your loss. The cause of death was wounds received in action. If any articles of private property left by the deceased are found, they will be forwarded to this Office, but some time will probably elapse before their receipt, and when received they cannot be disposed of until authority is received from the War Office …[123]

Catherine O'Donnell of Deptford in Sunderland did receive more details of her husband's death from two former comrades, Sergeants

Brammer and Halpin. They wrote to her on the day Martin, who'd worked for fifteen years before the war in Shorts' Shipyard, was killed:

> I regret to have to break this sad news to you regarding your husband, whom I'm sorry to tell you was shot through the head this morning by a sniper; he was unconscious until he died. It has been a sad blow to me and all his chums for he was well respected by all with whom he came into contact with. We did the best we could for him when we saw there was no hope of recovery, his platoon sergeant and chums knelt and said the Rosary and de Profundas and a few acts of contrition as we were Roman Catholics like himself. He died the death of a hero; he was a soldier and a man. Please accept the sympathy of myself and all his comrades: Gone but not forgotten.[124]

The humour of the Tommies was proverbial; it needed to be, the horrors of war could not be contained by fine sentiments, which were all too soon corroded. For every Robert Graves, Siegfried Sassoon or Wilfred Owen, there was a thousand, less elevated or less bitterly reflective:

> BE IN THE FASHION
> Why have cats, dogs, canaries, rabbits, parrots etc
> LICE!
> Every conceivable shade supplied – blue backs, black backs, red backs, grey backs, white backs; also in a delicate pink shade and with variegated stripes; pure thoroughbreds from our own seams, most clinging, affectionate and taking ways; very prolific, hardy and will live anywhere. Once you have them you will never be without.
> In dainty pochettes at 2s per thousand![125]

Private Jack Wilson, who served throughout the war with 13th Battalion NF, was a livestock agent. He came from North Tynedale, a wild upland dale, home to the notorious Border Reivers of the sixteenth century. Jack was cast in similar mould: dour, pragmatic and with no trace of subservience. His diary, which he maintained till 1936, reads as we might expect from one of his moss trooper ancestors, had any troubled to record his daily round. Like many from the rural uplands, Jack came from a hard school, inured to cold and wet, long hard hours and meagre rations. War was an extension of civilian life with the added danger of sudden and violent extinction.

Jack's style is laconic. He combines brief references to illness (he is quarantined, along with twenty other men suspected of having smallpox, in August 1915) with information about where he was staying, the nature of his training and travelling arrangements. Feet are clearly a preoccupation – hardly surprising when you consider the notoriously uncomfortable design of the army boot of the period. He manages to get two pairs within a fortnight, suggesting that he was more than capable of making the state of his feet known and getting something done about it! Then, in the midst of recording the most prosaic of events, there is a sudden departure from form:

24 September 1914: ... billeted with Mr and Mrs C. Smith, 20 Charles Street where I was very well off in a private houses in Berkhampstead.

14 October 1914: Marched from Halton to Northampsted and back with rifles, 18 miles, and some very sore feet on return.

25 October 1914: Received one pair of boots.

2 November 1914: Sent to Leighton Buzzard VAD hospital suffering from Tonsillitis.

2 November 1914: Received another pair of boots. [Jack kept the pressure up – a third pair are handed over in May 1915, along with another suit of khaki.]

24 December 1914: Battalion manoeuvres, defending Tring reservoir, here we learned about picket duty, scouts patrols, supports, patrols, visiting, examining and reconnoitring.

24 December 1914: Arrived home to Burdon side, 25th – supper and dance at H. Green. At Sundaysight and stayed overnight at Smeddywell Rigg.

28 December 1914: Norman Wilson died at Burdon side aged six months. [It is not known who Norman was.] I returned to Wilstone (near Tring) via Newcastle, Leeds, Crewe, arriving Wilstone 6.30 on 29th.[126]

We can only presume that his religious convictions were a source of consolation: his diary is peppered with references to services and he made a habit of visiting Baptist Chapels in the towns he passed through. Through the winter of 1915, into spring and summer, he and his comrades in Kitchener's New Service Battalions were in training, sometimes using facilities they had built themselves. The diary describes how a new rifle range at Aston Clifton was constructed by the trainees themselves in January 1915 – Jack spent three days on the job. Reviews and parades in front of commanders such as Kitchener add a little excitement to their routines and there were regular football games and other sports events to keep them entertained. Training itself was physically demanding, something which must have been tough for those who were not very fit to start with.

Despite the public health improvements of the nineteenth century, the physique and fitness of recruits was often poor. Poverty, malnutrition and poor housing took their toll. During the Boer War, the poor standard of volunteers was a public scandal, with journalists and politicians having much to say. In 1904, a working party was set up, the Inter-Departmental Committee on Physical Deterioration – but to little effect: over 15,000 recruits were rejected as unfit between 1902 and 1911. As the Committee noted, 'sturdy' countrymen like Jack were usually a bit healthier than their urban cousins, 'the ill-fed, anaemic, under-sized and somewhat neurotic lads' of the cities.[127]

But the country bred could not escape that scourge of the period, tuberculosis:

3 April 1915: My brother William died in a sanatorium at Edinburgh and was buried at Thorneyburn on April 6th. I was unable to attend funeral.

As winter closed, their routine continued; the war would wait, there would be no movement till spring:

June 1915: We had a divisional march for 21st Div via Halton, New Mill, Ivinghoe, Cheddington, Longmartin & Aston Clinton, very hot trying day, very few managed to do the full distance.

2 July 1915: Received service rifle No 280B; the whole of the month was spent on the rifle range near to Acton Clinton firing our course of musketry.

High summer and the routine dragged on.

1 August 1915: I was isolated with 20 other men suspected of having smallpox.

6 August 1915: We marched to Tring under Sergeant George Bell where we had our clothing disinfected.

8–12 August 1915: 21st Division left Halton, marching to Whitley Surrey via Wycombe, Maidenhead, Sunningdale, Windsor, Guildford a very trying march with full pack, the days were extremely hot. At Whitley we were under the command of General Sir F C Forrestier-Walker. Most of our time was spent in route marches, trench digging.

About the 4 September there was considerable trouble over leave, much damage being done to the camp. Such events are not often recorded; Kitchener's Tommies might be willing warriors but they were still civilians in uniform, averse to the random abuses of the system.

As summer waned, the battalion prepared to move to France.

9 September 1915: we sailed to France – Folkestone to Boulogne, to a small village near Watteau.

12 September 1915: Sick, 13th Battalion did long route march.

Jack's undoubted marksman's skills, his background as a countryman was perfect, meant he was eligible to volunteer for sharpshooter duties.

16 September 1915: sniper parade under Lieutenant Elton.

17 September 1915: we had a field day by Insule, 8 a.m.–6 p.m.: no dinner.

20 September 1915: lay all day waiting for order to move, marched off at 6 p m, marched till 1 a m, slept in open field 7 hours.

21 September 1915: rested all day, at 8 p.m. marched another 11 miles.

22 September 1915: marched all the night of 22nd/23rd moving up to Lozingheim where we disposed of most of our surplus kit.

24 September 1915: we marched close to firing line, slept in turnip field in artillery formation, heavy rain.

On 25 September 1915, Jack's battalion was approaching the cauldron of Loos, a first and terrible test for Kitchener's men.

Early in the morning 9.30 we set off toward the line, soon we began to meet wounded men of the Scottish Div 15th coming down with glowing reports of the battle, reached Mazingarbe about midday where we saw the effects of the first shell and got orders to load up for action.

We formed up and marched towards Loos in column of route and today four and a half years later, I often wonder we were allowed so easy a march up a main road; three and four streams of traffic close to the battle area.

Then it was time for action. True to his roots, Jack gives scant detail of the fighting with no reflection; neither he nor his upland ancestors had been much given to analysis.

26 September 1915: Repulsed several attacks, Captain Agnew killed.

27 September 1915: Relieved by Guards Div, rested in field over to Vermelles and Sailly Labourse.

28 September 1915: I went out with a small party to the battlefield to salvage rifles etc, got a slight dose of gas, marched to Loos, Le Grince and took train for new front.

Summer waned and the battlefield of Loos reverted to relative calm. The Allies had sustained some 50,000 casualties and gains had been meagre.

13 October 1915: Commenced our march to line again staying overnight at Bailleul.

14 October 1915: From Bailleul to Armentieres and billeted in the asylum district of the town.

Between 17 October and 2 November Jack and his comrades moved between trenches 88, 89, 74, 75 ('whizz-bang corner'), 79, 80 and back to billets.

> 5 November 1915: I took over sniper duties by request of Lieut. Hutchins, fireworks display [tantalisingly, he gives us no insight into his sniper role].

> 8 November 1915: We were heavily shelled; Sergeant Raisbeck shot through head by sniper.

As 1915 drew to a close, a year when the Allies had sought in vain and at steadily increasing cost to break the deadlock, Jack prepared for Christmas in the trenches. No hint of sentiment intrudes.

> 24 December 1915: Took over from 12 NF again, Private Duncan Smith killed by bullet which passed through the sentry box in which I was standing on RE Dump.

> 25 December 1915: Damp morning took top of our dugout and raised the walls one foot, had stew and Xmas pudding, leave commenced for 21st Division: Merry Christmas, Jack.

Between January and March 1916, Jack and his comrades were in and out of the line. On 8 March they were relieved by 15th DLI; twenty-six men got twenty-eight days' No. 1 Field Punishment for sleeping with their boots off.[128]

From 28 April to 8 May, Jack was on leave and returned to Tynedale.

> 8 May 1916: Cycled to Bellingham, then by train Newcastle and London, arriving Kings Cross 4.30 p.m. Waterloo 5.10 too late for boat special, so I got a taxi back to St Pancras arriving North Medburn 7p.m.

By 14 May 1916 Jack was back in the line:

Working party in 'Tambour' trench under Lieutenant Walker. In the evening I had a walk to Albert to see the ruins, the church with the overhanging 'Virgin Mary & Child'.

As build-up for the great Somme offensive continued, 13th NF prepared for a further, even harsher test.

On 23 May 1916, Jack was inducted into the art of operating the Lewis gun but, within a week was back to sniping over no man's land. As the Calvary of the Somme erupted on 1 July, his battalion went over the top at Fricourt, where their bravery earned a general's commendation. Any rest was shortlived and they were soon back in action at Mametz Wood. In the desperate fighting they lost Jack's section leader Sergeant Butteridge, who was killed along with two of the company officers, Captain Godber and Lieutenant Baring. During the heavy bombardments at Mametz Wood, many more were killed. While engaged in the doleful chore of burying the dead, Jack himself was nearly suffocated by a random gas shell.

Jack and his comrades continued to endure the torments of the Somme.

4 August 1916: Old French ammunition dump on fire at Candle Factory, great explosions all day and flying debris all over the place.

19 and 20 September 1916: Heavy rains, awful mess of mud.

26 September 1916: Shelled from Trones Wood moved on to Delville Wood & High Wood Road, Death Valley.

War and slaughter he could cope with but the matter of officers' frequent leaves seemed to rankle: '11 January 1917: Major Masahia-Palmer goes on his 5th leave. I was sweeping roads at the Chateau; snow fell all day.' He had previously recorded other officers going on third and fourth leaves (9 November 1916, 6 November 1916). By now it had been eighteen months since Jack last went home.

On 12 January 1917 he proudly records the 62nd Brigade transport competition, judged by General D. C. Campbell. First prize for clean transport went to 13th NF as did first prize for cobs (that owned by Lt Darzie); Major Masahia-Palmer came fourth.

Through 1917 the litany of war continued. Jack did not reflect, just got on with the job be that horse transport, service in the line or sport.

20 January 1917: D Company 13NF scored four goals, C Company 13NF one goal, won tug of war 1st prize 1st Lincoln Regiment, 2nd 13th NF.

6 February 1917: A mule killed in stable by dud anti aircraft shell going straight down through it.

27 March 1917: 13th NF took over trenches occupied by the 58th Division City of London, PO Rifles etc. With Lewis & Hughes water filling.

31 March 1917: Lieutenant Ewins killed near Croixelles.

2 April 1917: 62nd Brigade made an attack and took two villages, Capt O B Haines & Lt Rittman wounded; Walter Hargreaves and Sergeant Hawkins killed.

11–14 April 1917: At trenches with rations on pack mules, great difficulties in reaching our men, dumped rations in Hindenburg line barb wire under shell fire, Matt Dickson killed. Sergeant Judge wounded, Joe Dodd wounded; transport moved up to Bequerelle and moved back again on the 14th when 21st Division relieved by the 33rd – Corporal Luke suffered shell shock.

Amid the random death of the trenches, he still notes the death of someone at home who died, we assume of natural causes, at the age of seventy-five.

The war continued. Jack was not or does not appear to have been ground down even as the steady attrition whittled down his battalion.

3 May 1917: Very heavy bombardment at 3 am, 110 Brigade and 18th Division attacked. Later on in the afternoon I set out to find headquarters, after many tries in several directions found them in narrow trench, then reported same to transport, same night I had to guide Lieutenants Darzie and Weldon to Headquarters; German shelling very heavy.

Duties with the transport, however arduous, must have seemed like a balm.

11 May 1917: 21st Division relieved by 33rd Division; reveille 4 a.m., moved from Bequerelle to Boisleux-St-Marc and immediately commenced washing wagons and polishing axle ends 6 p.m. harnessed up and moved on to Blairouille finished up at 9 p.m.

17 May 1917: 13th NF transport competition at Blairville … Field Marshal Sir Douglas Haig rode past 7.30 p.m.

On 28 May, still fretting over leave, he records, 'Lieutenant Darzie goes on his 4th leave'.

On 31 May, Major Mayhew has gone home with 'prisoner' Laude. The detail and nature of the offence are omitted. In the middle of June:

The Battalion moved from Harnlincourt to trenches preparatory to attack on Hindenburg Line. Attacked 2.30 a.m. and failed with severe losses. Transport shelled on dump, Porterfield and Humpreys killed, captains Evans & Ricky killed; Woodbridge and Casson with Sergeant Hardy wounded. Lieutenant Wright and Sergeant Donohue killed. Lieutenant Garry died of wounds.

It is hardly surprising Jack was longing for leave though his turn didn't come until that August. The war would wait for his return and his later entries are abbreviated:

[a] summary of events and places we were at in brief from Sept 9th 1917 till I was captured by the Germans May 28th 1918 when I destroyed my diary before falling into enemy hands. We went to Ypres in the middle of Sept in preparation for attack on Passchendaele Ridge where we had a great many casualties including Brigadier General Rawlings & G R Dix, at Hellblast Corner, Clapham Junction, Polygon Wood, Wist Rutte, Mic Mac Camp, Burr Cross Roads, ANZAC Camp, Fromelles, whilst here we were heavily bombed. I also acted as runner for Capt Darzie who was at this time B.T.O. Leaving him in the latter end of October we went to 'Merrivale' near Arras to get equipped ready to go to Italy.

The fusiliers would be in the thick of confused fighting as successive German hammer blows threatened to fracture the embattled Allied lines. He ended up in the trenches relieving the French along the River Aisne where, in May 1918, he was wounded. Jack, shot through the left thigh, was now a prisoner, 'surrounded by Germans and taken prisoner along with fifteen wounded comrades and four RAMC orderlies we were sent back to a hospital for some day then on to Marles for a couple of weeks'.

Having been treated and his wounded healed; he was sent east as a POW to a camp at Sporthau and eventually put to work on the land. He was accustomed to the fields of course and did not suffer any unduly harsh treatment, like a true Northumbrian meticulously recording his meagre pay awards.

Sent out on commando to Frau Ida Alkert, Prumkendorf, Kries Liegnitz, in Silesia; winnowing and mowing corn, mowing hay and clover, mowing grass and loading hay...

Letters and food parcels did arrive from home but even the war's end did not bring immediate relief. He was still in Germany at the end of the year.

> Christmas Day 1918: Rose at 7 a.m., made porridge and tea, fried bacon and bread. Snow fell all the forenoon. For dinner we had vegetable ration, sausage and pudding. At 2 p.m. we had an international football match, England v Scotland, grand game; the score England 4, Scotland – 2.

Jack would come home safe and, on the surface at least, not much changed. There would be another laconic entry a few years later: 'Today I got married.'

EIGHT

NO MAN'S LAND

FOO: Is this the best way to trench 31?

Jock Sniper: Yes, you go doon the ' Y' communication trench till ye come to the wee hoose and when you get past the wee hoose, you want to mind your 'P's' & 'Q's', as they've got a machine gun on it, and keep your stern up an' yer heid doon so if ye do get one, it's a Blighty one![129]

Sniper – Beating the Boche at his own game!

It may fairly be claimed that when hostilities ceased on 11 November 1918, we had outplayed Germany at all points of the game.
– General Lord Home, G. C. B.[130]

The art of the sniper, the battlefield predator, is an ancient one. As far back as Towton Field in the cold Yorkshire spring of 1461, John 'Butcher' Clifford was picked off by a keen-eyed bowman during a preliminary skirmish when he was foolhardy enough to remove his bevor and assuage his raging thirst. Next day, Lord Dacre was similarly accounted for by a youthful archer; it is said, hidden in a tree. It was with the development of rifled guns that the sharpshooter came into his own during the American Civil War and Austro-Prussian conflict: 'Austrian sharpshooters were used against the soldiers of Frederick the Great, and were so effective that at times the ex-Kaiser's ancestors found it difficult to bring his Hussars, armed only with short sabres, out of the camp.'[131]

Initially, the Germans, once mobile warfare had bogged down in stalemate, enjoyed a significant advantage. They had more trained shots. Their near monopoly on the manufacture of precision optical instruments meant they had more and better telescopic sights available. British sharpshooting officers such as Major Pemberthy, who ran the 3rd Army's sniper training school, rejected any claims of innate superiority: 'Reports of the deadly work done by the Boche snipers gave the world the impression that German soldiers were better shots than we were. The German never was a better shot, or even as good a shot as the Britisher.'

Pemberthy did concede that the enemy had focused more clearly on the value of sniping:

> When both sides settled down to trench warfare, the Boche sniper showed the value of his special training. Often behind his trench line as well as in it, and from cunningly constructed and concealed posts, he kept a vigilant watch on our lines. He picked off sentries and observers who carelessly or sometimes unavoidably exposed themselves.

Major Hesketh-Prichard, who was Pemberthy's contemporary in charge of 1st Army sniper training, divided the war of marksmen into four phases: the German ascendency 1914–15; a more even-handed dogfight 1915–16, as the Allies struggled to match their opponents; 1916–18 when the Germans reacted to increasing British skills by adopting new tactics and, finally, the more fluid warfare of 'the Hundred Days' in 1918.[132]

At first, the British response was often rather ad hoc. The army contained many fine shots and British marksmanship in battle was rightly feared:

> On one occasion several runners had been sniped and at last Major-General Hughes went round the cook-house and called the cook noted for his marksmanship and winner of the DCM in South Africa. He said 'take your rifle and shut up that sniper'. The cook

dropped his spoon and was away some twenty minutes. He came
back with a grim smile and the Hun sniper was silent for ever.[133]

At the outset, the lack of 'accurised' (improved) infantry weapons,
meant that many privately owned, high-quality sporting rifles were
hastily sent out and turned against the most dangerous game: 'By
the irony of fate, one privately owned rifle, fitted with telescopic
sights, which did great execution in the hands of a sniping officer
of the Staffords, was a pre-war gift by the Kaiser to a well-known
British general.'

Many British soldiers, coming from an urban environment,
lacked the basic hunting instinct and tracking skills necessary for
the successful sniper. Hunters, gamekeepers (and poachers) were
inevitably better equipped. The Canadians, many of whom inhabited a rugged outdoors environment, proved particularly adept:

> One of the finest snipers I ever met was a full blooded Red
> Indian, John Ballantyne. He applied all the methods of the chase,
> so familiar to him from his beloved Canadian forests, to hunting
> the Boche sniper. He had been known to wait patiently for seven
> days in a wonderfully prepared and concealed sniper's post for a
> valuable target – a Hun officer whom he finally killed.[134]

An Ojibwa Indian from Ontario, Francis 'Peggy' Pegamagabow,
who was credited with 378 kills, was the highest scoring Canadian
sniper of the war.

For the front-line infantryman of both sides, the sniper was
feared and hated. They could not expect quarter when taken. There
was something underhand about sniping, unsporting, terrifying.
Nowhere in the line was safe:

> …the same sniper fired again from the village to our left and a
> man called Pratt dropped like a stone just where the corporal
> had fallen. He too had a small round hole in his temple and the
> back of his skull blown away. Pratt was beyond hope. His head

was shattered; splatterings of brain lay in the pool of blood under him; but, though he had never been conscious since the shot was fired, he refused to die. An old corporal looked after him, held his body and arms, which writhed and fought feebly as he lay. It was over two hours before he died.[135]

Inevitably, great exertions would be made to dispose of a particularly troubling enemy sharpshooter:

Opposite the front line of one Canadian battalion, there was a particularly clever sniper. For a long time, he defied us to discover his lair, all the while taking toll of officers and men. At last, by persistent and systematic observation, he was discovered but so well was his lair protected that ordinary rifle fire could not silence him. At last, the help of the gunners was sought, an 18-pdr was detailed to help and the sniper was driven out but not killed. I believe his bag up to that time had been two officers and seven men. He soon began operations from another well-concealed post. This was found by careful and patient observation, and he was again shelled and driven out. Some days later he resumed his sniping, and this time while the artillery shelled his new post, our snipers waited for his appearance and got him. He had probably been worth more to the Germans than a battery of field guns![136]

For those with the right temperament, the thrill of the hunt provided a terrific adrenalin rush: 'I have known cases where the doctor and even the padre were with difficulty restrained as non-combatants from taking a hand in this fascinating game of hunting the Boche.' Sniper duels were the most dangerous form of hunting. A skilled marksman who scored highly at the butts was not necessarily suitable. The instinct of the hunter and the cold nerve that went with it were the true sinews of the sniper's deadly art.

The colourful if rather disreputable Cesare Borgia was said to have hunted wild boar on foot and with sword rather than spear. One suspects he'd have been at home in the trenches:

The fact also that, in many cases, the Boche was shooting too made it a short, sharp duel, the winner being he who got his shot in first and the loser probably losing his life as well as the trick. The realisation of this called for nerve and courage of a high order. All the same, some snipers will tell you that it was this very risk which gave the game its greatest fascination.[137]

Despite the inherent risks the sniper became recognised as an elite soldier, one who could by the standards of trench warfare be pampered, excused debilitating fatigues and guaranteed more rest than his lowlier comrades. Such preferential gifts often led many who had no particular aptitude to volunteer simply for a perceived 'cushy number':

On Hill 60 in 1915, I remember a young officer who was not altogether innocent of 'eye-wash' telling me that he had killed several Huns by the simple method of firing through the enemy's sandbag breastworks with a Rigby Express Rifle. He could not see his targets, so I asked him how he could tell when he scored a hit. 'Oh,' he said, 'those trenches are very wet and I hear the bodies splash when they fall into the water'.[138]

Some were prone to wildly exaggerate their kills, many of which were very hard to verify:

Sir, I have the honour to report that six little wooden crosses will be required in the Hun trenches this evening, making a total of eleven this week. I have the honour to be sir, your obedient servant ... Private X. Such cavalier claims were not always believed and this particular hawk-eye received a rather cynical reply from his sniping-officer: In future, the left ears of all Huns killed by Private X will be attached to his reports please![139]

Even the most highly motivated newcomer was often infected by a brand of wishful thinking. Masters such as Major Hesketh-Pritchard, an accomplished big-game hunter, tended to adopt a more cynical stance:

> New snipers were nearly always optimistic, and it was quite a common thing for them to think they were doing the enemy much more damage than was really the case. A conversation has been known to run as follows:
>
> 'Morning, you two' [sniper and observer].
> 'Good morning, sir.'
> 'Anything doing?'
> 'Smith got a Hun this morning, sir.'
> 'Good, how do you know?'
> 'He gave a cry, threw up his hands and fell back.'
>
> Now this may have been correct but, as a matter of fact, continued observation showed that a man shot in ordinary trench warfare very rarely either threw up his hands or fell back. He nearly always fell forward and slipped down. For this the old Greek rendering is best. 'And his knees were loosened.'[140]

Bravado aside, sniping was not for the faint-hearted. At all times German marksmen were formidable, resilient and deadly. For a sharpshooter, there was very often no second chance. One moment of carelessness, of complacency or error would most likely have fatal consequences.

> At a certain spot in our lines, not very far from Auchonvillers 'Ocean Villas', a German sniper had done fell work. It is hard to say how many British lives he had taken, but his tally was not small. He lurked somewhere in the mass heaps of earth, rusty wire and sandbags which there formed a strongpoint in the German line; there were twenty or thirty loopholes from which he might be firing. The problem was, from which of these did his shots actually come?

It was an old enemy trick to throw up a number of steel loop-holed plates, a sniper's mantlet which gave some measure of security, though a round from an express or high-velocity weapon might slam through a single layer of plate.

On our side there was no loophole whatever covering the area in which this German sniper worked, and any attempt to spot his post had perforce to be done over the top of the parapet. As he was simply waiting and watching for people to look over, it was only a very hurried and cursory glance that could be taken. At length, however, the Hun was located by an officer, in the vicinity of two enormous steel plates set near the top of his parapet.

Major Hesketh-Pritchard then set up a British loophole opposite the enemy's steel. Barely had dawn crept over the parapet than the German sniper put a round through the new device.

The trap was now ready, and the officer whose duty it was to deal with the matter went one hundred yards down the trench to the right flank, whilst an assistant protruded the end of a black stick which he happened to have in his hand, keeping at the same time well to the side. At the same moment the officer on the flank shot at the right hand of the two big plates once, and then again. The bullets rang loud upon the plates, and the German sniper at the second shot betrayed himself. Thinking as he did that the shots were fired from the open loophole opposite to him, he fired at it, and the gas from his rifle gave away his position. The two big plates were of course, dummies, and he was firing almost from ground level and from an emplacement cleverly concealed by a mass of broken wire. The loophole was now shut for a moment or two, and then once again opened, the officer on the flank having moved to a position where he could command the German sniper's loophole. His cap had fallen off. He had a bald head. The sniper was soon dealt with.

As the British developed both the theory and practice of sniping, every battalion would appoint a number of marksmen and observers whose job it was to spot and range targets. All reported to the designated battalion sniping officer. Sniper and observer alternated roles but always worked as a pair. Their function was not limited to the finer art of removing the King's enemies. They had a vital intelligence role:

> …the accuracy of information given by snipers was really wonderful. On one occasion the snipers of the 33rd Division reported that two Germans had been seen with the number 79 on their helmets. This information went from battalion, through brigade, division and corps, to army, who rather pooh-poohed the snipers' accuracy as the 79th, when last heard of, had been on the Russian front. Within a day or two, however, the Germans opposite the battalion to which these snipers belonged sent a patrol out of their trenches one misty morning. The patrol fell in with our scouts, who killed two and carried back the regulation identifications. These proved the snipers to be correct!

Killing the enemy was not the only means of inflicting loss:

> Another great duty of snipers was the blinding of the enemy. Thus, if the Germans bombarded any portion of our front, their artillery observers almost always did their work from the flank, where very often from the front line or from some other point of vantage they spotted and corrected the shell bursts of their gunners. On such occasions, our snipers opposite both flanks of the bombardment area broke the periscopes of the German observers and thus often succeeded in either rendering them blind, or forcing them to take risks.

Inevitably, German snipers aimed for British periscopes in retaliation but Hesketh-Pritchard was ahead of them. Dummy scopes were set up to provide easy, expendable targets. By judging the angles of shooting, the British could get a line on the German snipers themselves. Ominously he observed, 'there were many methods by which the man could be rendered harmless!'

Dominating no man's land, gaining ascendancy over the enemy in any particular sector was never just about fire supremacy. Much of the 'game' revolved around psychology and the native character of the combatants involved:

> The English were sound, exceedingly unimaginative, and very apt to take the most foolish and useless risks, showing their heads unnecessarily and out of a kind of unthinking optimism ... The Welsh were very good indeed, their 38th Division keeping a special sniper's book, and their sniping officer, Captain Johnson, was very able. I think that in early 1918, the snipers of this division had accounted for 387 Germans in trench warfare. The Canadians, the Anzacs and the Scottish regiments were all splendid, many units showing an aggressiveness, which had the greatest effect on the morale of the enemy.

A sniper, like the Russian Vasily Zaytsev at Stalingrad in the war to come, can generate his own legend, earning grudging respect from an enemy who never sees him but is left, all too often, to count the cost. One such figure was 'Willibald the Hun'.

> The officer turned, and the stretcher party resumed its way. He stood watching them for a little, his thoughts roving from the horrible way in which a pointed bullet, fired from a rifle with a muzzle velocity of 3,000 feet per second, will at times [be so accurate] ... to the deeds and too-haunting personality of Wilibald the Hun.

By this point Willibald was a public nuisance – he had accounted for nine in the battalion and more from their relief. The British sniping officer, known as 'Red', could not get a fix on this scourge. Red had a team of observers stationed along the length of the front-line trench, each straining to gain a tell-tale glimpse when the sniper fired.

In the late afternoon Red, 'having passed down an old, disused trench in the rear of the British position, crawled cautiously out behind the parados: here was an area seamed with shell-holes, each half-full of green, scummy water, rotting sandbags, rusty wire, nettles and coarse grass'. Crowning a slight rise, one larger crater, left by a very large shell, offered an ideal vantage. This was best avoided in the morning when light favoured the Germans and their much superior optics. By afternoon, the situation was reversed.

Methodically, Red quartered the ground, examining all likely lairs in the trench, in the spinney, in the scarred wilderness of no man's land. Nothing. Broken wire, shell-holes, sandbags, pulverised bricks and mortar, men lying in queer positions, men whose ragged tunics the evening wind stirred strangely, men who would never move again.

In the chill of pre-dawn, Red, after his fruitless search the previous day, had an idea. He dressed and moved along the trench, grey light filtering. Approaching one of his posts, No. 16, he instructed the guard to open his loophole at 5.15 a.m. Red himself would resume his former eyrie to the rear. He synchronised his watch with that of the sentry. The time approached, 5.15 – bang! Red saw a wisp of gas, clear in the cold dawn air, rise from the remains of a garden a mere seventy yards away.

Very cautiously, he wrapped a torn section of sandbag round his telescope, and focused on the little plot of turnips. At first he saw nothing. Then he became aware of some turnip tops moving when all the rest were still. A moment later he made out the top of Willibald's head, garlanded with turnip tops and the upper part of his square German face. This then was the explanation of the accurate shooting and long casualty list. Willibald had been firing at short range, less than a hundred yards. Red now had to

regain the British trenches. No easy matter at that most dangerous time of day. He would be perfectly silhouetted for part of his
crawl. Last evening the light had worked in his favour. Now, the
German would have a perfect opportunity to add to his already
impressive bag.

Red started off. As he neared the thistle (one he'd marked as the
fringe of the danger zone) his heart beat fast and quick. He passed
the thistle. He felt very like a fly crawling over an inverted plate
while someone with a flytrap waited to strike. He was crawling
straight away now. The thistle was behind him. Another four yards
– two – one – still Willibald did not fire and, with a deep sigh of
relief, Red hurled himself into the disused sap and safety.

This momentary lapse, failure to remember the gas cloud would
rise in cold dawn air, has just cost the sniper his life. Red has him
spotted and retribution followed remorselessly. So Willibald was
brought in. His cap, some letters in his pocket, and his shoulder-
straps were forwarded to his brigade; but his rifle, beautifully fitted
with a Zeiss telescopic sight, which had taken over twenty British
lives, turned its muzzle eastwards instead of west, and began to take
German lives instead.

Even as the war ended and both sides could claim equal honours
in the field of marksmanship, Major Pemberthy was not about to
concede that the enemy might ever have edged ahead:

Compared with the average Boche post of a similar character
which I have inspected since November 1918, we were certainly
not behind the Germans in this respect. The use of camouflage
was also practically illustrated. Demonstrations were given in the
use of such devices as sniper's suits, painted in different colours,
to merge into the ground; dummy heads for exposing above the
trenches and drawing Hun sniper's fire in order to detect his position by flash or smoke of his rifle, white suits for night patrols
when snow lay on the ground. The Boche of course used many
similar devices but I think we beat him at the game.

Gunner

'The Battery Horse'

He whinnied low as I passed by,
It was a pleading sort of cry;
His rider, slain while going back,
Lay huddled on the muddy track.
And he, without a guiding hand,
Had strayed out on the boggy land;
And held there by the treacherous mire,
Lay exposed to shrapnel fire.

He was a wiry chestnut steed,
A type of good Australian breed;
Perhaps on steep Monaro's height,
He'd followed in the wild steer's flight,
Or out beyond the great divide
Roamed free where salt bush plains are wide.
Or, through the golden wattle groves
Had rounded up the sheep in droves,
Then shipped away to feed the guns,
And help the boys to strafe the Huns.
– Lance-Corporal E. R. Henry[141]

'The primacy of the guns' … this largely defined the war on the Western Front which was never, as some accounts might suggest, a purely static conflict. Each year of the war was very different to the last and it was the guns and their gunners who emerged as true arbiters on the field. British artillerymen had much to learn and much of that learning was painful. But learn they did and the science of gunnery advanced in prodigious bounds. At the outset at Mons, Le Cateau and Ypres, the Royal Field and Horse Artillery fought over open sights as infantry support. The Germans had already moved on to indirect fire which endowed them with a significant advantage.

Stark failure on 1 July 1916 was followed by an increasing professionalism. Realisation dawned that for any assault to succeed, the enemy front-line defences must be drowned in fire and the surviving garrison so traumatised they would lose the capacity to resist further. German batteries had to be knocked out, however well camouflaged. Effective creeping barrages were necessary to lay down a curtain of drenching fire ahead of the advancing troops. The Royal Flying Corps performed outstandingly in terms of aerial observation. Increasingly sophisticated techniques such as 'sound ranging' and 'flash spotting'[†] were developed to pinpoint enemy batteries. The British, by 1917, were moving towards the fully integrated all-arms battle which would bring final victory in 1918. Nonetheless, as Peter Hart and other authors point out, German *Landseers* would remain utterly formidable until the very end.[142]

In 1914, Newcastle-born George Russell Elder was working for W. H. Smith. His wages were 28s (£1.40) per week. With a wife and child to support, the household budget remained extremely tight. His motivation for enlisting was simple: his employers deducted a full day's pay for a day's absence; he was already working an average sixty-hour week. He enlisted on 27 March 1915. W. H. Smith continued to pay Mrs Elder 15s (£0.75p) per week while George was in khaki.[143]

George had joined the Royal Field Artillery, whose batteries were equipped with the 18-pounder 'quick-firer' and was selected to undergo training as a telephonist and signaller. As the battery horses began to arrive, the aspiring gunners had to learn how to work with their new equine comrades. As for the guns themselves, all they possessed were a dozen ancient French 90mm cannon. Training with the ordnance alternated with learning the ropes as

---

† A method of pinpointing enemy batteries derived from the sound of his guns or mortars, pinpointing the muzzle flash as the enemy fires.

a signaller, the complex, precise language of flags and battlefield telecommunications, very much in its infancy.

George found the work stimulating, though confined to the safe reaches of South Northumberland. Field telephones were the principal means of communication. Absence of tactical radios was to hamstring gunnery throughout the war. Transport for the guns was primarily horse-drawn, though traction engines had been employed in the South African campaign: 'Every morning before breakfast, the rule was to take all horses for exercise. One particular morning, all horses had been saddled up and formed up outside the stables, with the exception of one beautiful grey mare.' George was given the mare which proved rather more wilful than her calm demeanour suggested. First she bolted back towards the stables. He brought her round 'all of a lather and prancing about like a duck on hot bricks'. Order restored he was congratulating himself on his equine skills when 'she let off a neigh like an elephant, took the bit between her teeth and went off into the field like a racehorse'.

Unnecessary galloping was a disciplinary matter but equally so was sawing at the bit, no matter really in this case as it had absolutely no effect whatsoever. George clung on for grim death. His sergeant, after some frantic waving, useless in the circumstances, attempted to head George's wild ride off and both mounts came very close to a huge collision or horseflesh and riders. The incident concluded with George being dumped unceremoniously onto the largely unyielding turf by his disobliging charger.

Dazed and bruised, he found himself before the battery commander. The hearing was not unsympathetic and it was the sergeant who was reprimanded for allowing a novice onto the back of a spirited horse '… so ended my first serious baptism into horse management'.

An artillery battery is a complex, multi-faceted organism, guns, limbers, ammunition and supply wagons, baggage carts, cookhouse stores, tools and impedimenta all drawn by horses. Routine training was enlivened by impromptu parades and exercises. As most recruits were native Northumbrians, training in Gosforth Park so near to Newcastle had its drawbacks. The Geordies proved prone to lateness and absenteeism and, as 1915 closed, they moved lock, stock and baggage to York where they swapped quarters with a West Riding Brigade who were prone to identical deficiencies. Here, they took delivery of brand new 18-pounders manufactured by Armstrong-Whitworth (now BAE Systems).

Not only were the guns new, George was equipped with full battery telephone and signalling equipment: flags for Morse code and semaphore, telephones for field work, micrometers and angle of sight instruments, telescopes large and small, field glasses of various sizes and lastly reels of DII and DIII insulated steel wire for field communications.

Life in training had its livelier moments. A group of half a dozen Geordie gunners-to-be went out for an evening's refreshment which involved what might now be termed a pub crawl. 'We made our way to a pork shop, where the pease pudding, pigs trotters, saveloys and black puddings were all in the window, steaming hot.' For Geordie this fare promised a sumptuous feast. Rations were procured and the team sat down on the tram to enjoy. However a group of Yorkshire Hussars were sharing their conveyance and took exception to the gunners, a traditional rivalry exacerbated by differing accents. A drink, a pie and a fight was manna indeed to the Geordies and battle was joined on and off the tram, 'pease pudding, black pudding and ducks were all used as missiles'. Only the universal alarm of 'Here come the MPs' disrupted the fun. York was out of bounds for a week thereafter.

Live firing exercises revealed the fact that none of the signallers had actually been trained in their mysterious art and George was selected for expert instruction. This was at Fulford outside York: 'I was trained in branches of signalling and telephony with the HQ staff, who were more advanced than us in signalling.' From Fulford down to Retford where the gunners received more intensive training from the RE who were the acknowledged masters: 'On the Monday both of us [he travelled with his officer] were at the signalling school of the RE and were examined in every branch of signalling and telephony.' From Retford to Otley and more training: 'Altogether I was at the school for six weeks, passing through all the parts of signalling, connected with an army in battle.'

Though in the UK, the Brigade did witness some enemy action. Late evening on 2 May 1916, a Zeppelin L21 bombed York and its vicinity. The raider had mistaken his target for the more industrialised centre of Middlesbrough; tumbling from their cots the gunners, some in a marked state of undress, set about repelling the aerial invader. Across the night sky the sinister silver cigar-shaped Zeppelin moved with stately grace, ready to rain death though not, for this night at least, upon George and his comrades. Nonetheless, the attack resulted in both loss of civilian life and structural damage to the ancient city. York suffered two more airship raids in 1916.

More training, further exercises, continual gruelling work in the saddle followed. On 25 June, the brigade moved by train from Codford to Southampton and so to France. Like so many others, the great monster of the war was sending out its siren call, drawing George and his mates into its embrace. All of the gunners from 63rd (2nd Northumbrian) Division were being sent to join the Royal Naval Division, an anomalous formation which, having been extensively blooded at Gallipoli was being part integrated into the army for service in the forthcoming Somme campaign. The sailors very much resented army interference with hallowed naval custom and particularly disliked General Shute, their CO, regarded as something of a martinet.

Sir Alan Patrick Herbert (1890–1971) was a humorist, playwright and author, perhaps most famous for his *Misleading Cases*. He served in the RND throughout the Somme, and was moved to scurrilous verse by intense dislike of his commanding officer:

> The General inspecting the trenches
> exclaimed with a horrified shout,
> 'I refuse to command a Division
> Which leaves its excreta about.'

But nobody took any notice
No one was prepared to refute,
That the presence of shit was congenial
Compared to the presence of Shute.

And certain responsible critics
Made haste to reply to his words
Observing that his staff advisors
Consisted entirely of turds.

For shit may be shot at odd corners
And paper supplied there to suit,
But a shit would be shot without mourners
If somebody shot that shit Shute.[144]

After the hardship of bringing all the guns and stores ashore, George Elder and his comrades travelled to France, steaming very slowly at the creeping paces Tommies had come to know so well. So leisurely was the pace that men alighted to walk alongside, picking fruit as they passed with gangs of raucous boys prancing alongside the lumbering wagons, yelling in broken English words they had picked up ... 'bully beef, bully beef'. They de-trained at Pernes, west of Bethune. By degrees they came closer to the front, 'large dumps of shells of all sizes were lying by the roadside and there were bales of barbed wire by the trenches. To make certain we were near to war, we eventually saw large and small batches of infantry in battle order, going towards the line.'

Shortly afterwards they marched to Bully Grenay, close to the battlefield of Loos in Artois. The village, despite severe batter-ing, still functioned with civilian life and commerce continu-ing. Here they found 'six gun pits, each of them containing an 18-pounder gun. This was our first sighting of the British artillery in the Great War.' Here, the Northumbrians were to understudy the more experienced gunners of 47th London Division. Finally, the Londoners left their pupils in charge while they departed to claim the new ordnance the Geordies had sweated prodigiously to bring from England!

George was responsible for a daily inspection of the telephone wire, pegged into the sides of the infantry trenches, extending for four and a half miles to the observation post or 'Oh Pip' as they called it. The OP was the eyes of the guns. The forward observation officer (FOO) was responsible for identifying and marking targets, calling down fire like divine wrath. Clearly if the wires were severed, this vital artery of communication was lost. At one point George with one gunner and an officer were on duty for several days in the OP, merely a shelter dug into the trench with an aperture for the observer's telescope. George's officer lost his sang-froid when, having observed two close misses, he wondered aloud if the Germans were ranging on their position. They were and the next rounds came uncomfortably close covering them in mud and debris. A rather undignified exit from that position ensued!

Now officially attached to the RND as 315th Brigade Royal Naval Division Artillery, they were moved towards Saint-Pol, training with their new comrades for an expected attack. Being Northumbrian, hard work and long marches did not deter the gunners from enjoying such recreations as were to be found. Marching six miles each way from their camp into the town in search of ale and the ubiquitous pork shop was no obstacle, 'as we walked back, we were in a pretty poor state'. George experienced problems with a particularly difficult horse called Mr Fagi, a bad-tempered beast which nearly broke his leg with a particularly vicious kick. Mr Fagi generally made himself so objectionable a bullet proved the only remedy.

'Something was in the wind.' By creeping stages they moved up towards the front. As they drew closer the dragon's breath of war reached out towards them, German guns stonked the road ahead, 'we could see by the flash and the bursts that they were getting nearer to us'. George and his pal Michael dived for cover just as a shell burst directly over their heads. All was confusion. 'All I could remember immediately after, was staggering across the road through the mud and hearing a confused sound of galloping horses, men shouting and after that, clank, clank and blackness deeper than night.'

George later found he'd been stunned by shrapnel. Michael had fared rather worse, half delirious from his wounds. 'I cut his topcoat sleeve off, taking no notice of the way he was shrieking and crying, I had to set my teeth against the sound of screaming shells which were hurtling through the air…' The wounded man, bleeding staunched, had still to be got to the first aid post 'but when we moved him the poor chap let out some of the most awful yells and screams I have ever heard, or ever wish to hear again'. Michael survived but his wounds guaranteed a ticket back to 'Blighty'.

After the briefest of rests George went up to the gun line. On reporting to his CO he was furnished with details of his signal communications, wires etc., and who was connected with him by phone, a list of secret code words and abbreviations. This was a regular procedure at every new gun position the battery took. As the time for attack came closer, the gunners established their routine, synchronising watches so that in the laggardly dark of pre-dawn the gun commanders could rouse their resting warriors as one to leap to their guns and be ready.

At the appointed time, with all guns loaded, the order to fire would ring out. The air would then be rent by the roar of shells as each gun loaded and fired for a full quarter of an hour, stopping exactly at 6.00 a.m. This drill was carried out down the line for a distance of some fifteen miles. For a full fortnight this ritual bombardment took place, regular as clockwork. The Germans were to be denied rest, unnerved, and yet there was no infantry assault following on, fostering, it was hoped, an element of complacency.

The moment was drawing nearer. George, alongside one of the section officers, was chosen to go in with the infantry as liaison officer and signaller; vital, though scarcely enviable roles. They would go over at 06.00 next morning. This meant both had to move forward into the assault trenches rather sooner to find their bearings: 'At about midnight, the officer and myself went away from the battery to proceed to the trenches, my sole equipment consisted of tin hat, gas mask, a reel of thin telephone wire, telephone earth pin on my leg and a couple of signalling flags.' George was about to become a participant in the Battle of the Ancre, the last big 'push' on the Somme, launched in the depths of mud-deluged autumn on 16 November by Gough's 5th Army. The RND's objectives comprised the village and station at Beaucourt. Most of these were taken though at fearful cost: 100 officers and 1,600 men died; nearly 3,000 were wounded. Serre, of evil repute, was not taken.

As zero hour approached, the pair was making their way up through the reserve trenches, constantly checking the fragile umbilical of telephone wire. George was assigned to a deep dugout where RE signallers were in charge of telecommunications. He plugged into their system and spoke to his colleague back with the battery. All was well, thus far anyway. Despite the tensions, George managed to doze in the small hours. As the clock crept towards six in the morning, the steady tattoo of the German bombardment reached a tempo, like a distant drumbeat so many feet below ground.

At 5.35 a.m. George's officer bade him make ready. The infantry were standing against the side with fixed bayonets and smoking their inevitable fags. Occasionally they would hear the cry 'make way for the stretcher-bearers' and struggling along the narrow trench would come the stretcher with some fresh victim writhing in agony.

As he and his officer moved along the trench, George played out the wire behind him. This flimsy and vulnerable link was all that allowed the artillery to coordinate with attacking infantry. While it might survive in fixed trenches, once the signaller moved into the maelstrom of no man's land, it was certain to be chopped into fragments. As they reached their jumping-off point the German barrage died away. Silence like a benediction descended briefly over the vast canvas of conflict. Then it was over as a British hurricane bombardment drenched the enemy front line, drawing immediate retribution: 'Mr Fritz was then retaliating but where they were dropping I couldn't say, as we were all taking advantage of whatever availed itself in the trench side … "Get ready boys, only a few minutes to go…"'

Then, 'over you go boys and the best of luck!' George went over the top with the rest, telephone wire snaking behind as he reeled it out like Ariadne's thread. Around, a crescendo of enemy shells, rifle grenades and a storm of small arms, 'one could see men throwing up their hands and dropping down dead or badly wounded. Several of the men in my immediate vicinity got it pretty bad, how I was missed, I can't say.' Into the German front line and survivors were surrendering. These were sent to the rear while the more recalcitrant, deep within their dugouts, were winkled out by threats or, failing that, a deluge of Mills bombs. The creeping barrage lifted as though by the hand of God and marched on across the blasted ground. George, like any seasoned Tommy, found time for some profitable looting: 'I went on a souvenir hunt in the dugouts and obtained a lovely German officer's peacetime sword. It was all inscribed on the handle, blade and scabbard. When I found it I hid it down my trouser leg.'

Any attempt to contact their battery by telephone proved futile. The thin umbilical cord of wire had clearly been severed and minced by enemy fire. No man's land was a scene of utter carnage, British and German dead thick by the parapet. Neither wire nor flags worked and the pair was unable by any means to communicate with their fellow gunners. There was nothing for it but to trudge back over the dearly purchased ground, through the trench maze to their battery by now so far behind the scene of the infantry action. The enemy was now completely out of range.

No rest for George, however; the guns were immediately dragged out of their pits, harnessed up and the battery cantered off to pursue the foe. They bounced and rattled by the tortured ground at Beaumont Hamel. The road they were struggling along was nothing but a broken track. Great pot-holes were everywhere making the going for horses and guns practically impossible. Most of the damage had been caused by British heavy guns during the attack. Dead horses and men were lying all along the road where they had been caught by shellfire as they attempted to get away. There was a prevailing, noxious stench hovering everywhere; rising from the broken, spilt corpses, laced with the odour of gas.

George Elder was to have many adventures with the gunners after the end of the Somme fighting. He came home safe and resumed working for W. H. Smith – a job he held for over half a century after. He died in 1980 at the age of eighty-eight.

Tunnellers

'Getting Back'

I've heard men say when in the camp,
Or on the sea or on the tramp,
The tales they'll tell to folks at home
If they win through and cross the foam
And get safe back.

Some carry with them day and night,
A souvenir of some big fight,
To show to friends where they have fought,
On fields where victory's dearly bought –
If they get back.

While thunderous cannon rend the skies,
They face the foe with steady eyes;
Though some get through, there's some must go,
Who try conclusions with the foe,
All can't get back.

Our boys who fell have left a name
Upon the priceless lists of fame;
The memory of those brave hearts dear,
All I ask is a souvenir,
If I get back.
– Lance-Corporal E. R. Henry[145]

'Into the mouth of Hell' … the Western Front was a parallel war. While millions burrowed beneath what had been fields and lanes to make trenches, others dug far deeper. Since Joshua brought down the walls of Jericho and King John sacrificed pigs to tumble Rochester's corner tower, mining has been a feature of siege warfare. The Western Front was the greatest siege in history. As trench lines hardened, as troops became used to this static, submerged existence, both sides sought to gain advantage by burrowing under the other's lines. This became a new dimension of conflict. Miles of subterranean galleries were dug, partly defensive to intercept an enemy doing the same and partly offensive. Mines packed with explosives would be detonated under key bastions in the enemy line to clear the attackers' path. The results of these huge detonations were often mixed.

Sir John Norton-Griffiths, better known to Imperial and Great War contemporaries as 'Empire Jack' or 'Hell-Fire Jack', had served in the Matabele and Second Boer Wars. He became a successful engineer and, in 1914, raised a volunteer battalion at his own expense and was promoted Major. He was the Tommy's Vauban, directing the construction of fortifications all along the line which he toured in a Rolls-Royce, suitably equipped with a first-rate travelling cellar. When German mining commenced in earnest during the early months of 1915, Kitchener immediately sought out Norton-Griffiths:

As early as November, 1914, I laid a scheme before the War Office and begged to be allowed to take out a handful of men whom I described as 'moles' and make a start. Although the scheme was listened to sympathetically and indeed was sent out to France for approval, it went no further until, early in 1915, I got a telegram to report immediately to Lord Kitchener. Well do I remember that interview. Alone in his room at the War Office, he showed me the urgent dispatches which had been coming from Lord French to the effect that unless some means could be found of checking the mining efforts of the Germans he (French) would probably have withdraw certain sections of the line. Lord Kitchener [who of course knew Norton-Griffiths from South Africa] asked me to amplify my suggested mining scheme – we had lost heavily to German mines at Ypres.

To his demand, I replied that the only thing I could suggest would be to use 'moles' … 'clay kickers' or 'workers on the cross' – using a north country expression for the class of small tunnel mining.[146]

An impromptu demonstration followed. Borrowing a fire-shovel, Norton-Griffiths lay on his back and mimed digging with the shovel between his feet, not something Kitchener was likely to have witnessed previously. The major 'showed him, lying on the floor, what a clay-kicker really was and what a small-hole he could work in. Kitchener turned round and said to me: "Get 10,000 immediately!"'

Very nearly a century on and a remarkable archaeological project, the La Boisselle Study Group, is actively engaged in excavating and renovating a complex of tunnels near the village of that name on the Somme battlefield. The site lies adjacent to but unconnected with the nearby Lochnagar Crater and was labelled by Tommies as 'the Glory Hole'. The diggers have shed significant light on life and death in the tunnels, a high-risk occupation at best. A photograph of Ezekiel Parkes shows a man who might have come from any pre-war group of miners (in his case from Derbyshire), stolid and unmilitary with calloused hands of iron. He and another sapper, John Lane, were killed deep underground when Germans blew the mine. Their bodies were never recovered.

Frederick James Mulqueen DSO MC, a Canadian by birth and civil engineer by profession, served firstly with 172 and latterly 182 Tunnelling companies on the Western Front. In the summer of 1914, he was working in South America on the engineering staff of the Sao Paulo Tramway, Light and Power Company. Pre-war recession diminished the opportunities and he transferred his skills to the Anglo-Brazilian Iron and Steel Company. Their order book was

equally diminished and, on 4 July 1914, he embarked for Liverpool
on the *SS Darbo*.

Wireless reports spoke of the worsening situation in the Balkans
but no hint of fear seemed to cling to Liverpool docks. The English
were enjoying a warm summer and he went by train to Alnmouth
on the Northumbrian coast. Here, the countdown to war was spent
fishing and golfing. Due to the influence of his host, Mr Vaughan,
Frederick was taken on by Redpath, Brown and Co. in Edinburgh.
It was now August and war fever proved contagious:

> As one walked the streets of the city, one could feel a desire to get
> at the Germans. The fever which was prevalent everywhere was in
> my bones. I wanted to join up Troop trains filled with cheering
> soldiers were passing through the city's stations and I wanted to
> be with them.

A Clyde-side friend had offered his 45-foot steam yacht *Lady Lel*
to the Royal Navy as a pinnace and Frederick, together with the
owner's son, were to sail the boat and join a squadron at anchor in
Loch Ewe. This would earn both temporary commissions in the
Royal Naval Volunteer Reserve (RNVR). Mulqueen was a keen
sailor though his friend appeared unwilling to part with the helm
as they steamed up the west coast towards their rendezvous. On
sailing blithely into Loch Ewe they did not realise certain naval
protocols applied and that the warships might decide their diminutive craft was hostile. Having very nearly been blown out of the
water, they managed to establish their bona fides. Frederick was
perhaps not a natural sailor. His attempts at the maritime version of
the three-point turn ended in ignominy, davits shorn away. Rother
worse, a libidinous excursion ashore turned to tragedy when their
longboat capsized and several officers drowned. Their Lords of the
Admiralty now had second thoughts about the proffered commission which indeed proved very temporary.

And so to London, living modestly in digs and lobbying for a
commission in one of the Canadian outfits. This was accompanied

by some riotous living at Simpsons or the Savoy, served by the head waiter Jimmy, something of a wartime legend in *Casablanca* mode. Still, no luck with recruiting. Finally, he was offered a subaltern's role with the gunners. On 12 January 1915 he received his admission to the ranks of temporary gentlemen. Equitation proved the next stumbling block. Frederick who had ridden in Canada was given a spirited seventeen-hand Argentine mount. His lack of visible prowess sparked the wrath of the riding master – an ex-ranker made up to major: 'The major had without exception, the loudest and most commanding voice I have ever heard, furthermore his range of adjectives was phenomenal.'

On 15 February, Mulqueen dined with an acquaintance who had returned from war work in the Far East, an engineer who spoke of the increasing need for skilled professionals at the front. A transfer to one of the new tunnelling companies was discussed but, in the short term, led nowhere. By March he had orders for France as a gunner and landed at Le Havre on the 27th. Barely a week later, he was sent up to the front via Bailleul. It was in the course of his baptism with the guns that he decided to switch to engineering, 'on my return to the battery, I reported what I had done and I was looked upon as quite insane. To join a tunnelling company was considered sheer suicide.' Nonetheless, by 22 April he had orders to join 172 Company RE.

On that same day he met and was briefed by Norton-Griffiths himself, already something of a titan. It was a dark time. The Germans had used gas for the first time in the Salient and opened a gap in the line; the Major had encountered 'the remnants of a Zouave battalion some distance behind the lines with gas in their lungs and fear in their eyes'. The war had entered a newer, even more terrible phase. Sappers were already burrowing beneath Hill 60 in the sector but Mulqueen was sent to Company HQ in Dickebush. He was to relieve a Lieutenant Hickling in the line. The British position dug in amid the ruins of St Eloi, was compromised by German control of the 'Mound' overlooking the shattered huddle: 'A heading had been started from the village toward the Mound,

and was about half way there at that time. Our orders were to
charge a mine in the heading which was to be fired in the event of
an adverse situation developing.'

That evening Frederick moved up towards the front line,

in those days there were no communication trenches or, if there
were, we didn't use them. The night was dark and the road was
muddy. I had thought the vocabulary of the ranker major
was complete but I can assure you that, on that night, I was to
learn it was far from it!

The night sky was lit by the fitful glare of arcing Verey lights and
livened by the zip of spent rounds coming close. Rumour insisted
German snipers had infiltrated and lurked in cover ready to pick
off the unwary.

Eventually we arrived and reported to Lieutenant Hickling
whom I found to be a first rate fellow. The place was alive with
men, shoulder to shoulder in a position which consisted mostly
of barricaded buildings, half-demolished and shallow trenches.
Hickling showed me the shaft and heading and the mine which
he had laid but which was not completely tamped. The electric
leads from the detonators had been carried to the surface and
run behind a stout wall to a cellar to the north. I have forgotten
the exact details of the charge or its distance from the shaft but
my recollection is that the former was more than ample and the
latter far from it! The exploder was ready and waiting but it was
not connected.

The relief completed, Mulqueen was now very much on his own.
He was a civil rather than a mining engineer, 'I had never been in
a mine!'

The depth of the shaft was probably 14 feet and the gallery leading from it was exceedingly small, possibly 3'6" x 2'0". It was

much smaller than that which was later made standard. The sergeant and I explored it and, following Hickling's instructions, we outlined to the men the amount of additional tamping to be placed. Sandbags filled with clay were used for this purpose … there was room for only one person at the 'face' at any time. The sandbags were passed from hand to hand along the length of the gallery and securely packed adjacent to the charge where the tamping was completed, a check was again made of the leads, exploder etc.

Mulqueen was under the immediate orders of the infantry commander in his sector, a lieutenant-colonel of 4th Battalion Northumberland Fusiliers. It was the infantry officer who would give the order to fire the mine. Meantime, the Fusiliers were crammed into an isolated post, the infantry's strength concentrated in the forward positions.

German gunners were active. Desultory shells came over but there seemed no fear of imminent assault…

The term whizz-bang is an extraordinarily effective description of the type of high velocity shell. In the case of a round fired from a howitzer, one could hear the explosion of the gun some seconds before the shell arrived. Not so the whizz-bang; one hears a whizz and then the bang almost simultaneously. We tunnellers were well established in dugouts adjoining the shafts. Fusiliers were ready and determined, machine guns well sited to enfilade any attacks on the battalion front. In daylight the position appeared even more precarious; the Germans occupied the other half of the village. The Mound dominated the whole position and the Germans had captured this after exploding a mine of their own on 14 March.

Since the first use of gas, much talk revolved around its lethal effects.

There was a great deal of discussion on the use of gas by the Germans and the best way of combating it. It was agreed that it could only be used when wind conditions were favourable and, at such times, extra sentries should be posted. The Germans were known to have used masks and it was understood we would eventually get them. Pending their receipt there was little one could do ... one unique suggestion was that one should urinate on one's handkerchief and place it over one's nose. It was stated that urine (ammonia) neutralized the chlorine. I can say I never tried it!

Meanwhile, the business of digging continued:

I spent the following day in the line with Hickling and he explained his plans to protect the post underground. Already difficulties were being encountered in that the disposition of the soil proved a problem. The clay was filled into sandbags underground, hoisted up the shafts by winches and the sandbags piled outside the so-called dugouts which had been built over the shaft-heads.

For the infantry, most materials were in short supply, but the engineers fared rather better, drawing on precious stocks of timber and cannibalising the wrecked buildings around.

The infantry lived in makeshift dugouts but Hickling had designed a more rugged affair to cover our shafts and to house the men who were off shift. He scrounged timbers from the destroyed houses and used them as uprights to support wooden joists (also from the houses) on top of which he placed corrugated iron sheets and protected the top and sides with layers of sandbags containing the earth brought up from below. These dugouts were relatively safe from shrapnel. In any event one had a sense of security in them and psychologically, they helped the men.

Hickling had decided that the dimensions of the shaft and heading of the first mine were wrong and should be enlarged. It is probable that the subject had been considered at Company HQ and also with the other tunnelling companies. In any event, standards were agreed upon; the shaft was 6'0" x 4'0" and the galleries 3'6" x 2'6". The ground was sandy clay and was wet, therefore at the bottom of the shaft a sump was dug and a double acting, hand-operated pump installed over it. The pump was worked by an infantry fatigue party and, as the men usually hated the job, the pump received some pretty rough treatment. It was also necessary to supply fresh air to the working face and this was delivered through a three- or two-inch airline connected to a Rootes hand operated blower placed at the top of the shaft. The blower was also operated by an infantry fatigue party and it was not a rare occurrence for the officer on duty to find both the pump and the blower idle!

Hickling had been feeling his way downwards, seeing if he could probe deeper before hitting the water table. The engineers were beginning to master the practice of this branch of their profession. Geologists, hydrologists and other experts were co-opted and a new science was developing, embodying such eclectic elements as crater formulae, explosives, mining theory, listening instruments and mine rescue. At 35 feet the diggers encountered drier clay and the original charge was lifted from the first, shallow mine and deposited deeper. The first shaft was converted into a listening post to detect counter-mining operations.

The mine in this heading had been placed directly under the junction of the roads leading to Ypres, Voormezeele, Wytschaete and Hollebeke. The road junction consisted of an area of heavy pave, i.e. oblong granite blocks approximately 10" x 4" x 6". Based on our subsequent experience, had we fired the mine, the pave would have been thrown in all directions and would probably have destroyed not only the Germans but also many of our troops including the officer who exploded the mine! Some of us were born under a lucky star!

Under Hickling's able administration our section commenced a series of galleries which not only protected the St Eloi post but subsequently forced the Hun into defensive action close to his own lines. A ready use was found for the sand-bagged soil. It was built into an extension of the trench system both to left and right.

It was customary to stack the sandbags by day and leave the more exposed work of building trenches till night-time. Mulqueen came across a party working blithely by day. They were convinced their area was in dead ground and couldn't be overlooked by German marksmen. Frederick decided to cautiously investigate. No sooner had he peeped out than a sniper round passed clean through his hat (this was prior to the issue of 'tin' helmets), a lucky star indeed.

'Tunnellers were not very popular with the infantry, largely because the spoil from underground was easily spotted by the Germans and drew fire. Also water, pumped from diggings, tended to flood the trenches.' On 6 May Mulqueen endured what he laconically describes as a 'rather one-sided talk' with the infantry CO after the latter had descended rather precipitously into the run-off.

Wisely, he decided to seek a solution. Behind the main front-line trench ran an older irrigation drain or channel, much choked. If this could be cleaned out and restored to function, it could provide the necessary additional drainage to absorb the waste from the diggings. That night he went out with a small working party. Despite darkness and diligence, the enemy twigged to their presence and began throwing grenades. One 'sank into the muddy water between the three of us and exploded about two feet from my head'. Miraculously, he emerged largely unscathed though both his companions suffered wounds.

Despite his apparent escape, Mulqueen suffered headaches and dizziness. This was doubly unfortunate as he was, at this point, responsible for the positioning of a 'collar' over a newly dug shaft. This was a tricky business. The collar itself was fabricated in the rear and from timber. It then had to be carefully and exactly located over the head of the shaft. Planks lining the opening were suspended from the collar, so correct siting was of the essence. With his head-ache rampant Frederick had been obliged to leave the fine detail to his sappers whose efforts were less than outstanding. The unfortunate result was 'a hell of a mess' and Hickling, proud architect, 'as mad as a hornet'. Obviously, his injuries from the grenade blast were more severe and he was obliged to report sick. Here he first heard of the sinking of *Lusitania* engendering 'a further loathing of the Huns if that was possible'.

An initial period of four weeks' rest was extended by a further six weeks. He did not return to St Eloi till 24 July. His comrades had not been idle. The underground labyrinth had progressed prodigiously and new drainage carried away the excess water. His luck held when another German rifle grenade missed by a whisker but the shock caused an unexpected nervous reaction, legacy of his previous close shave.

Their work continued:

The respective shafts and underground workings at St Eloi were lettered in accordance with a general working pattern in vogue on the front. Headings were driven from our front line towards the German trenches at varying depths of 15 feet – 35 feet. As those headings approached their objectives, they encountered German defensive operations. Alternatively, in some places, they forestalled German offensive workings. On some other fronts, shafts were sunk in the support trenches and were less vulnerable to enemy raids, attacks etc. these were connected by lateral galleries running beneath or slightly in front of the front-line trench system. In August 1915, we had not managed to build any laterals at St Eloi, as the Hun did not give us time to develop such refinements!

Listening was the key, the key to what was becoming a deadly subterranean game of cat and mouse, of hunter and hunted, one where the roles could be reversed in an instant, the price of inattention, death or entombment.

[Listening] was accomplished by a carefully controlled system. While there were several different kinds of listening instrument, the first with which we were supplied and, in my opinion the best was the geophone, constructed on the principle of the ordinary medical stethoscope. It consisted of a circular wooden disc, about three inches in diameter and an inch thick within which was enclosed a flat mass of mercury held in place by two mica discs. Two small nipples led to air spaces on the outside of the upper and lower mica discs respectively. Rubber tubes connected the nipples to the ears. To obtain direction of sound, two instruments and a compass were used.

This business of listening was both highly complex and infinitely subtle. Sound ranges differed in changing soil conditions. Operators had to become adept in filtering out extraneous noise, work which became the province of highly specialised elites,

whose acumen was uncanny. I remember in one of our headings on the Vimy Ridge which was in chalk, we traced the German operator from over 90 feet away to within 10 feet of our position. In the early days listeners were trained 'under fire'. It was a dangerous undertaking. If the neophyte's judgment failed him, he and his comrades were apt to find themselves buried under tons of clay with little hope of rescue. Not all volunteers were temperamentally suitable. The successful listener must be a cool personality. Often he will find himself alone in a dark gallery. He must not allow his imagination to run away with him. On the other hand, he must not overlook even the slightest sound indicative of any activity.

The moist gallery, 35 feet below ground, half-lit with a flickering candle, apparently remote in its very stillness and yet, was it remote? Was the dull sound which the geophone picked up the burst of a distant shell or was it clay carelessly dropped in a nearby German gallery. The two geophones were shifted along the floor until the sound reaching each ear was uniform. The compass was set midway between the two instruments. Had sounds been heard previously from that general direction? Were the sounds coming from a higher or lower level? The instruments were shifted up and down the face of the gallery, up and down the timbers. Moments of indecision, one must not become 'windy'!

Yes, the Germans were working forward, to the left and slightly higher but how much higher and how far away? The sergeant took the instruments. What did he think? Should we let the Hun come closer or should we blow? A hasty check of the distance from our trenches, and from the German – a hasty review of previous listening records; how quickly was he working forwards – were we too distant from both and should we concentrate on the destruction of his gallery by firing a camouflet [an early sapper's version of, in modern parlance, a shaped charge].

Only the officer could make the final, vital decision. Once made, a process unfolds. The 100lb camouflet had to be located within a bored out chamber, some 16 feet in length. Normally, the sergeant worked the auger; silence is, in every sense, golden.

The mining officer must advise the infantry of his decision and its probable effect. He must have the explosives and canisters brought forward from the magazine. He must warn the shifts working in nearby galleries. He must assemble the electric leads, detonators and exploders. Possibly, some two or three hours after the decision was made the mine, completely tamped would be ready to fire!

As the underground war intensified and mining operations ballooned, the choice of suitable explosives was modified:

From the day when I joined the Tunnelling Companies in April 1915 to the day we fired our last mine in December 1916, we thought and dreamed explosives and their effect. Black powder was the first, followed by wet gun cotton, then blastine and, finally, ammonal; of these ammonal was by far the most satisfactory.

Major Norton-Griffiths quotes an exchange of memoranda concerning the explosive ammonal:

> To 5th Corps HQ
>   Can you please say if you have made use of any ammonal and, if so, whether the results are satisfactory?
>   Signed, Lieutenant-Colonel G. F. Farmer etc

> To Camp Commandant, 5th Corps
>   For report please.
>   Signed, Lieutenant-Colonel W. H. James etc

> To AG & QMG, 5th Corps
>   This is not understood. For what purposes is ammonal used please? Is it a drug or an explosive?
>   Signed, Lieutenant-Colonel J. Fryer etc

> To Camp Commandant, 5th Corps
>   Perhaps the medical officer attached to Corps HQ will be able to give you all required information?
>   Signed, Lieutenant-Colonel W. H. James etc

> To AG & QMG, 5th Corps
>   In accordance with your previous minute, I have consulted the MO in command of 5th Corps HQ. He informs me that ammonal is a compound drug extensively used in America as a sexual sedative in cases of abnormal sexual excitement. So far as I am able to ascertain, this drug is not in issue to Corps HQ. Under the circumstances, I regret that I am unable to report as to the results of the use of ammonal being satisfactory or not and, at the present moment, the MO states that no cases have occurred among 5th Corps HQ personnel indicating the necessity for administering the drug.
>   Signed, Lieutenant-Colonel J. Fryer etc.

NINE

SINEWS OF WAR

Angels of Mercy

'Who?'

Who doubles round both morn and eve,
The wounded soldiers to relieve,
Without the slightest word of thanks from privates, corporals
and other ranks –
The trolley boy.

Who may not smoke, nor curse, nor swear
Because the nurse is ever near,
And may not spill upon the floor,
A drop of water maybe more –
The trolley boy.

The patients at him swear and curse
And treat him like a Hun – or worse,
The say his hands are cold as death,
And mutter swear words beneath their breath –
At the trolley boy.
– F. V. Barnes, 1/15th London Regiment, 9 December 1916

Katherine Harley is buried in the Allied War Cemetary in
Salonika, the only woman amongst thousands of fallen soldiers.
The headstone in English and Cyrillic reads:

On your tomb instead of flowers.
The gratitude of the Serbs will blossom.
For your wonderful acts,
Your name shall be known from generation to generation.

Monica Krippner, in her superb book about women's efforts in Serbia between 1915 and 1918, quotes a letter from one of her colleagues at the Scottish Women's Hospital.

On the afternoon of 7 March [1917], after a busy day, Mrs. Harley was sitting by the window in her house having a cup of tea when a shell burst nearby. As a reflex action everyone threw themselves flat on the floor. Then Edith scrambled to her feet and saw her mother still in the chair. 'Mother, get down please!' she pleaded. But there was no response.

Mrs Harley was already dead – a piece of shrapnel had struck her in the middle of the forehead as neatly as a well aimed bullet.

Her funeral was conducted with full military honours and was attended by representatives of the Serbian, British and French armies. In Monastir a street was named after her and, within months, the Serbs unveiled a memorial which can still be seen today.[147]

Just what was this 62-year-old ardent suffragette doing in Serbia? Like so many other supporters of the women's cause, she had decided to suspend her political activities for the duration of the war, swept up by patriotism, the desire to support the men on the front line and the opportunity to exercise some of those long-denied skills women were not supposed to have. Nor was she the only member of her family to get involved. Her brother was none other than Field Marshal John French. Her sister, Charlotte Despard, was a leading light in the pacifist movement. As that intrepid American journalist, Molly Potter Daggett, reported:

In the historic chapel, the wall at the back of the altar behind the great gold cross was hung with battle-flags. Men in khaki and women in khaki listened with bowed heads. It was the memorial service for Katherine Mary Harley, of whom the London papers of the day before had announced in large headlines, KILLED AT HER POST OF DUTY IN MONASTIR.

In that other world we used to have before the war, Mrs. Harley was known as one of England's most distinguished constitutional suffragists, not quite so radical as Mrs. Despard, her sister, who is the leader of the Woman's Freedom League. One of her most notable pieces of work in behalf of votes for women was the great demonstration she organised a few years ago in that pilgrimage of women who marched from all parts of England, addressing vast concourses of people along the highways and arriving by diverse routes for a great mass meeting in Hyde Park. You see, Katherine Harley was an organiser of tried capacity. And she, too, comes of a family of soldiers. She was the daughter of Captain French, of Kent. Her husband, who died from the effects of the Boer War, was Colonel Harley, chief of staff to General Sir Leslie Rindle in South Africa. Her brother is Viscount Sir John French, former Field Marshal of the English forces in France. And her son is now fighting at the front. With all of this brilliant array of military men belonging to her, it is a curious fact, as her friends in London told me, that Mrs. Harley did not believe in war. 'Katherine was a pacifist,' one of them said at the International Franchise Club the night that the announcement of her death was received there in a hushed and sorrowful silence. 'But she believed if there must be war, someone must bind up the wounds of war.' And it was with high patriotic zeal and with the fearless spirit of youth, albeit she was 62 years of age, that Mrs. Harley in 1914 enlisted with the Scottish Women, taking her two daughters with her into the service. She went out as administrator of the hospital at Royaumont. And when that was in successful operation, she was transferred to Troyes to set up the tent hospital there. Then she was called to Salonika. It was at Salonika that she commanded the famous transport flying column of motor-ambulances that went over precipitous mountain roads right up to the fighting line to get the wounded... They buried her like a soldier and she lies at rest with the Croix de Guerre ... on her breast out there at the front of the conflict.[148]

They had responded in their thousands, those women. Not just the suffragettes: women of every class and background flocked to help, driven by a sense of adventure and duty. What better way to do your bit than by aiding the wounded?

> It was in the autumn of 1913 ... I saw a snapshot of a girl astride on horseback leaping a fence in a khaki uniform and topee. Underneath was merely the line 'Women Yeomanry in Camp', and nothing more. 'That', said I, pointing out the photo to a friend, 'is the sort of show I'd like to belong to: I'm sick of ambling round the Row on a Park hack. It would be a rag to go into camp with a lot of other girls. I'm going to write to the Mirror for particulars straight away.'[149]

Catherine Marguerite (Pat) Beauchamp Waddell was twenty-one when she joined the First Aid Nursing Yeomanry (FANY). The daughter of woollen manufacturer Cranston Waddell, she was the youngest of three children and the only girl. Her mother had died in the year of her birth. It is easy to imagine her as the spoilt darling of the family but her memoir, published in 1919, shows a woman of great verve, humour and compassion. She hailed from Wetheral in Cumberland and described herself as speaking with a broad Cumbrian accent.

An early volunteer, by 1915 she was working as a VAD (Voluntary Aid Detachment) for the Lamark Hospital in Calais doing everything from cooking to nursing. She transferred to a FANY ambulance unit working for the Red Cross in 1916 and spent much of the next year ferrying supplies and wounded with the aid of 'Susan', a four cylinder Napier given to the Red Cross by a Mrs Herbert Davis. Susan had been converted from a private car to an ambulance and was, Pat tells us: 'battle-scarred, as her canvas testified, where the bullets and shrapnel had pierced it. She had a fat comfortable look about her, and … always came up to the scratch, that car, and saved my life more than once.'

Nursing was one of the jobs already open to women, medicine one of the few professions. Some 700 nurses worked in military hospitals before the war. By 1918 this had jumped to 13,600. There were only 200 or so women doctors in 1900. One source suggests that over 70 per cent of them volunteered for war work, often to find themselves rejected by both army and Red Cross. Elsie Inglis was fairly typical. Famously, her offer of assistance was met with: 'My good lady, go home and sit still.' Her response was to set up the Scottish Women's Hospitals which would go on to provide medical care in Belgium, France, Russia and Serbia. Funded, organised, and staffed by women, it offered medical attention for all: soldiers, refugees and civilians.

Royaume, thirty miles north of Paris, was typical. Between 1915 and 1919 it dealt with 11,000 casualties, most of them French. Katherine Harley was its first administrator. A newsreel film still exists which shows her welcoming stretcher cases. She walks along the lines of newly arrived litters handing out cigarettes; all eagerly received. It was a not uncommon spectacle. Pat Beauchamp recalled a similar scene in Calais. She had boarded a hospital ship bound for Cherbourg:

The floor of the saloon was packed with stretchers all as close together as possible. It seemed terrible to believe that every one of those men was seriously wounded. The stretchers were so close together it was impossible to try and move among them, so I stayed on the bottom rung of the ladder and threw the cigarettes to the different men who were well enough to smoke them.

Often the men could only speak Flemish, but I did not find much difficulty in understanding it. If you speak German with a broad Cumberland accent I assure you, you can make yourself understood quite easily! It was worth while trying anyway, and it did one's heart good to see how their faces lighted up.

A flood of private hospitals, ambulance services and welfare agencies run by women followed the declaration of war. Rejected by the War Department, they were much sought after elsewhere:

> When war broke out in August 1914 Lieutenant Ashley Smith lost no time in offering the Corps' services to the War Office. To our intense disappointment these were refused. However, F.A.N.Y.'s are not easily daunted. The Belgian Army, at that time, had no organised medical corps in the field, and informed us they would be extremely grateful if we would take over a Hospital for them. Lieutenant Smith left for Antwerp in September 1914, and had arranged to take a house there for a Hospital when the town fell; her flight to Ghent where she stayed to the last with a dying English officer, until the Germans arrived, and her subsequent escape to Holland have been told elsewhere.

Tommy Atkins (or even Pierre Poilu) was rather more positive. And more helpful when he got the chance:

> The weather became atrocious as the winter advanced and our none too water-tight huts showed distinct signs of warping. We only had one thickness of matchboarding in between us and the elements, and, without looking out of the windows, I could generally ascertain through the slits what was going on in the way of weather. I had chosen my 'cue' looking sea-ward because of the view and the sunsets, but then that was in far away Spring. Eva's was next door, and even more exposed than mine. When we happened to mention this state of affairs to Colonel C., he promised us some asbestos to line the outer wall if we could find someone to put it up.
>
> Another obliging friend lent us his carpenter to do the job – a burly Scot; the fact that we cleaned our own cars and went about the camp in riding breeches and overalls, not unlike land-girls' kit, left him almost speechless.
>
> The first day all he could say was, 'Weel, weel, I never did' – at intervals.

The second day he had recovered himself sufficiently to look round and take a little notice.

'Ye're one o' them artists, I'm thinkin',' he said, eyeing my panthers disparagingly. [She had painted the wall of her hut.] 'No, you mustn't think that,' I said apologetically.

'Ha ye no men to do yon dirty worrk for ye?' and he nodded in direction of the cars. 'Scandalizing, and no less,' was his comment when he heard there were not. In two days' time he reported to his C.O. that the job was finished, and the latter overheard him saying to a pal, 'Aye mon, but A've had ma outlook on life broadened these last two days.' B. 'phoned up hastily to the Convoy to know what exactly we had done with his carpenter.

Sometimes the assistance was rather more unofficial:

Tommy is certainly a nailer at what he terms 'commandeering'. I was down at the M.T. yard one day and as I left, was told casually to look in the box when I got to camp. I did so, and to my horror saw a wonderful foot pump – the pneumatic sort. I had visions of being hauled up before a Court of Enquiry to produce the said pump, which was a brand new one and painted bright red. On my next job I made a point of going round by the M.T. yard to return the 'present'. I found my obliging friend, who was pained in the extreme at the mere mention of a pump. 'Never 'eard of one,' he affirmed stoutly. 'Leastways,' he said reminiscently, looking at me out of the corner of his eye, 'I do seem to remember something about a stawf car bein' in 'ere this morning when yours was' – and he smiled disarmingly. 'Look 'ere,' he continued, 'you forget all about it, Miss. I 'ates to see yer puffing at the tyres with them old-fashioned ones, and anyway,' with a grin, 'that car's in Abbeville now!'

Increasing shortages of medical personnel wore down Army resistance and by 1916 the War Department was recruiting women doctors to the RAMC, largely deploying them overseas.

Women drivers and ambulance bearers freed up men for the war effort and, to her joy, Pat Beauchamp was finally able to work with her own countrymen.

Attitudes to women were slow to change, though:

A priceless article appeared in one of the leading dailies entitled, 'Women Motor Drivers. – Is it a suitable occupation?' and was cut out by anxious parents and forwarded with speed to the Convoy. The headlines ran: THE LURE OF THE WHEEL; IS IT NECESSARY?; THE AFTER EFFECTS. We lapped it up with joy. Phrases such as 'Women's outlook on life will be distorted by the adoption of such a profession, her finer instincts crushed,' pleased us specially. It continued 'All the delicate things that mean, must mean, life to the feminine mind, will lose their significance' – (cries of 'What about the frillies you bought in Paris, Pat?')

'The uncongenial atmosphere' – I continued, reading further – 'of the garage, yard, and workshops, the alien companionship of mechanics and chauffeurs will isolate her mental standing' (shrieks of joy), 'the ceaseless days and dull monotony of labour will not only rob her of much feminine charm but will instil into her mind bitterness that will eat from her heart all capacity for joy, steal away her youth, and deprive her of the colour and sunlight of life' (loud sobs from the listening F.A.N.Y.s, who still, strangely enough, seemed to be suffering from no loss of joie de vivre!) When the noise had subsided I continued: 'There is of course the possibility that she will become conscious of her condition and change of mind, and realize her level in time to counteract the ultimate effects(!). The realization however may come too late.

The aptitude for happiness will have gone by for the transitory joys of driving, the questionable intricacies of the magneto–' but further details were suspended owing to small bales of cotton waste hurtling through the air, and in self-defence I had to leave the 'intricacies of the magneto' and pursue the offenders round the camp! The only reply Boss could get as a reason for the tumult was that the F.A.N.Y.s were endeavouring to 'realize the level of their minds'. 'Humph,' was Boss's comment, 'First I've heard that some of them even had any', and retired into her hut.

Training could be rather ad hoc, depending on the individual. Amalgamation of the Red Cross and St John's Ambulance to form the Joint War Committee provided expertise to the 46,000 women who formed Voluntary Aid Detachments. The VADs were to be trained 'in the art of improvising and in coping with emergencies'. Basic skills in first aid and nursing equipped them for a huge range of functions. Those deemed as unskilled started out as cleaners, drivers and orderlies. Facilities such as food and dressing stations were staffed by VADs on ambulance trains, clearing hospitals and railway stations. Others ran small hospitals and convalescent homes.

For Pat Beauchamp, training would involve a driving test if she were to take up the chance to work with British troops:

I was naturally anxious after a year with the Allies, to work for the British, but ... I was dubious as to whether I could pass the test ... Though I had come out originally with the idea of being a chauffeur, I had only done odd work from time to time at Lamarck ... I went round to the English Mechanical Transport in the town for the exam., the same test as the men went through. It was a very greasy day and the road which we took was bordered on one side by a canal and on the other by a deep and muddy ditch. As we came to a cross road the A.S.C. Lieutenant who was testing me, said, 'There you see the marks where the last man I tested skidded with his car.' 'Yes, rather, how jolly!' I replied in my agitation, wondering if my fate would be likewise. We passed the spot more by luck than good management, and then I reversed for some distance along that same road. At last I turned at the cross roads, and after some traffic driving, luckily without any mishap, drove back to hospital. I was questioned about mechanics on the way, and at the end tactfully explained I was just going on leave and meant to spend every second in a garage! I got out at the hospital gates feeling quite sure I had failed, but to my intense relief and

joy he told me I had passed, and he would send up the marks to
hospital later on. I jumped at least a foot off the pavement!

A wounded soldier would pass down a series of care points before
arriving at Base Hospitals. Stretcher-bearers would transport anyone
who could not carry themselves to the Regimental Aid Posts. From
thence to Dressing Stations, and on to Casualty Clearing Stations,
at every point encountering women providing medical and nursing
care. Evacuation back to a Base Hospital might be carried out via
ambulance train. For some, the end of the line was a Red Cross
hospital ship which would take them back to Britain, for others
treatment and convalescence would be arranged in France.

21 August 1914 – The whole system of Field Medical Service has
altered since South Africa. The wounded are picked up on the
field by the regimental stretcher-bearers, who are generally the
band, trained in First Aid and Stretcher Drill. They take them to
the Bearer Section of the Field Ambulance who take them to the
Tent Section of the same Field Ambulance, who have been getting
the Dressing Station ready with sterilisers, &c., while the Bearer
Section are fetching them from the regimental stretcher-bearers.
They are all drilled to get this ready in twenty minutes in tents,
but it takes longer in farmhouses. The Field Ambulance then
takes them in ambulance wagons (with lying down and sitting
accommodation) to the Clearing Hospital, with beds, and returns
empty to the Dressing Station. From the Clearing Hospital they
go on to the Stationary Hospital – 200 beds – which is on a
railway, and finally in hospital trains to the General Hospital,
their last stopping-place before they get shipped off to Netley and
all the English hospitals. The General Hospitals are the only ones
at present to carry Sisters; 500 beds is the minimum, and they are
capable of expanding indefinitely.[150]

These ambulance trains which carried the wounded on the first
stage of their journey were astonishing vehicles: fourteen carriages

long with an operating theatre, pharmacy and medical store. They allowed both for triage on the way to a base hospital and for emergency high-quality medical care. They undoubtedly saved the lives of many casualties who could not have waited for treatment. Six carriages were bedded wards (occupants being referred to as 'liers'), with another for the 'sitters' (i.e. walking wounded). Accommodation for the permanent medical and nursing staff took up two more with a cookhouse, dining room and ancillary facilities in the remainder.

Sister Katherine Evelyn Luard typified the ambulance train nurse in some ways, although she was unusual in being a member of the Army Nursing Service Reserve rather than Queen Alexandra's Imperial Military Nursing Service (often known as 'QA's). Evelyn (as she was known) was forty-two in 1914 and had already served in South Africa during the Boer War. Her memoir, *Diary of a Nursing Sister on the Western Front 1914–15* was published anonymously – typical of this calm and unassuming woman. She went on to work in some of the most exposed casualty stations of the Western Front, only resigning in 1918 when her father became seriously ill. The diary was based on her letters home, often it seems Evelyn is talking directly to her reader.

Her entry for Thursday 24 September 1914 gives an all-too-vivid impression of the evacuation trains in use before the fully equipped ambulance versions came into service. These were often box freight cars which took supplies to the front and brought the wounded back in. Evelyn was never one to pull her punches, even if she rarely complains on her own behalf:

24 September 1914, 3 p.m. – Taking 480 sick and wounded down to St Nazaire, with a junior staff nurse, one M.O., and two orderlies. Just been feeding them all at Angers; it is a stupendous business. The train is miles long – not corridor or ambulance; they have straw to lie on the floors and stretchers. The M.O. has been two nights in the train already on his way down from the front (four miles from the guns), and we joined on to him with

a lot of hospital cases sent down to the base. I've been collecting
the worst ones into carriages near ours all the way down when
we stop; but of course you miss a good many. Got my haversack
lined with jaconet and filled with cut-dressings, very conveni-
ent, as you have both hands free. We continually stop at little
stations, so you can get to a good many of them, and we get
quite expert at clawing along the footboards; some of the men,
with their eyes, noses, or jaws shattered, are so extraordinarily
good and uncomplaining. Got hold of a spout-feeder and some
tubing at Angers for a boy in the Grenadier Guards, with a
gaping hole through his mouth to his chin, who can't eat, and
cannot otherwise drink. The French people bring coffee, fruit,
and all sorts of things to them when we stop.

We shall have to wait at St Nazaire all day, and come back by
night to-morrow.

This is in scraps, owing to the calls of duty. The beggars simply
swarm out of the train at every stop – if they can limp or pull up
by one arm – to get the fruit and things from the French.

Her luck was about to change though:

27 September 1914 – I am for permanent duty on No[ ] Ambulance
Train (equipped) which goes up to the Front, to the nearest point
on the rail to the fighting line. Did you ever know such luck?
There are four of us, one Army Sister and me and two juniors; we
live altogether on the train. The train will always be pushed up as
near the Field Hospitals as the line gets to, whether we drive the
Germans back to Berlin or they drive us into the sea ... We shall
have two days and two nights with wounded, and two days and
two nights to rest on the return empty. The work itself will be of
the grimmest possible, as we shall have all the worst cases, being
an equipped Hospital in a train. It was worth waiting five weeks
to get this; every man or woman stuck at the Base has dreams of
getting to the Front, but only one in a hundred gets the dream
fulfilled.

We are able to form a clear picture of the arrangements on the train from her description of Tuesday 13 October 1914:

> We each have a bunk to ourselves, with a proper mattress, pillow, and blankets: a table and seat at one end, lots of racks and hooks, and a lovely little washing-house leading out of the bunk, shared by the two Sisters on each side of it: each has a door into it ... The train is one-third mile long, so three walks along its side gives you exercise for a mile ... Had an excellent night, no sheets (because of the difficulties of washing), my own rug next me, and lots of blankets: the view, with trucks on each side, is not inspiring, but will improve when we move: have only been allowed walks alongside the train to-day because it may move at any minute (although it has no engine as yet!), and you mayn't leave the train without a pass from the Major.
>
> M.O.'s and Sisters live on one waggon, all our little doors opening into the same corridor, where we have tea; it is a very easy family party. Our beds are all sofas in the daytime and quite public, unless we like to shut our doors.

Evelyn also provides an insight into some of the drawbacks as well as the ways one might get round them. Ever practical, she was well up to a spot of railway maintenance:

> 13 November 1914, Boulogne – We have been all day in Park Lane Siding among the trains, in pouring wet and slush. I amused myself with a pot of white paint and a forceps and wool for a brush, painting the numbers on both ends of the coaches inside, all down the train; you can't see the chalk marks at night.
>
> Sunday, 20th, 6 p.m. – At last we are on our way back to Boulogne and mails, and the News of the War at Home and Abroad. At Rouen, or rather the desert four miles outside it, we only see the paper of the day before, and we miss our mails, and have no work since unloading on Friday. This morning was almost a summer day, warm, still, clear and sunny. We went for a

walk, and then got on with painting the red crosses on the train, which can only be done on fine days, of which we've had few.

Clearly, at times, there was an air of unreality about their situation:

13 October 1914 – In between the actual dealing with the wounded, which is only too real, it all feels like a play or a dream: why should the whole of France, at any rate along the railways and places on them, be upside down, swarming with British soldiers, and all, French and English, working for and talking of the one thing? Everything, and every house and every hotel, school, and college, being used for something different from what it was meant for; the billeting is universal.

You hear a funny alternation of educated and uneducated English on all sides of you, and loud French gabbling of all sorts. By day you see aeroplanes and troop trains and artillery trains; and by night you see searchlights and hear the incessant wailing and squawking of the train whistles. On every platform and at every public doors or gates are the red and blue French soldiers with their long spikey bayonets, or our Tommies with the short broad bayonets that don't look half so deadly though I expect they are much worse.

Even with greatly improved facilities on the new train, conditions were still difficult, giving some sense of the daily horrors faced by all involved in caring for the wounded, soldiers, civilians and nurses:

16 October 1914, 2 p.m. – Have had a very busy time since last entry. The shelling of the village was aimed at the church, the steeple of which was being used by the French for signalling. A butcher was killed and a boy injured, and as the British Clearing Hospital was in the church and the French Hospital next door they were all cleared out into our train; many very bad cases, fractured spine, a nearly dying lung case, a boy with wound in lung and liver, three pneumonias, some bad enterics (though the

worst have not been moved). A great sensation was having four badly wounded French women, one minus an arm, aged sixteen; another minus a foot, aged sixty-one, amputation after shell wounds from a place higher up. They are in the compartment next three wounded officers. They are all four angelically good and brave and grateful; it does seem hard luck on them.

I stayed up till 3 a.m. and then called the others, and we got up again at 8 and were all busy all the morning. It is a weird business at night, picking your way through kitchens and storerooms and wards with a lantern over the rickety bridges and innumerable heavy swing-doors. I was glad of the brown overall G. sent me, and am wearing the mackintosh apron to-day that N. made me...

We have a great many washings in the morning, and have to make one water do for one compartment – (the train ran out of water this morning – since refilled from the river alongside); and bed-makings, and a lot of four-hourly treatment with the acutes. The enteric ward has a very good orderly and excellent disinfecting arrangements ... Lack of drinking water makes things very difficult.

I thought things were difficult in the hospitals at Le Mans owing to lack of equipment, but that was child's play compared to the structural difficulties of working a hospital on a train, especially when it stands in a siding several days. One man will have to die on the train if we don't move soon, but we are not full up yet. Twenty-seven men – minor cases – bolted from the church yesterday evening on to the train when the shells were dropping, and were ignominiously sent back this morning.

Pat Beauchamp also experienced such moments:

We had a lot of work that autumn, and barges came down regularly as clockwork. Many of these cases were taken to the Duchess of Sutherland's Hospital ... One night, taking some cases to the Casino hospital, there was a boy on board with his eyes bandaged. He had evidently endeared himself to the Sister on the train, for she came along with the stretcher bearers and saw him safely into my car. 'Good-bye, Sister,' I heard him say, in a cheery voice, 'thank you a thousand times for your kindness – you wait till my old eyes are better and I'll come back and see you. I know you must look nice,' he continued, with a laugh, 'you've got such a kind voice.'

Tears were in her eyes as she came round to speak to me and whisper that it was a hopeless case; he had been so severely injured he would never see again.

I raged inwardly against the powers that cared not a jot who suffered so long as their own selfish ends were achieved.

That journey was one of the worst I've ever done. If the boy had not been so cheerful it would have been easier, but there he lay chatting breezily to me through the canvas, wanting to know all about our work and asking hundreds of questions. 'You wait till I get home,' he said, 'I'll have the best eye chap there is, you bet your life. By Jove, it will be splendid to get these bandages off, and see again.' Was the war worth even one boy's eyesight? No, I thought not.

There were still horrors to contend with once the men had reached the safety of the Base Hospitals. Frances Cluett was a Newfoundlander who became a VAD at the age of thirty-three. In 1917 she was stationed at the 10th General Hospital in Rouen:

Groves has had to undergo another operation. I hear there are talks of sending him to his home in Canada. This morning Sister was syringing his leg; then she put plugging into it. Plugging is put on one side of the leg and pulled through the other side. It is awful.

Poor Rodgers has had his hip cut open again to take a piece of bone that was floating around in the wound out: that wound is awfully deep. Goswell is able to hop around the ward: I expect he will soon be sent to his home in London. He went yesterday down to Theatre Royal. It seems so nice to see those poor things able to get up again. Four have died in Gallishaw's ward.[151]

The army steadfastly refused to allow women on the front line although some did make it through – like Elsie Knocker and Mairi Chisholm who ran a first aid post within 100 yards of the Ypres line. For others, the distinction between trench and aid station must have seemed a little blurred when the guns opened up. There are numerous accounts of women under fire, not necessarily aimed at them, but dangerous enough all the same. This from Evelyn Luard:

> 15 October 1914 – We ... are having quite an exciting afternoon. Shells are coming at intervals into the village. I've seen two burst in the houses, and one came right over our train. Two French soldiers on the line lay flat on their faces; one or two orderlies got under the train; one went on fishing in the pond close by, and the wounded Tommies got rather excited, and translated the different sounds of 'them Jack Johnsons' and 'them Coal-boxes' and 'Calamity Kate', and of our guns and a machine gun popping. There is a troop train just behind us that they may be potting at, or some gunners in the village, or the R. E. camp.
>
> There have been two aeroplanes over us this afternoon. You hear the shell coming a long way off, rather like a falsetto motor-engine, and then it bursts (twice in the trees of this wood where we are standing). There is an endless line of French horse transport winding up the wood on the other side, and now some French cavalry. The R. T. O. is now having the train moved to a safer place.
>
> The troops have all gone except the 1st Division, who are waiting for the French to take their place, and then all the British will be on the Arras line, I believe, where we shall go next. (There's another close to the train.) They make such a fascinating purring noise coming, ending in a singing scream; you have to jump up and see. It is a yellowish-green sound! But you can't see it till it bursts.

What unites all these women is their regard for the men in their care and the spirit they show in the face of sometimes appalling conditions:

And now I have seen war. Every way I turn I am looking on men with broken bodies and women with broken hearts. War is not merely the hell that may pass at Verdun or the Somme in the agony of a day or a night that ends in death. War is worse. War is that big strong fellow with eyes burned out when he 'went over the top', whom I saw learning to walk by a strip of oilcloth laid on the floor of the Home for the Blind in London.

They're teaching him now to make baskets for a living! War is that boy in his twenties without any legs whom I met in Regents Park in a wheel chair for the rest of his life! War is that peasant from whom to-day I inquired my way in one of the little banlieues of Paris. There was the Croix de Guerre in his coat lapel. But he had to set down on the ground his basket of vegetables to point down the Quai de Bercy with his remaining arm. You know how a Frenchman just has to gesture when he talks? The stump of the other arm twitched a horrible accompaniment as he indicated my direction![152]

War Horses

Sergeant George Thompson was a bluff Wearsider. Born in 1893, he joined the Territorials at seventeen. George's grandfather and father had both worked at Vaux Breweries all their working lives. Had it not been for the war he would have followed them. As it was he served in 1/7th DLI with horse-drawn transport throughout the war. He was twice mentioned in Despatches and awarded the Military Medal. He wrote up his wartime diary ten years after Armistice as a memoir for his infant daughter, born in 1926.

That summer, August 1914,

our battalion got horses and wagons belonging to a local contractor. Then we started to train for war service. I was stationed in the drill hall for a while whilst the government was buying up horses. I can still remember the old drivers saying 'take care of him, he is quiet and a good worker and will go anywhere'. Little did anybody think what was in store for them, same about myself!

The horse I was in charge of was a rank bad one. Nearly every time I took him for a drink, I used to get into trouble. He used to kick, bite and bolt![153]

When the call for volunteers for service overseas went out, the whole battalion responded, around 600 of them soon augmented by a further draft of another 400.

We were fitted out with real service gear. Each man had to manage two horses. We went over to Newcastle to collect a pair and a limber wagon for each driver. I was to be No. 1 driver. There were around sixty horses and mules on our strength and perhaps fifty men. All drivers were taken to 50th Division RFA and went through a hard week's training to learn both to ride and to drive. They gave us some stick, I can tell you! First came riding bareback and then with saddles on; we were sore for days afterwards.

The locals who the Durhams were billeted with took the Wearside men to their hearts; 'there were some tears shed the day we left them for France. After the war was over, I went to see them. Some had lost husbands and some, sons.'

The Battalion entrained from Gateshead, their destination Southampton with plentiful halts to feed and water the horses. On 17 April 1915 they sailed for France and the great cauldron of the Western Front. 'The name of the ship was SS *Dunkirk* and a very big ship she was. So we started putting our transport on board ship and some game we had with some of our mules … It was a grand night, full moon.' To counter any menace from lurking U-boats a quartet of sleek destroyers darted restlessly amongst the wallowing fat-bellied merchantmen, 'to see them sweeping around us was a grand sight'. From Havre, another long train journey. French rolling stock was already notorious amongst the BEF for squalor, disrepair, discomfort and aching sloth. 'We had a job with one mule though; he would not come off the ship. So some sailors cured him, hoisting him out of the hold a real "tuff-un" they said!'

From Boulogne the transport joined with the battalion, a mere two days after leaving the north-east then moved northwards again, crammed into the increasingly and depressingly familiar French rail wagons. Finally they reached billets, transport being accommodated in a large farm. Here the main problem was in persuading the stubborn and contrary mules to endure shoeing.

> We had to throw them and fasten their four legs together before we could get a shoe on them. The war was getting closer. On our way up to the line we met Canadians coming down the road and the sights we saw were enough for us. They told us what it was like up the line and they were right too. Now we could hear the heavy guns firing.

They drew nearer the crucible. Up to bustling Poperinghe and spring nights under canvas. From there, the short journey into the maelstrom of ravaged Ypres. 'The smell of the place was awful. We were now under shellfire. Our battalion went straight into the line while the transport went to a place named White Chateau.' Now the lives of George and his fellows in the transport section began to take on a shape that would be familiar for the hard months and years to follow. Ammunition and supplies had to be taken up to the front trenches under cloak of darkness. To move by daylight was simple suicide. The wagons had to set off, travel, arrive, unload and get back before dawn.

> The RSM attempted to camouflage our horses with cut branches. If we had stayed there till daylight I don't think I would have lived to tell the tale. There was shells bursting all around us and rifle bullets came whipping passed us. Happily a staff officer came up and sent us back.

Those of George's comrades who had not yet experienced the reality craved to know what it was like. Their induction was not long delayed, 'some of them who went up that road failed to return. It was Whit Monday 1915 and our battalion was in the thick of it. The Germans sent over some gas, a yellowish cloud and we had to don gas masks sharpish.' By now, their base at White Château was becoming uncomfortably exposed and they decamped to St Jean.

> At this place there was what was left of a battalion of KOSB, about three hundred of them. They were in an awful state. St Jean is not far from Hell's Corner and I saw a spy shot there. A Canadian Field Battery stationed next to the KOSB spotted suspicious movement in a church, they arrested a man soon identified as a spy, they soon put him out of the road. A few of us went to have a look at him. He was a very tall chap with French clothes on top of his German uniform. They buried him near where our lines were.

Next day,

> one of our wagons went up for rations, the poor fellow had not long started on his journey when a shell burst right on top of him and blew him and his horses to pieces … That same road I have seen with my own eyes strewn with dead, the worst road to be on in Belgium. At St Jean, the horses never had their harness off. We slept under the wagons and we got shelled all day long. We were pulled back towards Ypres, finally able to take the harness off and clean down our horses. They looked a bit better. The horses had their own gasmasks too and we had some game on with them!

Drivers might not be in the line but their routine journeys back and forth exposed them to equal risks.

> One night I was going up with rations to Zillebeke. I was the first wagon to get unloaded and I was just turning round when a shell burst just beside me and a lump of shrapnel dropped just beside my left foot and sank into the ground. I dug it up and my father still has it as a souvenir. The shell holes I have seen, you could easily have chucked in a wagon and pair of horses.

Casualties amongst both men and horses were high. Ypres, with its tortured stump of cathedral tower, remained the epicentre of the never-ending storm of fire and steel: the Calvary of the BEF.

Winter:

> When the winter came on, it was awful both for horses and men. I have many a time wondered how those poor horses stood it so long. I have seen them standing up to their knees in mud and for days. It was not an easy job being a transport driver. Every time we went up with rations we always heard bad news, so many had been killed or wounded.

Now they moved to Armentières and found billets in a large, purpose-built riding stable, 'a fine place'. Despite these more pleasant surroundings, death was always on hand.

> One of our best horses was killed in a stupid accident. The driver came back late from delivering rations. Now there were high iron railings around the site and, having fed his horse, he fastened the head rope high up on the railings. Well, he forgot to tell the picket to halter the rope. When they went by, the horse had hung itself!

George had not enjoyed any home leave for fourteen months at this point. His journey to Boulogne was a purgatory all to itself, achingly familiar to Tommies: 'Thirty men to a truck and the trains so slow you could get off and walk alongside for a bit of exercise. Seven days leave, what an awful feeling when you had to go back again … always wishing the rotten war was over.' As ever the front was waiting, 'I remember going up one night with rations to the trenches, and one whole street of houses was on fire. What an awful sight it was. We had to go full stretch and gallop. The horses were very frightened. We got through it.'

Horses were much in demand, attrition and disease constantly winnowing the stock. The RFA, distinctly a cut above mere transport, relieved the section of a score of their best at Kemmel. 'They

gave us twenty mules in their place and they left us some right
beasties. We had some game on to get them broken in.'

> O mule with voice so shrill and hide so hard
> We've always thought you were strictly barred,
> From classy cavalry
>
> Just now you are content
> But when your shoes get bent
> And to the forge you're sent
> There'll be some revelry!
> – *Plum & Apple*, October 1915

Remounts were much sought after and when the Durhams heard
a train load would arrive, a team of drivers under an NCO took
a motor truck and drove down to the railhead. They were first in
the queue.

> We unloaded twenty of the best horses and moved them out into
> a field. As we were about to leave the transport officer came up
> and demanded to know by what authority we'd removed these.
> Our NCO replied that when he saw our unit's name on the list
> he assumed it was in order. Nice try; Well that officer didn't half
> give us some stick. He made us unload the whole train and set up
> a picket line. He said this would be a lesson for us in the future.
> Finally he gave us the worst twenty horses, all that was left and we
> were the last to leave. One of these was so wild we couldn't get a
> saddle on for a week! We really cursed that officer.

George and the other drivers were always looking out for their
horses, as best they could.

> The first thing I used to do, if possible, was to look for shelter
> for my horses, same thing with the other drivers. One out of the
> two horses that I took away from Newcastle was still with our

battalion when I left them after the war was over. They were soon re-formed as pioneers; we got extra pay for this, more horses and more wagons. We now had ninety-five wagons and limbers, all full of different tools for various types of work either in the trenches or on the roads. Our job was to take materials, wire and duckboards, from a central supply depot to working parties in the line.

George Thompson was now promoted to corporal.

As ever, we had to wait until dark before moving. I used to make our wagons get well apart from each other so if any shelling started they had a bit of a chance to get off the road. There was a stretch of the road where the Germans used to shell pretty often, 'Cafe Belge' they called it, as it used to be a cafe in peacetime. We used to gallop past it as we'd had a few of our drivers wounded and numbers from the battalion killed here.

They came to the little town of Albert, lying just behind the great Somme battlefield; 'I remember while we were passing through Albert there was a large memorial and an top of this memorial was a bronze woman and she was lying right down and it looked very dangerous, many a time I passed and it was still hanging there.' Albert had been badly mangled by the whirlwind but there was still valuable booty to be had.

We spotted a large covered in wagon which must have belonged to some show people. One night, it was very foggy; we took a few horses down and brought it clear away. About thirty of us could sleep in it. Our camp was near Fricourt and we camouflaged the wagon with trees but nobody ever asked.

Next they moved up to the infamous High Wood, chalk roads churned by the passage of countless men and animals.

The horses were permanently caked in dust. The first thing I saw when I went into the line was a village full of German dead, and also British, the whole place was full of dead, smell was awful, horses and wagons lying about all over.

Part of a vast infrastructure created to sustain Haig's army in the Somme 'Department' was large stocks of core construction materials. The transport drivers were regular customers at the dump in Albert. 'When we first got inside we found hundreds of German prisoners working there. Some of these spoke English very well and one knew Sunderland, he used to go there for holidays before the war.' The Somme battlefield was a test even for the Durhams steady nerves. At Contalmaison,

I saw a trench full of German dead; you would think some of them were still alive as they were crouched in a sitting position and looked as though they were ready for a jump. They were all gassed. I think some of them were only boys, they looked so very young.

George earned a mention in Despatches around this time. He was leading a convoy when a battalion of the South Wales Borderers ahead of them on the road were badly raked by German shellfire. George used his wagons as impromptu field ambulances to get the many wounded clear, galloping furiously in and out of the bursting shells, dragging injured men from the inferno. The Germans were using balloons to guide their gunners and he had to anticipate when the salvos were due. Having done all they could the drivers calmly reverted to their original supply mission.

Animals like men are prone to disease. I remember when we were stationed at Fricourt there was a skin disease came out among our horses and an officer in the AVC came up one morning and ordered about fifteen horses to go down the line and one of them was one I had brought out from England and he had to go as well. So instead of sending him away, we sent another in his place and we built a stable for him away from all the other horses and looked after him ourselves and in a month we had him working again. Those horses they took from us we never saw again.

For sale: A desirable villa situated in Vermelles;
Ideal for anyone fond of fresh air;
Every inconvenience;
Latest War news;
Battlefield attached.
– *Plum & Apple*, October 1915

Next they were re-deployed to the Arras sector, at that point a relative haven, at least compared to the Somme. Nonetheless, horror was still a frequent caller,

I remember going by Arras station and seeing a gun with all its horses and belonging to the RGA. There were eight heavy horses and the four drivers all blown to pieces; they must have caught a salvo of shells. We saw, in a shell hole, two British and two German soldiers, all four of them with their throats cut. It looked to me as though someone had done this with a knife.

There was no let up, no way to avoid seeing the full horror of battle and its aftermath. Near the village of Tilloy,

we came to where our cavalry had been cut up. As far as the eye could see there was nothing but dead lying about. I saw something which caught my eyes; it was just like a large tree stump. You went inside then you could climb up and look through a hole and see round for miles; it was a disguised German artillery lookout.

Death was often whimsical.

I remember one night our transport officer Mr Walker who came from Sunderland went up with our convoy. He got off his horse and tied it behind one of the wagons and then began walking ahead of the convoy. Poor chap, he had not been in front for more than five minutes when a shell burst right in front of him and blew him to pieces. He was a fine fellow and everyone felt sorry for him, everybody had a good word for him.

George was given regular command of the nightly convoys, a most dangerous series of assignments.

On one occasion at night we were trapped by accurate shellfire in a very narrow valley, the Germans were plastering the road both in front and behind of us as though they knew we were there. Our horses were going mad with the noise. We thought our time had surely come. It was no use making a dash for it as the shells came over so regular. Finally, it eased up just for a while and I gave the order to get out at the gallop. As we rode one shell burst squarely on the last vehicle though miraculously both driver and horses escaped unhurt. We even managed to get back later and salvage the load!

Enemy aircraft were now adding to the routine stresses of bombardment:

A German plane flew over and was engaged by ack-ack fire. It appeared to go into a deep dive but straightened out almost at tree level and began strafing us. We had to start diving for cover. British planes gave furious chase but the Boche seemed to get away. By now such strafing was commonplace and we all used to have a go with rifles, everybody on the road had a shot at the planes.

We didn't lose any horses to the fliers but we lost one of our best by accident at Arras. We'd taken a well dug German trench which housed a large tank, probably used for bathing. There was a fresh outbreak of skin disease amongst the horses and we were given fluid with which to wash them down by the AVC officer. So we converted the tank for use by our horses so they could walk straight through. One slipped and broke his leg. We moved him into a shell hole, shot him and filled in the hole.

Navigation in the night dark labyrinth of trenches proved a navigational nightmare. One senior NCO, despite great experience, managed to get a whole convoy lost, heavy laden wagons nose to tail down what turned out to be a blind alley. The transport was hemmed into a sunken road with dawn not far off, a perfect gunner's dream. Now the drivers

> had to unhook the horses out, unload the wagons, laden with timber and ammunition, drag the wagons back so far up the narrow valley and then manhandle them round as best we could. It was very hard and heavy work, took us hours to get back on track and then we ran into heavy shell fire.

The men were not deprived of spiritual sustenance though they were apt to be diverted by more material needs.

> Our chaplain used to visit the lines and we had a little canteen just a few yards away. Well he'd been speaking to us for half an hour when he said, 'I can see all eyes are on that canteen, so I think I will say no more'. He told our officer to dismiss us and he did. He was right to, there was a rush for the canteen – we used to get a barrel now and then if we were lucky.

Hopefully, for the Wearsiders it was Vaux ale!

Now the Durhams were moved, horses and men, into the St Quentin sector in time to experience the German spring offensives of 1918.

> We had been playing a football match and had just finished when a dispatch rider came in like an express train, telling us to retreat at once to a certain town. Then, down came our battalion runner to tell us to pack up at once to pack up at once, not a minute to spare. For ten full days we retreated and everybody was getting funny [nervous] about it. I thought our number was up. There was that much traffic on the road it became blocked. We had a

canal to cross by a very small bridge and it took ever so long to get all the transports. We could see the German infantry advancing and their spotter balloons.

We were now frequently attacked from the air, low level passes, so we had to get off the road and disperse, returning their MG fire with our rifles. Our retreat was made yet more difficult by hordes of refugees, the towns were full of people, it was awful to see, taking with them as much as they could and their little children crying over the homes they might never see again. Some of these poor people were getting killed as the Germans advanced. We passed a large wooded area and there were Portuguese infantry running away, some of them had no boots.

Near Merville, the Durham battalion was making a stand. George was ordered up with rations and ammunition. This meant the supply convoy had to pass along a Roman straight section of road, closely bordered on both sides by trees, an unenviable prospect. Germans were filtering into the woods and the tempo of shells falling on the highway was increasing. The 'convoy' in this instance comprised George himself, mounted, with a single wagon and driver. Their outward journey passed easily enough, they located their infantry guide and unloaded their precious cargo however, 'the worst was yet to come'.

As they retraced their approach, shells began falling in mournful abundance. 'Follow me Harry,' bellowed George.

Harry was alright, he belonged to South Shields. We galloped off the road, cross country, forded a stream and came up to a large, abandoned farm, going hell for leather. We heard a voice shouting and thought at first this might be a German but it turned out to be and NCO from our MG section. Poor fellow, he was shot all down his back. He was left lying on an old bed in a passageway. 'Come here Harry' and we lifted him into the wagon, 'don't leave me, don't leave me', he was pleading.

Again they careered off cross country, agony for the badly injured man. As they regained the shattered road a quartet of shells exploded directly in front, blast slewing horses and wagon right around. Amazingly, neither men nor horses were injured.

'Are you alright Harry?' 'Well, I think so.' We turned the team around again and set off at the gallop. We thought the injured NCO must have died but we took him on to the ADS at Hazebrouck. Our ordeal was not over for we came under yet more shell-fire, 'Coal boxes' this time. When we got there, everybody was getting ready to pull out but we managed to get him into a field ambulance at last.

This action earned George a second mention in Despatches.

'After the war was over I met that NCO in Sunderland and he shook my hand. He said to his dad, "this was the corporal that saved my life". I felt sorry for him as he was on crutches.' George returned to his native Sunderland and became the third generation of his family to work at Vaux Brewery. For the next forty years, he was employed as a foreman, retiring either in 1958 or the following year. One of those horses he had taken out returned with him.

'The Orderly Officer'

When at the stables you're kept slaving
And the day is cussed hot
The horses are ill-tempered
And the Sergeants swear a lot
Don't curse the British Army
Or sing the hymn of hate
Just strafe the orderly officer
For keeping you so late!
– *Plum & Apple*, October 1915

TEN

COMFORT ME, OH LORD, PRESERVE ME FROM MY ENEMIES...

Historians, blessed with hindsight, have frequently pointed out the manner in which politicians and generals tend to refight previous conflicts. The tactics and strategies of 1914–18 were, we are told, preceded by those of the American Civil War. The implication is that politicians and generals are incapable of carrying out historical analysis. By 1914 one lesson of both the Crimea and the War Between the States had been taken to heart: the impact on public opinion and morale of the media.

The Defence of the Realm Act (DORA), issued in August 1914, gave government the power to impose censorship and control communications as well as the right to detain suspects without trial. In that same month the War Office Press Bureau was established. Essentially it focused on what we would now term 'spin', controlling what could and would be reported and working with publishers and newspaper proprietors to ensure the war effort was portrayed in a positive light, while emphasising the moral repugnance of the enemy. Demonising the foe, showing how bestial they were, was nothing new of course and German atrocities in Belgium provided a propagandist's gift of sure provenance.

Journalism and reportage were to be regulated and controlled. Initially this could be rather heavy handed (as witness Kitchener's arrest of Phillip Gibbs for unauthorised reporting). Gibbs was released, having been cautioned he would be 'put up against a wall and shot' if he were caught 'at it' again. However, the Bureau rapidly came to see the value of enlisting wider support and moved from appointing its own recognised war correspondents to issuing limited licences to foreign journalists. This was particularly the case with the Americans. The British administration was keen to enlist US support and appointed a Canadian, Sir Gilbert Parker, to disseminate favourable publicity there. It was a decision welcomed by Mabel Potter Daggett. Mabel was an American journalist and suffragette, a campaigner on a range of social issues. At the age of forty-four she had decided on a trip to Europe to investigate the impact of the war on women's lives:

> It was on a summer's day in 1916 that I rushed into the office of the Pictorial Review. 'Look!' I exclaimed excitedly to the editor at his desk. 'See the message in the sky written in letters of blood above the battlefields of Europe! There it is, the promise of freedom for women!'
>
> He brushed aside [the] 'lay-out' before him, and lifted his eyes to the horizon of the world. And he too saw. Among the feminists of New York he has been known as the man with the vision. 'Yes,' he agreed, 'you are right. It is the wonder that is coming. Will you go over there and find out just what this terrible cataclysm of civilisation means to the woman's cause?'[154]

Never one to sit quietly on the Home Front, she was determined to reach France, something which proved more difficult than anticipated:

> So, this is not to be the simple life for research work. And though I come through all the submarines and the lines of steel, and the Zeppelins have not got me yet, what shall it profit me to save my life and lose my assignment? I am bound for the front ... Now, what should a journalist do?
>
> Well, a journalist, I discovered, should get one's self personally conducted by Lord Northcliffe. There were those of my masculine contemporaries already headed for the front whom he was

said on arrival here to have received into the bosom of his news-paper office and put to bed to rest from the nervous exhaustion of travel, and sent a secretary and a check and anything else to make them happy ... nothing like that was happening to me.

The short cut to a war office is through a press bureau. But a press bureau modestly shrinks from the publicity that it purveys. You do not find it on Main Street with a lettered signboard and a hand pointing: 'Journalists, right this way.' And you can't run right up the front steps of a war office and ring the bell.

My soul is all curled up with the cold while I am trying to determine which letter (of recommendation). This to Sir Gilbert Parker was the 84th letter handed me by the editor of the Pictorial Review as I stepped on the boat. The next evening at 6 o'clock I am on my way to Wellington House.

'Sir Gilbert,' speaks the attendant in resplendent livery. And I find myself in a stately English room. There, down the length of the red velvet carpet beneath the glow of a red shaded electric lamp, a man with very quiet eyes is rising from his chair. 'Do you know where you are?' he asks with a smile, glancing at the letter of introduction on his desk that tells of my mission. 'This,' he says, 'is the headquarters of the English government's press bureau for the war and I am in charge of the American publicity.' ... Who cares for Lord Northcliffe now!

Official sanction may have got her to the front but it was not necessarily going to get her back again. Her descriptions begin to give a sense of the restrictions on movement and travel that had become commonplace:

All my journey apparently is going as pleasantly as a summer holiday planned by a Cook's Agency, when at length I come up with a bump against the British Control office in the Rue Cheveaux Lagarde. And the going away from here requires some negotiations. The British lieutenant in charge reads my nice French letter and without comment tosses it aside. 'You wish to go to London?' he asks in great surprise. 'Now, why should you wish to go to London?' He gives me distinctly to understand this is not the open season for tourists in England. 'We don't care to have people travelling,' he says in a tone of voice as if that settles it. 'Why have you come over here in these difficult and dangerous times, anyhow?' he asks querulously and a trifle suspiciously. 'The best thing you can do is to go home directly. And America is right across the water from here.'

'But, Lieutenant,' I gasp, 'my trunk is in England and I've got to have a few clothes.'

'No,' he says, 'personal reasons like that don't interest the British Government. Neither am I able to understand a journalistic mission which should take a woman travelling in these days of war.' He looks at me. 'The New Position of Women! It is not of sufficient interest to the British Government that I should let you go,' he says with finality.

'I know, Lieutenant,' I agree. 'But surely you are interested in the Allies' war propaganda for the United States?' The light from the window shines full on his face and I can see a faint relaxation about the lines of his mouth. 'Now I wish to go to England so that I may tell the story of the British women's war work. The readers of Pictorial Review are four million women who vote.' The lieutenant stirs visibly. His sword rattles against the rounds of his chair.

Censorship could be far more subtle than simply banning unauthorised reports. Newspaper proprietors adhered to guidelines about presentation of the news: deaths were referred to as 'wastage' and heavy casualties a 'baptism of fire'. Victory was always close and the dangers of combat or the miseries of trench life were to be presented with heroic deprecation. Occasionally, the reports were doctored to get a message home. F. E. Smith, head of the War Office Press Bureau personally added a line to Arthur Moore's 'Times' report on the battle of Mons: 'The BEF requires immediate and immense reinforcement. It needs men,

men, and yet more men. We want reinforcements and we want them now.'

Nor were journalists and writers the only ones to be monitored. Officers were responsible for reading and editing the letters their men sent home. The contents must have seemed occasionally bewildering (and comic) to young men with little experience of life and a limited social circle. The diaries of officers routinely refer to this activity – we already heard George Purvis describe it as 'an awful business'. His brother encountered it as well:

19 July 1916 Wednesday. No breakfast. Adjutant, at 10. Censoring letters gets humorous. The boy whose mother was dead, the wife who wouldn't write. Animalism, faith hope and cheerfulness.[155]

Human nature being what it is, discretion was not always maintained, even by the censoring officers:

A baby lieut. with measles showed me some marvellous sketch-maps of German trenches and positions he'd made from observations through a periscope. He also had the very latest thing in sectional war maps, numbered in squares, showing every tree, farm, and puddle and trench: a place with four cross-roads was called 'Confusion Corner', leading to a farm called 'Rest-and-be-Thankful'.[156]

Images were as fiercely controlled as the written word. Personal cameras were banned and only a limited number of official photographers could provide images. These were not to include pictures of mass deaths or of the more gory injuries. War artists such as Paul Nash complained of similar restrictions. Of course, the existence of small, pocket-sized, cameras did allow some men to flout the rules and profoundly disturbing photos from the period can be seen today. The order applied to everyone including VADs. Pat Beauchamp recorded the reaction when they heard the news:

To our great disappointment an order came up to the Convoy
that all cameras were to be sent back to England, and everyone
rushed round frantically finishing off their rolls of films. Lowson
appeared and took one of the cook-house 'staff' armed with kettles
and more or less covered with smuts. It was rightly entitled, 'The
abomination of desolation' – when it came to be gummed into
my War Album![157]

Somebody who did manage to get himself in front of an official
camera was journalist Albert Rhys Williams. A compatriot of
Mabel's, he had obtained leave of absence from his post as minister
at the Maverick Congregational Church in Boston to travel to
Europe. Albert was a radical. A friend of Lenin, he both witnessed
and participated in the revolution of 1917. But in 1914 he was
covering the war in Belgium. Having narrowly avoided execution
by the Germans, who had suspected him of spying, he was in the
mood for light relief:

'Wouldn't you like to have a photograph of yourself in these war-
surroundings, just to take home as a souvenir?'

That appealed to me. After rejecting some commonplace sugges-
tions, he exclaimed: 'I have it. Shot as a German Spy. There's the
wall to stand up against; and we'll pick a crack firing-squad out of
these Belgians. A little bit of all right, eh?'

I acquiesced in the plan and was led over to the wall while a
movie-man whipped out a handkerchief and tied it over my eyes.
The director then took the firing squad in hand … 'Aim right
across the bandage,' the director coached them. I could hear one
of the soldiers laughing excitedly as he was warming up to the
rehearsal. It occurred to me that I was reposing a lot of confidence
in a stray band of soldiers… 'Shoot the blooming blighter in the
eye,' said one movie man playfully.

'Bally good idea!' exclaimed the other one approvingly, while
one eager actor realistically clicked his rifle-hammer. That was
altogether too much. I tore the bandage from my eyes, exclaiming:

'It would be a bally good idea to take those cartridges out first.' Some fellow might think his cartridge was blank or try to fire wild, just as a joke in order to see me jump. I wasn't going to take any risk and flatly refused to play my part until the cartridges were ejected. Even when the bandage was readjusted 'Didn't-know-it-was-loaded' stories still were haunting me. In a moment, however, it was over and I was promised my picture within a fortnight.

A week later I picked up the London Daily Mirror from a newsstand. It had the caption:

Belgian Soldiers Shoot a German Spy Caught at Termonde

I opened up the paper and what was my surprise to see a big spread picture of myself, lined up against that row of Melle cottages and being shot for the delectation of the British public...

'The Belgians have a short, sharp method of dealing with the Kaiser's rat-hole spies. This one was caught near Termonde and, after being blindfolded, the firing-squad soon put an end to his inglorious career.'

One would not call it fame exactly, even though I played the star-role. But it is a source of some satisfaction to have helped a royal lot of fellows to a first-class scoop. As the 'authentic spy-picture of the war,' it has had a broadcast circulation. I have seen it in publications ranging all the way from The Police Gazette to 'Collier's Photographic History of the European War.'[158]

Albert never did return to the ministry. A lifelong communist and apologist for the Soviet Union, he made his career as a writer and journalist until his death in 1962.

Official demonisation of Germany went hand in hand with a rising level of xenophobia in the early months of the war. Germans living in Britain faced hostility, even violence and internment in camps like those at Knockaloe on the Isle of Man. Despite the hysteria, only 20 per cent of those living in Britain were actually considered dangerous enough to lock away, a fact which did not necessarily penetrate the national consciousness. It was common for people to change their name to something more 'English' (like

'Windsor' instead of Saxe-Coburg-Gotha), there were attacks on German-owned businesses and even dachshunds were at risk.

The hysteria was particularly rabid over the business of spies. Even the head of Special Branch was later to recall that spy mania was a real problem in 1914 as reports flooded in of German agents working in Britain. It gripped the population like an epidemic – 'spy fever' it might be called. Of the twenty-one alleged German suspects arrested only one was brought to trial.[159]

Mabel Potter Daggett was well aware of the problem as she made her preparations to come to Britain:

> I began to be written down in the great books of judgment which the chancelleries of the nations keep to-day. Hear the leaves rustle as the pages chronicle my record in full. I must clear myself of the charge of even a German relative-in-law. I must be able to tell accurately, say, how many blocks intervene between the Baptist Church and the city hall in the town where I was born. They want to know the colour of my husband's eyes. They will ask for all that is on my grandfather's tombstone. They must have my genealogy through all my greatest ancestors. I have learned it that I may tell it glibly. For I shall scarcely be able to go round the block in Europe, you see, without meeting some military person who must know.
>
> Even in New York, every consul of the countries to which I wish to proceed, puts these inquiries before my passport gets his vise. It is the British consul who is holding his in abeyance. He fixes me with a look, and he charges: 'You're not a suffragist, are you? Well,' he goes on severely, 'they don't want any trouble over there. I don't know what they'll do about you over there.' And his voice rises with his disapproval: 'I don't at all know that I ought to let you go.'
>
> But finally he does. And he leans across his desk and passes me the pen with which to 'sign on the dotted line'. It is the required documentary evidence. He feels reasonably sure now that the Kaiser and I wouldn't speak if we passed by. And for the rest? Well, all governments demand to know very particularly who goes there when it happens to be a woman.

She did not exaggerate the degree of concern:

And they are so particular about journalists. One friend of mine back from the front a month ago had his clothes turned inside out and they ripped the lining from his coat. Then there is the lemon acid bath, lest you carry notes in invisible writing on your-skin. They do it, rumor says, in Germany. But who can tell when other War Offices will have adopted this efficiency method? Oh, dear, what is the use not to have been drowned if one must face an inquisition? And they may turn me back on the next boat. My thoughts are with the lemon acid bath. How many lemons will it take to fill the tub, I am speculatively computing, when 'Next,' says the soldier. And it is I.

And on what least incidents does human judgment depend. Perhaps they'd like me better if my hat were blue instead of brown. Thank heaven I didn't economise on the price of my trav-elling coat. I step bravely forward when the officer at the head of the table reaches out his hand for my passport ... Well, what is he going to do about me?

Molly made it home safely. She continued her work as a journal-ist until her death in 1927. Campaigning till the end, she devoted herself to Unitarianism and the temperance movement. The inscription on her gravestone reads, 'She Loved Humanity'.

Of course, paranoia about spies and fifth columnists (as they would be called in a later conflict) does not mean there were not really people ready to carry out these roles. The better known ones like Carl Lody and Margaretha Zelle (Mata Hari) have been well documented but many more are casually referred to in diaries and letters. Evelyn Luard came across some of them:

22 November 1914 – Left B. early this morning and got to Merville about midday. Loaded up and got back to B. in the night. Many wounded Germans and a good lot of our sick, knocked over by the cold. I don't know how any of them stick it. Five bombs were

dropped the day before where we were to-day, and an old man was killed. Things are being badly given away by spies, even of other nationalities. Some men were sleeping in a cellar at Ypres to avoid the bombardment, with some refugees. In the night they missed two of them. They were found on the roof signalling to the Germans with flash-lights. In the morning they paid the penalty.

28 November 1914 – A sergeant of the 10th Hussars told me he was in a house with some supposed Belgian refugees. He noticed that when a little bell near the ceiling rang one of them always dashed upstairs. He put a man upstairs to trace this bell and intercept the Belgian. It was connected with the little trap-door of a pigeon-house. When a pigeon came in with a message, this door rang the bell and they went up and got the message. They didn't reckon on having British in the house. They were shot next morning.

28 December 1914 – This turned out to be one of the German communication trenches. They stayed in that all Wednesday, Wednesday night, and Thursday, living on some biscuit one man had, some bits of chocolate, and drinking the dirty trench water, in which was a dead German dressed as a Gurkha.[160]

New Places: New Faces

It was a cunning German ruse to think of utilising Gurkha uniform. For many, Imperial troops were unfamiliar and potentially inexplicable. Any apparent discrepancies in their knowledge or behaviour would be put down to their 'foreignness'. Even Evelyn Luard, who had served in South Africa found Indian and Gurkha troops puzzling. Initially, she reflects the attitudes of her time but, as she meets more and more of these men, a greater understanding emerges. She is never lacking in pragmatism and compassion:

30 October, Boulogne – After filling up at Nieppe we went back to Bailleul and took up 238 Indians, mostly with smashed left

arms from a machine gun that caught them in the act of firing over a trench. They are nearly all 47th Sikhs, perfect lambs: they hold up their wounded hands and arms like babies for you to see, and insist on having them dressed whether they've just been done or not. They behave like gentlemen, and salaam after you've dressed them. They have masses of long, fine, dark hair under their turbans done up with yellow combs, glorious teeth, and melting dark eyes. One died. The younger boys have beautiful classic Italian faces, and the rest have fierce black beards curling over their ears.

25 November – … Loaded up at 7.30 this morning, all Indians, mostly badly wounded. They are such pathetic babies, just as inarticulate to us and crying as if it was a crêche. I've done a great trade in Hindustani, picked up at a desperate pace from a Hindu officer to-day! If you write it down you can soon learn it, and I've got all the necessary medical jargon now; you read it off, and then spout it without looking at your note-book. The awkward part is when they answer something you haven't got!

The frost has broken, thank goodness. The Hindu officer said the cold was more than they bargained for, but they were 'very, very glad to fight for England'.

(Advent) 29 November – On the way down from Chocques. We have got Indians, British, and eight Germans this time. One big, handsome, dignified Mussulman wouldn't eat his biscuit because he was in the same compartment as a Hindu, and the Hindu wouldn't eat his because the Mussulman had handed it to him. The Babu I called in to interpret was very angry with both, and called the M. a fool-man, and explained to us that he was telling them that in England 'Don't care Mussulman, don't care Hindu' – only in Hindustan, and that if the Captain Sahib said 'Eat,' it was 'Hukm,' and they'd got to. My sympathies were with the beautiful, polite, sad-looking M., who wouldn't budge an inch, and only salaamed when the Babu went for him.

Monday, November 30th, Boulogne. – We were late getting our
load off the train last night, and some were very bad. One of my
Sikhs with pneumonia did not live to reach Boulogne. Another
pneumonia was very miserable, and kept saying, 'Hindustan
gurrum England tanda'. They all think they are in England.

The Gurkhas are supposed by the orderlies to be Japanese. They
are exactly like Japs, only brown instead of yellow. The orderlies
make great friends with them all. One Hindu was singing 'Bonnie
Dundee' to them in a little gentle voice, very much out of tune.
Their great disadvantage is that they are alive with 'Jack Johnsons'
(not the guns). They take off all their underclothes and throw
them out of the window, and we have to keep supplying them
with pyjamas and shirts. They sit and stand about naked, scratching for dear life. It is fatal for the train, because all the cushioned
seats are now infected, and so are we. I love them dearly, but it is
a big price to pay.

2 December – We got to Chocques very late last night … We
wandered past a place where Indians were busy killing and skin-
ning goats – a horrible sight.

9 February – Again they unloaded us at B. last night, and we
are now, 11 a.m., on our way up again. The Indians I had were
a very interesting lot. The race differences seem more striking the better you get to know them. The Gurkhas seem to be
more like Tommies in temperament and expression, and all the
Mussulmans and the best of the Sikhs and Jats might be Princes
and Prime Ministers in dignity, feature, and manners.

When a Sikh refuses a cigarette (if you are silly enough to offer
him one) he does it with a gesture that makes you feel like a
housemaid who ought to have known better. The beautiful
Mussulmans smile and salaam and say Merbani, however ill they
are, if you happen to hit upon something they like. They all make
a terrible fuss over their kit and their puggarees and their belong-
ings, and refuse to budge without them.

16 March – ... just getting into Boulogne ... One of the Sikhs wailed before, during, and after his hand was dressed. A big Mussulman stuffed his hanky between his teeth and bit on it, and never uttered, and it was a much worse one. What was he to do with crying, he said; it was right for it to be done. May God bring blessings on my head; whereas it was full of pain, lo, now it was atcha.

17 March – On the way down a little Gurkha happened to get off the train for a minute, and when he looked round the train had gone past him. He ran after it, and perched on one of the buffers till the next stop, when he reappeared, trembling with fright, but greeted with roars of amusement by the other Gurkhas.

We had some more to-day, including twelve with mumps, and one who insisted on coming with his mumpy friend though quite well himself![161]

The arrival of exotic strangers was a phenomenon the French and the British shared. Only sometimes, the exotics described lived closer to home:

At Amiens a dainty Parisienne stepped into the compartment. She was clad in a navy blue tailleur with a very smart pair of high navy blue kid boots and small navy blue silk hat. The other occupants of the carriage consisted of a well-to-do old gentleman in mufti, who, I decided, was a commerçant de vin [a wine merchant], and two French officers, very spick and span, obviously going on leave...

After a little general conversation between the officers and the old commerçant the latter suddenly burst out with: – 'Ha, what I would like well to know is, do the Scotch soldiers wear the pantalons or do they not?' Everyone became instantly alert. I could see la petite dame bien mise was dying to say something. The two French officers addressed shrugged their shoulders expressive of ignorance in the matter. After further discussion, unable to contain herself any longer, la petite dame leant forward and addressing herself to the commerçant, said, 'Monsieur, I assure you that they do not!'

The whole carriage 'sat up and took notice,' and the old commerçant, shaking his finger at her said: 'Madame, if you will permit me to ask, that is, if it is not indiscreet, how is it that you are in a position to know?'

The officers were enjoying themselves immensely. La petite dame hastened to explain. 'Monsieur, it is that my window at Amiens she overlooks the ground where these Scotch ones play the football, and then a good little puff of wind and one sees, but of course,' she concluded virtuously, 'I have not regarded, Monsieur.'

They all roared delightedly, and the old commerçant said something to the effect of not believing a word. 'Be quiet, Monsieur, I pray of you,' she entreated, 'there is an English young girl in the corner and she will of a certainty be shocked.' 'Bah, non,' replied the old commerçant, 'the English never understand much of any language but their own' (I hid discreetly behind my paper).[162]

Mentioned in Despatches…

All the diaries mention the discomforts of war, atrocious living conditions, poor food and, of course, the high probability of death or injury. The capacity of human beings to find comfort in these situations is astonishing and the ways in which it is done are varied. Recognition and the chance to be valued for your efforts make a huge difference (as witness the experience of US Vietnam veterans during the campaign for their memorial). Medals and honours are of real significance. And are well earned. Pat Beauchamp's description of receiving the Croix de Guerre in her hospital bed is deeply moving. Sometimes, though, you can only guess at how much it meant. Newspaper articles of the period give you a vivid sense of the discomfort but tend not to be accompanied by the intensive interviews required of today's veterans.

Sister Kate Maxey earned more decorations than most: the Royal Red Cross, 1st Class and a Military Medal for bravery under fire. A Northerner (born in Spennymoor, County Durham), she did her training in Leeds and enrolled as a Territorial Force Nurse in 1912. She was forty-one on the night of 21 March 1918 when bombs began to land on No. 58 Casualty Clearing Station. The *London Gazette* of 4 June 1918 recounts:

His Majesty the KING has been pleased to approve of the award of the Military Medal to the undermentioned ... for distinguished services in the Field as recorded... For gallantry and conspicuous devotion to duty displayed during a recent hostile bombing raid on a Casualty Clearing Station. Although severely wounded herself, she went to the aid of another Sister, who was fatally wounded, and did all she could for her. Later, although suffering severe pain, she showed an example of pluck and endurance which was inspiring to all.[163]

Her commanding officer gives us a vivid picture of what it took to earn that medal:

... Miss Maxse's tact, zeal for work, and influence for good are of the highest. On the night of 21.3.18 when lying wounded, she still directed nurses, orderlies and stretcher bearers and refused aid until others were seen to first. I have the greatest pleasure in giving this testimony to one of the finest Nursing Sisters I have ever met.[164]

Kate Maxey took some time to recover from her injuries – she was not fit to work until August of the same year. She was to serve in the Territorial Force Nursing Service until April 1931.

Calmly offering comfort when it was needed is one of the hallmarks of those nurses who worked in such frequently terrifying conditions. Sue Light quotes an article from one of the newspapers of the time which gives us a vivid picture of life on No. 27 Ambulance Train. It was the night of 10 November 1916:

'Boom' – a bomb dropped in a field. Up went a shower of earth, which came pattering down like heavy rain upon the roof of the coaches. A second bomb dropped nearer. The coaches rocked and the wounded men began to moan. Another bomb fell. It seemed to fall right on the train itself, though actually it was some yards away. Crash went every window. Out went every handlamp. The train gave a heave that threw the patients out of their beds. They rolled pell mell – they and their wounds and their splints and their beds in the middle of the coach.

And then a woman's clear voice rang out in the coach. 'Now do be quiet and good boys till I light a lamp.' A hand struck a match and applied it to the wick of a handlamp. Sister Kate Mahony stood calm and undismayed in the entrance of the coach. 'Now just wait till I get this wretched little lamp to burn and we'll have you all in bed in no time; Corporal, you come along and give me a hand,' she added, still holding the match to the wick. And the men in that carriage say that the hand never even trembled. They lay huddled there, some in bed, some on the floor, fascinated by the sight. She got hold of orderlies by the arm. 'Here, you come and help,' she said, and orderlies obeyed.[165]

Getting By

For many there was comfort in faith. Evelyn Luard found her own deep religious conviction shared by others and was clearly moved by the experience:

27 September 1914 – Went to the Voluntary Evening Service for the troops at the theatre at 5. The Padres and a Union Jack and the Allies' Flags; and a piano on the stage; officers and sisters in the stalls; and the rest packed tight with men: they were very reverent, and nearly took the roof off in the Hymns, Creed, and Lord's Prayer. Excellent sermon. We had the War Intercessions and a good prayer I didn't know, ending with 'Strengthen us in life, and comfort us in death'. The men looked what they were, British to the bone; no one could take them for any other nation

a mile off. Clean, straight, thin, sunburnt, clear-eyed, all at their Active Service best, no pallid rolls of fat on their faces like the French. The man who preached must have liked talking to them in that pin-dropped silence and attention; he evidently knows his opportunities.

We are now going to turn out the light, and hope for the best till they come to look at the warrant or turn us out to change.[166]

Like so many others, contemplation of the natural world offered Evelyn a chance to focus on something other than the mayhem all around. Her letters and diaries are full of detail about the flowers she collected and packed into her tiny rail carriage sleeping quarters. Any opportunity to wander in peace was seized and savoured. And, lest we grow too maudlin, she also finds joy in that most prosaic of British treats:

18 March 1915 – We have had an off-day to-day at the place of woods and commons, which I hope and trust means that things are slackening off. It doesn't do to look ahead at what must be coming, now the ground is drying up before the job is finished; but we can be thankful for the spells of rest that come for the poor army.

We had a heavenly ramble this morning, and found blue periwinkles and anemones in the woods, but no primroses. Lots of palm and gorse. Robins, willow-wrens, and yellow-hammers were singing, the darlings, much prettier music than guns, and it is good to get away from the sound of motors and trains and whistles.

We also had home-made bread and butter to-day out of the village, which caused more excitement than the Russian successes. We are having much nicer food since the French chef left, and it costs us exactly half as much.[167]

She is an astute observer of morale, noting the way in which distancing unpleasant experiences by focusing on externals helps many people get by. Tommies are characterised as accepting what cannot be changed and being grateful for lucky escapes. Not fatalism, more a way of processing the situation. It appears that the tradition of stoicism may have its uses:

17 October 1914 – Four Tommies in one bunk yesterday told me things about the trenches and the fighting line, which you have to believe because they are obviously giving recent intimate personal experiences; but how do they or any one ever live through it? These came all through the Retreat from Mons … They even had to take the tea and sugar out of the haversacks of dead Germans; no one had had time to bury for twelve days – 'it warn't no use to them,' they said, 'and we could do with it'… And they never criticise or rant about it, but accept it as their share for the time being.

27 October 1914, Boulogne – The twelve sitting-up cases on each carriage are a joy after the tragedy of the rest. They sit up talking and smoking till late, 'because they are so surprised and pleased to be alive, and it is too comfortable to sleep!'

11 November 1914 – You can tell they feel like that from their entire lack of resentment about their own injuries. Their conversation to each other from the time they are landed on the train until they are taken off is never about their own wounds and feelings, but exclusively about the fighting they have just left. If one only had time to listen or take it down it would be something worth reading, because it is not letters home or newspaper stuff, but *told to each other*, with their own curious comments and phraseology, and no hint of a gallery or a Press. Incidentally one gets a few eye-openers into what happens to a group of men when a Jack Johnson lands a shell in the middle of them. Nearly every man on the train, especially the badly smashed-up ones, tells you how exceptionally lucky he was because he didn't get killed like his mate.

Thursday, December 3rd – They all get very pitiful over the Belgian homes and desolation; it seems to upset them much more than their own horrors in the trenches. A good deal of the fighting they talk about as if it was an exciting sort of football match, full of sells and tricks and chances. They roar with laughter at some of their escapes.[168]

Unofficial Orders

From Colonel MacEmfit, commanding the Umpteenth (Reserve) Battalion, County of London regiment (the London Skittish):

Parades – tomorrow being the day after tonight, there will, of course, be no parades.

Medical – men who wake up during the night suffering from 'Haggis Fever' are warned against dipping their heads in the fire bucket as the contact with cold water is extremely apt to bring on the dreaded 'Tartan Rush' which would, in all probability, necessitate the immediate transfer of the sufferer to some other highland regiment as his face would, of course, clash with the hodden grey!

Plank beds – men are warned that they should be careful to see that the three planks making up the bed, all bend evenly when lain upon, otherwise men may get nipped in the bud!

(London Scottish Regimental Gazette, December 1916)[169]

Comfort and Joy

Comfort for the troops took a practical form. In August 1914 it must have seemed as if every one of the 12.9 million women not in paid employment suddenly took up knitting. Socks, scarves, gloves, waistcoats and blankets were made up in the millions and shipped either to the troops or to refugees. Emily Galbraith was touring in Scotland with her minister father soon after war was declared:

Everyone started knitting for the war effort. I remember we were staying on the shores of Loch Fyne and the women were knitting and they appealed to my father if it was right or wrong to knit socks on Sundays for the soldiers, and my father said it was quite right and they were all very pleased.[170]

They were extremely welcome as Evelyn Luard attests:

21 December – Weather appallingly cold and no chauffage … How utterly miserable Indians must be in this eternal wet and cold. The fields and land generally are all half under water again … Five mufflers went this afternoon to five men on a little isolated station on the way here. When I said to the first boy, 'Have you got a muffler?' he thought I wanted one for someone on the train.

'Well, it's not a real muffler; it's my sleeping-cap,' he said, beginning to pull it off his neck; 'but you're welcome to it if it's any use!'

What do you think of that? He got pink with pleasure over a real muffler and some cigarettes. You start with two men; when you come back in a minute with the mufflers the two have increased to five silent expectant faces.[171]

It was not just mufflers. Women were the main volunteers in hundreds of supply depots, which served as collection and distribution centres for donations of clothes, bandages, medicines, books, cigarettes, handkerchiefs, soap and stationary. Pat Beauchamp had a stock of handknits in her toolkit:

Major R. hastened out and told us that his own men who had been in the trenches for four days were just coming out for a rest, and he wished we could spare some of our woollies for them. We of course gladly assented, so he lined them up in the street littered with débris in front of the Headquarters. We each had a sack of things and started at different ends of the line, giving every man a pair of socks, a muffler or scarf, whichever he most wanted. In nearly every case it was socks; and how glad and grateful they were to get them! It struck me as rather funny when I noticed cards in the half-light affixed to the latter, texts (sometimes appropriate, but more often not) and verses of poetry. I thought of the kind hands that had knitted them in far away England and wondered if the knitters had ever imagined their things would be given out like this, to rows of mud-stained men standing amid shell-riddled houses on a dark and muddy road, their words of thanks half-drowned in the thunder of war.[172]

The entire nation made an effort for Christmas 1914. Princess Mary, seventeen-year-old daughter of King George V and Queen Mary, was responsible for a public appeal that raised the funds to ensure that 'every Sailor afloat and every Soldier at the front' received a Christmas present. Princess Mary's Christmas Gift was a brass tin filled with tobacco, confectionary, spices, pencils, a Christmas card, and a picture of the princess. Some 426,000 boxes were distributed to all British and Imperial soldiers and sailors who were serving on Christmas Day 1914.

Xmas Day, 11 a.m. – On way up again to Béthune … Sharp white frost, fog becoming denser as we get nearer Belgium. A howling mob of reinforcements stormed the train for smokes. We threw out every cigarette, pipe, pair of socks, mits, hankies, pencils we had left; it was like feeding chickens, but of course we hadn't nearly enough.

Every one on the train has had a card from the King and Queen in a special envelope with the Royal Arms in red on it. And this is the message (in writing hand) –

'With our best wishes for Christmas, 1914.

May God protect you and bring you home safe.

Mary R. George R.I.'

That is something to keep, isn't it?

An officer has just told us that those men haven't had a cigarette since they left S'hampton, hard luck. I wish we'd had enough for them. It is the smokes and the rum ration that has helped the British Army to stick it more than anything, after the conviction that they've each one got that the Germans have got to be 'done in' in the end.

7 p.m. – Now on the way back; not many badly wounded but a great many minor medicals, crocked up, nothing much to be done for them. We may have to fill up at Hazebrouck, which will interrupt the very festive Xmas dinner the French Staff are getting ready for us. It takes a man, French or British, to take decorating really seriously. The orderlies have done wonders with theirs. Aeroplanes done in cotton-wool on brown blankets is one feature.

This lot of patients had Xmas dinner in their Clearing Hospitals to-day. Here they finished up D.'s Xmas cards and had oranges and bananas, and hot chicken broth directly they got in.

12 Midnight. – Still on the road. We (the medical staff) had a very festive Xmas dinner, going to the wards which were in charge of nursing orderlies between the courses. Soup, turkey, peas, mince pie, plum pudding, chocolate, champagne, absinthe, and coffee. Absinthe is delicious, like squills. We had many toasts in French and English. The King, the President, Absent Friends, Soldiers and Sailors, and I had the Blessés and the Malades. We got up and clinked glasses with the French Staff at every toast, and finally the little chef came in and sang to us in a very sweet musical tenor. Our great anxiety is to get as many orderlies and N.C.O.'s as possible through the day without being run in for drunk, but it is an uphill job; I don't know where they get it.

We are wondering what the chances are of getting to bed to-night.[173]

Christmas went on a bit longer that year:

26 December 1914 – We had Princess Mary's nice brass box this morning. The V.A.D. here brought a present to every man on the train this morning, and to the orderlies. They had 25,000 to distribute, cigarette-cases, writing-cases, books, pouches, &c. The

men were frightfully pleased, it was so unexpected. The processions of hobbling, doubled-up, silent, muddy, sitting-up cases who pour out of the trains want something to cheer them up, as well as the lying-downs. It is hard to believe they are the fighting men, now they've handed their rifles and bandoliers in. (It is snowing fast.) We have to go and drink the men's health at their spread at 1 o'clock. Then I hope a spell of sleep.[174]

News from home was highly sought after. Best of all were letters and parcels, in the case of our nurses, often containing gifts for distribution to the Tommies as well as personal items. Newspapers were also prized – even old ones had to be batched up and passed on to satisfy the hunger for a taste of that other life.

8 December – Got up to Bailleul by 11 a.m., and had a good walk on the line waiting to load up. Glorious morning. Aeroplanes buzzing overhead like bees, and dropping coloured signals about. Only filled up my half of the train, both wounded and sick, including some very bad enterics. An officer in the trenches sent a man on a horse to get some papers from us. Luckily I had a batch of 'The Times,' 'Spectator,' and 'Punches.' ... At B. a man at the station greeted me, and it was my old theatre orderly at No. 7 Pretoria. We were very pleased to see each other. I fitted him out with a pack of cards, postcards, acid drops, and a nice grey pair of socks.

6 December 1915 – The British officers on the station came and grabbed our yesterday's 'Daily Mails,' and asked for soap, so what you sent came in handy. They went in to the town to buy grapes for us in return. This place is famous for grapes – huge monster purple ones – but the train went out before they came back. We had got some earlier, though.[175]

The convalescent units offered respite from the stress of trench life as well as care after illness or injury:

23 March, 9 p.m. – Waiting all day at G.H.Q … We went for
a walk along the canal this morning with the wee puppy, and
this afternoon saw over the famous jute factory Convalescent
Home, where they have a thousand beds under one roof: it is
like a town divided into long wards, – dining-rooms, recreation
rooms, dressing station, chiropodist, tailor's shop, &c. The men
looked so absolutely happy and contented with cooked instead
of trench food, and baths and games and piano, and books and
writing, &c. They stay usually ten days, and are by the tenth day
supposed to be fit enough for the trenches again; it often saves
them a permanent breakdown from general causes, and is a more
economical way of treating small disablements than sending them
to the Base Hospitals.[176]

The 'wee puppy' remains nameless, one of the thousands of mendi-
cant canines that made their way to the front either to work or
as pets and sometimes as both. Even the most unsentimental and
pragmatic of animal owners can grow fond of a creature they spend
time with. Animals offer consolation and companionship in stress-
ful situations. Evelyn's puppy had been a gift:

4 December 1914 – At Bailleul on our last journey we took on
a heavenly white puppy just old enough to lap, quite wee and
white and fat. He cries when he wants to be nursed, and barks
in a lovely falsetto when he wants to play, and waddles after our
feet when we take him for a walk, but he likes being carried best.
Some Tommies on a truck at Railhead brought him up for us;
they adore his little mother and two brothers.
   Tuesday, March 30th – . This cold wind has dried up the mud
everywhere, and until to-day there's been a bright sun with it.
The men clean the train and play football, and the M.O.'s take
the puppy out, and everybody swears a great deal at a fate which
no one can alter, and we are all craving for our week-old mails.[177]

Pat Beauchamp had pets too. She left London with a fox terrier by the name of 'Tuppence' who had to be smuggled onboard the transport ship. He had a tendency to wander:

> Then followed a hunt for rooms, which we duly found but in doing so lost 'Tuppence.' The rest of the time was spent looking for him; and when we finally arrived breathless at the police station, there was the intelligent dog sitting on the steps! I must here confess this was one of the few occasions he ever exhibited his talents in that direction, and as such it must be recorded.[178]

Tuppence disappeared permanently some time later – probably gone off with some Tommies was the likely supposition. Wuzzy turned up in March 1916:

> 'Wuzzy,' or to give him his proper name, 'Gerald,' came into existence about this time. He arrived from Peuplinghe a fat fluffy puppy covered with silky grey curls. He was of nondescript breed, with a distinct leaning towards an old English sheep dog. He had enormous fawn-coloured silky paws, and was so soft and floppy he seemed as if he had hardly a bone in his body. We used to pick him up and drop him gently in the grass to watch him go out flat like a tortoise. He belonged to Lean, and grew up a rather irresponsible creature with long legs and a lovable disposition.
>
> (Eventually) I became 'Wuzzy's' adopted mother … whenever I had time, combed and brushed his silver curls till they stood out like fluff. He could spot Susan miles away, and though it was against rules I sometimes took him on board. As we neared camp I told him he must get down, but he would put on an obstinate expression and deliberately push himself behind my back, in between me and the canvas, so that I was almost on the steering wheel. At other times he would listen to me for awhile, take it all in, and then put his head on my shoulder with such an appealing gesture that I used to risk being spotted, and let him remain. I grant you he had his bad days when he was referred to as my 'idiot son,' but even then he was only just 'peculiar' – a world of difference.

Our menagerie was gradually increasing. There were now three dogs and two cats in camp, not to mention a magpie and two canaries... There was Wuzzy, of course, and Archie (a naughty looking little Sealyham...) and a mongrel known as G. K. W.[179]

And then there was active service. It was Evelyn who would encounter one of the odder examples of animal life on the front line:

7.30 p.m., Ypres. – An armoured train, alongside of us ... manned by thirty men R.N.; three trucks are called Nelson, Jellicoe, and Drake, with guns. They look fine; the men say it is a great game. They are directed where to fire at German positions or batteries, and as soon as they answer, the train nips out of range. They were very jolly, and showed us their tame rabbit on active service. They have had no casualties so far.[180]

Evelyn Luard would go on to serve in a Field Ambulance post at Ypres and would only end her service in 1918 when the needs of her ageing father compelled her to offer her resignation. She was one of the few Nursing Reserves to earn a bar to her Royal Red Cross.

ELEVEN

THE LOST

You'd leave me cold though this our arguing
Endured till dawn, you lack the essential thing.
Healthy and leisured, pious, gentle, learned,
'You feel forbidden to fight' and thus unconcerned
With that vast horror which defeat would bring.

Hence, tho' you touched of David's lyre the string,
Or wrote with quill plucked from an angel's wing,
Unless you 'gave your body to be burned',
You'd leave me cold.

'You feel it wrong to nurse'. While others fling
Red life in the scale, what is your offering?
Levite! In you the milk of pity has turned!
For if sore wounded, and with eyes that yearned,
I lay in the Jericho Road a-perishing,
You'd leave me cold!
– H. M. W., 'To a Conscientious Objector', 30 December 1916[181]

'Shot at Dawn'

Few aspects of the Great War remain as contentious as those
Tommies executed by firing squad for various offences against
military law. Sometimes that is the consequence of an unfortunate mix: lack of historical understanding and an understandable
sense of pity for those cases where our modern sensibilities are very

different from those of the time. Some of the men who died should not have been shot. That is why so many of their names are now being added to memorials all over the country. But, in our haste to rightly exonerate the innocents, we also have to look realistically at those, who by the standards of their time, were property dealt with.

Blindfold and Alone – British Military Executions in the Great War by Cathryn Corns and John Hughes-Wilson, one of the most comprehensive works on the subject, tackles that other driver of the debate: the debate about how far class made a difference to the treatment meted out. The authors make the point that testimony against the accused rarely came from their officers but from NCOs and other ranks. Judgement may have been in the hands of officers but their attitudes and assumptions were shared by most of society at the time.

Martial justice was, in 1914, codified in the sixth edition of the War Office's *Manual of Military Law*. Courts martial were convened according to these rules. This was no summary justice: the sentence handed down was reviewed up the chain from battalion to brigade, through division, corps, army and finally to the commander-in-chief. In practice Haig commuted some 90 per cent of death sentences. It seems likely that over 350 men were shot for various crimes against military law from 1914 to 1920. A number of these would have faced the death penalty under civil law rules and many were repeat offenders. That there were injustices cannot now be denied, particularly since medical knowledge was considerably less advanced. Conditions such as post-traumatic stress disorder were not understood.

Towards the end of August 1916, 35th (Bantam) Division was moved from the Somme into 3rd Army sector around Arras. When deployed, 19th Battalion DLI[†] was positioned on the left before the battered shell of Roclincourt. Here the front line was essentially a series of old mine craters, linked and consolidated into a defensible

---

† 19th Battalion DLI was a bantam unit raised in Durham in January 1915, attached to 106th Brigade of 35th ('Bantam') Division. They were deployed in France during February 1916.

line of sorts, well-wired, with support and reserve lines behind in the usual way. A set of three communication trenches, Sunday, Wednesday and Cecil Avenues, linked the successive lines; both 'weekday' passages were heavily shelled.

Though the sector was nominally 'quiet', much raiding and counter-raiding went on. The defences overall were in poor shape. Deteriorating weather contributed to the overall squalor and disrepair. On 26 November, after days of shelling from both sides, 19th DLI were to mount a hefty raid. Nobody had asked the Germans – who were planning some diversions of their own, launching strikes against all three battalions along the brigade front. A key point was the rim of 'King' Crater a mere fifty yards from enemy lines. As 19th DLI were about to attack that night, the sentry posts at this point were relatively weakly held. At Post 'A' was Corporal Stevenson and a private; 'B' was manned by Lance-Corporal Hopkinson, and Privates Harding and Hunt; and Post 'C' by Lance-Corporal McDonald with Privates Ritchie and Spence. Another lance-corporal and three men were nearby in a dugout.

It was at 2.15 a.m. that Lieutenant Mundy and Lance-Sergeant Stones passed Post A on a routine patrol. En route to the next position, they were intercepted by a party of German raiders and shot up. The officer fell mortally wounded and Sergeant Stones bolted back to Post A. He continued along a communication trench till he reached the hub of Bogey and Wednesday Avenues. It was left to Corporal Stevenson to bring in the dying Lieutenant Mundy. At Post B, Private Harding was captured but his two comrades Hopkinson and Harding ran for it, yelling, 'The Germans are here!' Both Hopkinson and Stones were picked up by the battalion battle police[†] well to the rear of the action, both missing their personal weapons.

Meanwhile, the officer and NCO of the watch had also been bush-whacked by the enemy and injured by gunfire. Sergeant Stones, in

---

† These 'Battle Police' were not redcaps but provost detachments from the battalion itself.

his flight, had managed to alert the counter-attack platoon under Lieutenant Howes. This officer led his men forward towards the front line but found only four had followed. Meanwhile 19th DLI mounted their raid. This had resulted in costly fiasco, confusion and some casualties, mostly from 'friendly fire' as the raiders scurried back. The unfortunate events of this night's work underlined worries that the division, as a whole, was not up to scratch and that 'recently received reinforcements could not be trusted to hold the line'.

Zeal to impose martial law to the very letter was not a constant factor. Many infringements would be either overlooked or quietly dealt with at platoon level without any more being said. But when a division was perceived to be failing then the likelihood of examples being made increased significantly. In November 1916 the 35th Division fell squarely into this category. In consequence, no fewer than twenty-six death sentences would be handed down and three of those condemned, all NCOs, would actually face a firing squad.

Joseph William ('Willie') Stones was a stocky miner, classic bantam physique, and twenty-three years of age. He had enlisted at West Hartlepool in March 1915. He was a volunteer, a citizen soldier and his patriotic gesture left his wife and children in need.

As Lieutenant Howes would later testify, Willie Stones, who had been on active service for eleven months, had always been both steady and reliable. His company commander echoed this general approval and cited his coolness in action, one whom the officer would have deemed incapable of cowardice. Stones was accused of 'shamefully casting away his arms in the presence of the enemy' and of having run away from the front line. He was tried on Christmas Eve before a panel comprising one Lieutenant-Colonel and three captains, one an MO. Counsel for the defence was provided by Captain Warmington, an experienced and mature solicitor in 'civvy street' now also serving with 19th DLI. Willie Stones had the benefit of professional and dedicated counsel whose arguments were both skilled and structured.

Lieutenant Howes testified that as the alarm was raised he saw Sergeant Stones in the communication trench. This was about 150 yards in the rear. As NCO of the watch, and this was crucial, he should not have left his post at the front. The officer could confirm that the accused appeared to be 'very much upset'. Howes could not recall if he still had his rifle at that point. CSM Holroyd, Willie Stones's immediate superior, testified he had not seen him in the front line between 1.00 a.m. and 3.00 a.m., though he had relieved the previous NCO on time at 1.00 a.m. Important evidence came from Private Pinkney who was in the command dugout when Stones arrived to raise the alarm. The accused had then expressed urgent need to locate the company cooks before they were overrun. In was in the course of this fruitless search that Sergeant Stones became visibly unwell, having difficulty using his legs.

Private Pinkney was with Sergeant Stones as the NCO tried now to find the MO but, very soon after, the pair were intercepted and ordered back by the battle police. Sergeant Foster, on duty that night, stated that Stones was exhausted and trembling and that Lieutenant Mundy, when wounded, had ordered him back. Certainly by now Stones was unarmed and, when questioned, told Foster he'd jammed his rifle and bayonet crossways in the trench behind to provide an obstacle. In the divisional war diary, Willie Stones is initially described as being in a 'pitiable state of terror' – the word 'terrible' has been deleted. Foster continued his testimony as to the accused man's state of near nervous collapse.

Captain Warmington, opening his defence, adduced statements showing that Stones had twice reported sick with rheumatic pains in both legs. He then showed that there was no hard evidence to support an accusation that Willie Stones had deliberately cast aside his rifle and that only one witness saw him without it. Single witness testimony, if reliable, could be sufficient according to law but there was equally no evidence the NCO had fled in the first place. It was his duty to raise the alarm. In his own testimony the accused clearly stated that the mortally wounded Mundy had ordered him back to alert others and that his inability to continue was due to severe pain in his lower limbs. This was, at least in part, confirmed by Private Pinkney's own evidence.

What did emerge under cross-examination, and which may have been deemed critical, was the fact that when he left the dying officer he had assumed the other posts were still in place and was clearly unaware the sentries had stampeded. When he and Mundy were fired on, he stated his rifle was loaded but he didn't fire as not only was the safety on but so was the breech cover (designed to prevent mud and dust fouling the action). He had not fixed his bayonet. It seemed Lieutenant Mundy's revolver was still holstered and that neither man, being on a routine patrol, had anticipated sudden attack.

There was nothing wrong in this. The raid was totally unexpected and if being at the front with weapons other than at the ready seems unwise, the deep and constant mud clearly remained a potent factor. He also stated he had volunteered for the watch, despite being generally unwell. Both the CSM and MO testified for the defence. Willie Stones had attended the MO three days after the incident, complaining of rheumatic pains. Oddly, the fact the accused did not have a raised temperature was regarded as important medical evidence.

In summing up, Warmington reiterated his previous points and insisted there was insufficient evidence upon which to base a conviction. Character evidence, all favourable, was then given before the tribunal came to a finding. Willie Stones was found guilty of shamefully casting away his arms in the presence of the enemy, of leaving the front line and running away. He was sentenced to death with no recommendation for clemency. Both platoon and company commander reported very favourably upon his character and the battalion CO (temporarily acting as brigadier) favoured a reprieve. However the divisional, corps and army commanders, (the latter being General Allenby, destined for fame in Palestine) demurred and the sentence was allowed to stand.

As the authors of *Blindfold and Alone* point out, the case against Willie Stones was flawed at law. Even with the benefit of hindsight, a presumption must arise that the verdict was unjust. The presumption in military law must be the same as obtains in criminal law, namely that the defendant must be presumed innocent until found guilty. The prosecution had, evidentially, failed to establish that Stones's rifle had 'been shamefully cast away in the face of the enemy'. In terms of legal definition 'shameful' implies a 'positive and disgraceful dereliction of duty'. There is no concrete evidence of this and no witness testimony was adduced to prove Sergeant Stones had acted in this manner.

Furthermore, the prosecution was also required to prove the second limb of the allegation that the accused had 'left his piquet and run away'. His behaviour was perhaps erratic but given the established facts and medical evidence, there were no sustainable grounds. Lieutenant Mundy had, of course, died but no evidence was brought to show he had *not* ordered Stones to leave him and raise the alarm. Indeed any reasonable assumption would be likely to support this view.

This seems very much like a case of *pour encourager les autres* and one head was not going to suffice. The battalion, brigade and division's shortcomings were perceived as so deep and pervasive that further examples would be needed. Lance-Corporals Goggins and McDonald, with four privates, were tried on 28 December. Despite Captain Warmington's best efforts, all six were convicted and left facing the death penalty; only Private Ritchie was felt to be worthy of clemency as 'he is a person of low mental development…' Two days later a further eighteen trials were held and all of the accused were convicted and sentenced to death. Major-General Pinney, who had formerly commanded the division, wrote of the decisions:

The two NCOs [Goggins & McDonald] and four privates have been found guilty of a most serious crime. They appear to be all equally culpable as soldiers but the NCOs must be held as having especially failed in their soldierly duties and responsibilities. There are, however, some four thousand men in the division of whom 334 are in the DLI who are recommended for transfer as being unsuitable mentally and physically for infantry soldiers and it is probable that any of them would have behaved similarly under the circumstances described in the Court Martial. In view of the mental and physical degeneracy of these men I consider that although the sentence passed on all six is a proper one, the extreme penalty might be carried out in the case of the two NCOs only...[182]

In the courtyard of the *Mairie* in Poperinghe on the fringe of the Ypres Salient, a firing post still stands. In part the space remains as it was, hemmed in by proper Victorian provincial offices, though one side is much altered by modern rebuilding. The place is still narrow, undistinguished and utilitarian, less than a stone's throw from the pleasant centre. To one side are the cells in which the condemned men spent their last evening, in sight of the post which marked their final journey. Graffiti remains etched upon the walls, otherwise cramped and bare. The prisoners were taken there in the evening and held overnight. They were offered spiritual sustenance from a priest and/or more earthly solace in drink. Many went to their deaths insensible and needed to be lashed to chairs, too befuddled to stand upright.

Providing a firing squad was the responsibility of the officer commanding the military prison compound. The job was unlikely ever to appeal. It is one thing to kill your enemy in the heat of battle but to murder one of your own in cold blood in the clear dawn is another thing altogether. Volunteers would be sought, inducements – extra wages, leave or grog – offered. If this failed, then a set of petty defaulters would be conscripted. Standing in the firing squad provided ample means of absolution for minor crimes. On the night before, the shooters would be separated from their comrades. Training in their terrible chore was provided and enough drink given to dull the edges of sensibility.

Earlier in the war, executions were commanded by junior officers. This proved unreliable; many found the job unbearable. By 1917 the firing party would be directed by an experienced NCO who could be relied on, hopefully, not to funk the job. The condemned was brought forth in the early dawn and marched those few paces to the post, where he was tied and blindfolded. A dozen men formed the squad, each with his rifle loaded, the distance perhaps three metres. Each aimed at the breast and, contrary to movie versions, orders were given silently by signal. But there would be no mistaking the decisive click of bolts rammed home, a sound only too familiar to the condemned man. An MO was on hand to certify the man dead and, if he somehow still breathed, it was the duty of the NCO to administer a *coup de grace* with his .455 Webley revolver.

On 18 January 1917, at 07.35 on a winter's morning lined with freshly fallen snow, Sergeant Willie Stones with Lance-Corporals Goggins and McDonald was executed by firing squad at Roellecourt, near St Pol. At the distance of nearly a century, all may now be said to be casualties of war.

'The Deserter'

'I'm sorry I done it, Major'
We bandaged the livid face;
And led him ere the wan sun rose,
To die his death of disgrace.

The bolt-heads locked onto the cartridge;
The rifles steadied to rest,
As cold stock nestled at colder cheek,
And foresight lined on the breast.

'Fire!' called the Sergeant-Major.
The muzzles flamed as he spoke:
And the shameless soul of a nameless man
Went up in the cordite smoke.
– Gilbert Frankau[183]

POWs

'Waiting'

I wanted to beg you to stay; instead I smoothed my apron and watched you walk away.

I wanted to fall down on my knees and cry and scream and plead and plead and plead,

Instead I boiled water, made tea while you fastened braces, polished boots, shone buttons.

'I'm more likely to die down that bloody pit' you said, we both knew it wasn't true.

'This is our way out, our chance to get away, from the grime and the dirt and the same places/faces day after day.'

You always thought you were better than our little town, where we grew up side by side,

Always the tallest, strongest, fastest and bravest lad at school: Born for better things.

I knew you all my life, loved you since we were fifteen, and now I had to say goodbye.

'It's not for long love' you said 'we will all be home by Christmas love' you kissed me, held my gaze with those blue, blue eyes and turned and walked away.

I held that image in my mind till this day, you striding down the street, proud to be in khaki, prouder still of the red cap covering your sandy blond hair.

Played it over and over in my mind over the years, wondered if I could have changed things in anyway

Sixty-five years to the day I watched you stroll down our street round the corner, gone.

I'm old now Johnny, and now at last, I hope, soon, to see you again.

– Samantha Kelly

Drummer Joseph Dawson 2nd Battalion NF was captured at the 2nd Battle of Ypres (after being injured by shrapnel in the head): 'We were marched from the field of battle to a German field hospital by an escort of Uhlans, and though wounded, many a kick did we get.' Next they were marched to a Belgian school as a staging post: 'A sister of Mercy, having no love for Mr Tommy Atkins, gave us a very rough time: poor rations and cursory medical treatment.'[184]

On 20 May 1915, Dawson was evacuated by train to POW camp at Munster: 'A Red Cross nurse asked us in broken English if we would have anything to drink. Of course, being very thirsty we asked for water. She bent over me and spat in my face!' Civilians present also abused the wounded Tommies though he finally received rather better treatment afterwards including competent surgery to remove shrapnel from above his left eye. Finally Dawson was sent on to the POW camp in Munster.[185]

Private W. W. Hall was a POW from 1916–18. He was able to exchange letters with his wife Barbara:

Thursday, July 18th 1918:

My own dear Will,

I am still waiting of word of you but know it will not be your fault that I have got none. I got a card from the British Red Cross on Friday saying you were prisoner. I only hope you are going on alright and are quite well. I received an envelope from F last Wed and I thought it was from you at first, but when I opened it, it was from on your coy called W North, enclosed some franc notes, due to you for hair cutting the company and said that I would likely have got word that you were missing and most probably a prisoner as most of their lads were. I have been to Newcastle giving in your name and address in so they will be able to send your francs. Lieutenant W. Meldon is a prisoner at Baden I believe and a few more lads are missing from here. Well my love, I hope I will be getting a letter soon and that you are quite well as we all are at present. I will close with best love to my own lad from your own loving wife Barbara.[186]

16 North Burns, Chester le Street, Co. Durham, July 12th 1918:

My own dear Will

I hope you are going on all right as we are all quite well at present. We have had some very anxious weeks & I quite expect you will have been just as bad. Your father and all the others are going on all right. I am sending this in chance of you getting it as I know you will be hungry for news of us, as we are of you; hoping to have a letter from you soon, from your own loving wife Barbara. [Also signed, in a rather wobbly hand, Margarita Hall, and, more confidently, what looks like Tillie and Will. All three append numerous kisses.]

Bank Holiday, August 5th 1918:

My own dear Will

I have at last received your very welcome letter, it landed this morning, so must have taken 7 weeks to reach home. I think there is no need all for one to take such a time. Well, I hope you are going on all right and that you will have got some of my letters before now. I wrote 3 weeks ago as soon as I got the card through the British Red Cross saying you were reported a prisoner as I knew you would be longing for news from home, about the things you ask to be sent, the committee for the prisoners parcels sends underclothing, boots as well as the food parcels and I hope you will have got some before this. I am only allowed to send you 1 parcel in 3 months and am not allowed to enclose tobacco or cigs or any eatables except ½lb sweets…

You will be sorry to hear that Dodie Riddell was buried at Pelton on Sunday. He had been through 7 operations with his leg…

I got the money quite safe that you sent in your last letter from France, though little did I know that you were a prisoner before I received it. I mentioned in one of my other letters about receiving some cent notes from a chap called North in your company which was due to you for hair cutting. I have never changed it yet but think it would perhaps be better to get it changed now…

Best love from own loving wife Barbara…xxx

Sunday, August 8th 1918:

My own dear Will

I hope you are quite all right again. I am very glad to hear that you have met one of the Catterick chaps it will make the time go quicker when there is someone you know … It is our Tom's birthday today … I will have to be getting Tom into some trousers he is nearly too big for petticoats now but will wait till it is a bit colder. Willie is away with his aunt Jane at your cousin Phoebe's at Easington … I expect you will not have come across Trevor Dingwall or Longbottom's lad and Harry Witherspoon has not been heard of since March & Maggie is in an awful state. I am enclosing one of the photo's that we have had taken and hope that you will get it all right…

Sunday, August 18th 1918:

My own dear Will

…Mary Nevin died last Saturday night and was buried at Medomsley on Thursday… I have got a box ready to send and hope you will find it what you most require. The things I can send are very limited, it is not like sending a box to France where we can send anything we can get. Mrs Dingwall asked to be remembered to you. I think her son Trevor has been taken a prisoner on the same day as you. Also Longbottom's lad up beside your fathers,, just lads of 18½ years. Laurie Gettings has been killed and Mrs Gray has got word that Victor has been killed, a younger one than Billy, you know. The garden is looking grand just now and the roses on the rustic fence are out lovely and are nearly covering it … Your own loving wife Barbara xxx

Sunday, August 25th 1918:

… [Tom] is getting a bigger mischief than Will and is coming on, talking all right … The papers have had good news this week again and I hope it will soon be finished … I will have to draw to a close as it is nearly 11. That you are keeping well is my constant prayer so good night dear. God keep you safe and bring you back soon to your own loving wife…

Will and Barbara would not be re-united until 1919 when the POWs finally came home.

J. T. ('Tanner') Milburn was a native of Ashington in the southeast Northumberland coalfield, a breed famous for hardiness. He was a keen local sportsman and played football for Ashington AFC, a tradition begun by his father, Jackie. Tanner played in goal where he was renowned for stylishly saving penalties and for clearing corner kicks. He became a POW on 1 July 1916, serving with the Northumberland Fusiliers. These extracts are from a YMCA Friendship diary given to him on his return. Much of what he writes is couched in Geordie or Pitmatic[†] dialect. The authors have not sought to alter this.[187] Nor have we altered the dates, although they do not actually reflect the real timescale. Tanner was simply using the diary as a notebook. That means that events dated January 1919 actually happened in July 1916. We have, therefore, left the diary dates out to create a linear narrative.

January 1st (1919)

Were you treated brutally yourself or did you see anyone else treated brutally if so when and where. Answer: Yes; when taken prisoner behind the line at the Bapaume Road, where the Germans made footballs of us. I myself had to carry British Wounded 4 or 5 miles.

Do you know the names of the Germans soldiers or officials who committed such acts: No!

Were you confined in any working camp where the conditions were especially bad as regards accommodation\nature of work and general treatment: Give the names of every such working camp and, if possible, the name of the parent camp.

---

† Pitmatic or 'Pitamatic' – 'yakka' as it's known regionally – is a variable northeast dialect associated with the mining areas of south-east Northumberland and East Durham, in the former case a patois of Geordie and Northumbrian.

Yes in Heuberg camp, the conditions were very bad in 1916. The months of December till March 1917, we lay with two blankets on the bed and working from six in the morning till six at night. We had so much work for to do before we came into the camp again. It did not matter if it rained or snowed, you still had the same work to do.

Give the name, if you know it, of the commandant or of the feldwebel or unteroffizier in charge of each working camp while you were there. Answer: Field Officer Koch.

Have you any other statement, favourable or the reverse, to make with regard to your treatment as a prisoner of war?

Yes. This same officer spat in my face because I was bad [in Geordie dialect 'bad' means ill or unwell rather than misbehaved] and said the English prisoners should not be bad and the doctor in the hospital kept me in there from the 1st of September till 23rd September. The doctor said it was diarrhoea but it was none other than a poison stomach from German food. If it had not been for my comrade, Sgt Smithson 2 NF looking after me I should have died.

Tanner was taken prisoner on 1 July 1916. He had been buried for six hours by the burst from a British shell in the German's third line near La Boisselle.

After being dug out, there was about five Germans standing around me. I thought my time had come because one wanted to put the bayonet through me but the others would not have it. Which, many a time, I wish they had done me in.

January 10th

Well, I was taken from that line further behind. In a dug out were some Germans who were just going to stand to. Just as they got out, the English started a bombardment so the officer what was in charge of them, drove them out with his revolver. Some was fainting, others was crying so you see what sort of soldiers they are and what sort of officers they have.

This officer never said very much to me but asked me what regiment I was in. He could talk broken English. That was all he asked me. So I stayed in that dug out all night. Every moment I expected the British Tommy's to come over but they never came. So on the 2nd of July, I was taken to a chateau where there were a lot of British [wounded] lying.

On stretchers; wounded crying for help where no help would come. Do you know, I could have cried, to see these poor fellows dying who might have been saved if only they had been in our own men's hands. I saw one poor officer in there. He had, I would say, about ten wounds on him and only one shirt sleeve. All the rest was torn from him. I think with shrapnel. He died during the time I sat beside him. I asked him his name but he died with it on his lips. I saw lots of English wounded there but never say any doctor attending to them. Because, I tell you how it was, because everybody had the wind up. The English artillery was sending some stuff over.

So, on the 2nd of July, I was taken out of the trenches and on going out we met a German officer who pointed a revolver at my head because, he said, 'you are the swine'. I gave him a serious look. He rushed at me again, cut the numerals off my coat, took the ring off my finger and my jack knife. So he let us [me] go after that. I was not the least afraid. So, I tell you, me and the sentry got to the end of a communication trench on the Bapaume Road where an officer came up on horseback to speak to me, just as we were coming out of the trench. But this officer never spoke to me, yet just as he dismounted his horse, over came one of our shells and carried him and his horse into an open field. This was a horrible sight. I was beginning to feel hungry and a bit weak as I could not eat the German black bread.

So I tell you, when I came onto the Bapaume Road I had another experience. The Germans rushed out on me and made a football of me which I have already told to the English government. So they took me to a dressing station for the night where there were English and German wounded. This is where I saw some more English prisoners.

I fell in with a R.S. and another N.F. This N.F kid was very young, I should say about 18 years old. He was not wounded then but not so long after he was wounded: we passed another dressing station where some Germans rushed on us with sticks and stones and lumps of dirt, so we never spoke to them. The sentry was in the dressing station at the time, so one mad-brained German picked up a stone let it fly and it hit this kid right on the back.

This kid fell. I picked him up and asked him if he was much hurt and he said his back very sore. This square-head German stood and laughed. So we marched away from there where we came to a little village. I don't know the name but the people were willing to gives us bread, butter, eggs and cigarettes which the sentries would not let us have. But I managed to get a bit. So they took us into a church where I saw more wounded. This is where another young fellow in the Manchesters was wounded in the legs. So the cavalry took us away from here and this Manchester had to walk. Poor soul, I was sorry for him. I was a little bit stronger then because I had had a feed from the French people.

So I helped this fellow along the road for about 4 miles till the Cavalry took him off because he could not go hard enough for them. We left the poor fellow there, I suppose to die. Then we came across a German going along. This was a bit more luck for me. He took off his pack put it on to me for about two miles till we came to a big place where there were about 200 prisoners.

We were took to a camp and we lay here for 14 days. Every man jack of us was lifting with lice. It was awful. We were allowed a small ration of bread and we got soup. It was hell. Some were getting more than others. We were just getting to know what hunger was: we were selling our things. Some were selling watches for a slice of bread. Hunger is a very sharp thorn.

Every morning we inspected our shirts. He was a lucky man that only got score off him. I know men in the present day who have marks from scratching and will carry these marks to their graves. I may say I never had a wash with soap for a fortnight. [They were moved to another camp, where they were cleaned up and treated.] The next day we were inoculated … For 9 days we were isolated there, we were inoculated three times in 9 days. I tell you, we were all in a very bad state from the lice and lack of food.

Well, we had three meals a day at Dulmen. There were meals of two slices of bread a day, soup, barley water and coffee or tea beginning at 6 o'clock. I never tasted such horrible stuff in my life but what could a man do. You must eat it or die. As I said, hunger is a very sharp thorn. One who has been a prisoner under the Huns knows it well. I have seen a lot of men go about the camp eating the food from the pigs' bins that had been thrown away by other prisoners. Mouldy bread; [we] raked the bully beef tins and salmon tins out with our fingers. I used to get up at 6 o'clock and go about the camp on my hands and knees looking for cigarette tab ends. We used to smoke tea-leaves: that was a luxury.

We left on 14th August 1916, I think that's right, to go to a punishment camp. That camp was Heuberg in Baden where it was hell for English prisoners. This is where I fell in with this swine Field Officer Koch. Nice man what I hope is kicking the daisies up. Now this is where we got a loaf of bread ten inches long and five inches broad for five men. It was not enough for one. And the soup: it was made of grass and barley, sometimes potatoes which were planted before the flood. I saw one man get his soup one day and fetch a mouse out of it. That did me: I very near fetched all mine back again.

On 29th August 1916 I took very ill and went to see the doctor. He told me I must work. Every morning for three mornings I want and saw him. So on the 1st of September I was in a dying condition, I could hardly stand up. So we lined up for the doctor. So this is where the divine Field Officer Koch, he came to inspect us before we went to the doctor. So he said the English prisoners look all right. And he came to me and asked me, what was the matter with me? So I told him. So he called me a liar and a swine or pig and even spat in my face. He told us if the doctor signed our papers for work, we would all have to go in arrest for 7 days (my temperature was 38) and something else in German ... so I was sent up to the hospital.

If it had not been for a mate of mine doing a little bit for me, I should have pegged out. I saw about 50 Russians die in there – they were doing it left and right. So, it was very heartening in there for me. One day I got a parcel from my wife; this is what pulled me round. I got a bit of good old English food down me: and a bit meat...

I was on light duty for 8 days then I had to go out to work on a road which was very hard work. None of us was going to kill ourselves with work but the square-head ganger kept us out till our work was done. I seen it be 7o'clock when we got back into the camp. So they stopped that job and set us on to a stone quarry. This was a good job as the sentries were alright.

Then we went on to a garden setting drills and that kind of thing. We had a mad sentry. If we were having a smoke, he used to come rushing at us with his revolver or bayonet: mad. The asylum was the fittest place for him. There was about six of us standing talking: you should have seen him come over sacrament-ing and calling us all the names he could lay his tongue to. But this was the joke: everything he did, we did. When he swore, we swore: when he shouted, we shouted: when he ran we ran. Till, at the finish, he started to work himself [colloquialism for having a tantrum]. He was a star turn for to have a soldier's uniform on. I think if he had been in a Barnum and Bailey show; that should have been his place, in a lion's cage!

Tanner died in 1949 at the age of sixty-two and is buried in Seaton Hirst cemetery. His four footballer sons, George, Jack, James and Stan acted as pallbearers. The first two of these played for Leeds United for over a decade as full-backs, while their brother-in-law, Jimmy Potts, was goalkeeper. Together they were lauded as 'the Milburn Defence'. Brother James also played for Leeds. Tanner's nephew Jackie Milburn achieved legendary status as an England

International and Newcastle United striker, his fame only equalled by that of Tanner's two grandsons, Jackie and Bobby Charlton.[188]

Isaac Armorer Patterson was a native of Hexham. By 1914 he had already been serving as a Territorial for a decade. He was engaged to Daisy Barrasford, also of Hexham, who, when her fiancé went to war, became a nurse, based in Birmingham. The couple saw little of each other through four years of war though they corresponded religiously. Photographs show Armorer's tunic pockets bulging with bundles of Daisy's letters, as many as thirty at a time. On 22 August 1918, he was posted missing in action and it wasn't until October, as war's end loomed, that Daisy, who had kept writing, learned her faith had been vindicated; Armorer was a POW, he had been wounded in the leg and captured.[189]

The action in which Patterson (a subaltern) was wounded took place around 8.30 a.m. by a railway loop, just east of Happy Valley, and a mile north of Bray-sur-Somme. The Hussars had charged German defences, MG posts linked by infantry trenches, and Armorer's horse was shot from under him.

> Wounded be damned was what I said when I got hit. My next thought was to get into a small drain three yards from me. I made it to the drain and lay down full length. It was about nine inches deep and twelve wide but one can make oneself very small when only twenty yards from a German machine gun. During the first five minutes, I had hidden my sword. I stuck it into the side of the drain and covered the hilt over.
>
> What I saw when I looked out was not a pleasant sight; a German officer with his revolver drawn coming towards me. He looked at me and passed on to see if there were any more fellows lying about. Then he made signs for me to get up but I could not. He helped me up and called over one of his men to help me back to their gun line. I thought – I am both wounded and a prisoner, two things I never dreamt of.

The Germans stripped off Patterson's puttees to expose the damaged area of flesh. 'I had a look at my wound, a hole straight through the shin bone and out at the back of the knee, a little to the right.'

Soon, he was joined by more wounded captives from his regiment, Private Moore and Corporal Dance. The injured officer was despoiled of his surplus kit, revolver, ammunition, glasses and the badge of the cavalryman, his spurs. 'I had an awful time trying to walk back to the dressing station. It was a small hell. I had the German guard on one side and Cpl. Dance on the other, and used both as crutches.' Happily, the party ran into a Red Cross orderly who improvised a makeshift stretcher from branches and ground-sheet and, with a comrade, made up a stretcher party.

> They carried me about a mile to the dressing station at Bouvray Farm. We went through a lot of heavy shelling. During one of our halts, I saw one of our planes bring down a balloon and get clear of the German aircraft.
>
> We finally reached the ADS, located in an old dugout; I'd had a good dose of my flask by this time and gave the bearers a drink.

Next, he was conveyed by motor ambulance along the straight Roman road from Albert to Bapaume, through Mericourt. Then the operating theatre,

> the first thing I saw was a human leg lying under the operating table, it had been taken off above the knee. My own had swollen terribly and did not look at all well. I thought it was all broken to pieces, judging from the appearance. Now, I had my leg thoroughly examined and put into proper splints. The hospital was fairly clean and not badly looked after. My knee was about the size of a football and my leg about three time's normal size. I was on the serious surgical ward and most of the German patients had legs or arms off.

His next transfer was to a base hospital well behind the front. It was only a week since his capture and this unit proved 'one of the dirtiest places I have ever seen'. Here, he met an Irish NCO called Buckley. The latter was a senior man amongst the local British POWs, held in the nearby working camp. 'He told me how they were being treated and how they'd been treated since March and through the rest of the summer. He told me that since March, around 20 per cent of the prisoners had died.'

On 29 August:

I was put on a stretcher and loaded onto a Red Cross train, which was really quite clean … on 30th August we arrived at Valenciennes where I was taken to a POW hospital. On the ward there were eleven British officers all more or less wounded. The food here was very poor, thank goodness there were some Frenchmen in the hospital would sell their biscuits for ½ Mark each. September 6th; I had the splints taken off and was in a terrible funk, I thought my leg was going to fall off!

Just over a fortnight later he was moved to Antwerp and St George's Barracks which was being used as a POW hospital.

Food was a bit better here than Valenciennes. There was also a canteen where you could buy brandy, cigarettes and caramel. It was possible to have both a bath and haircut and, on Wednesdays we ate boiled meat and potatoes. I got a newspaper from our Belgian helpers and it showed the great advances our armies were making. I knew almost every village that was being taken; there was great excitement as first one place, then another fell.

25 October:

We left Antwerp for Karlsruhe. The Belgians provided us with a half-chicken each, two eggs, four apples and a bottle of John Crabbe's whisky (pre-war stuff). Had it not been for these gifts we would have been very badly off. We passed through Aachen, Cologne, Mainz, Heidelberg and Frankfurt. We arrived at around three in the afternoon on 27th October and were put up in the Hotel Europa. Next day we were marched to a temporary camp then, on 30th October made ready to move again. Before leaving we heard that Austria had signed an armistice. Our party comprised 58 officers and we had a second class carriage right through. We passed back through Hamburg and Frankfurt to Pillau [near Baltiysk] arriving on 2nd November.

We were marched to a small fishing village of about a hundred inhabitants, it was as near to the sea as was possible without being in the sea. The camp used to be a German hospital, it was a new camp, no canteen, no parcels, in fact nothing, hardly any rations. We were thoroughly searched and made to strip off. During the searching I found a German trying to pinch a packet of tea from an officer at which I spoke up and caused a bit of a stir. On 10th November, I went to Holy Communion, a thing I never dreamt of [Armorer was a good chapel goer] … the padre was a South African with one arm.

His single entry for 11 November simply says: 'Thank God.'

Armistice meant an end to hostilities but the POWs, as ever, were more immediately concerned with rations or, rather, the paucity of rations. Their daily allowance was meagre in the extreme; Germany was near destitute:

8.00 am – coffee and bread allowance for the day (275g)
1.00 pm – Potatoes & cabbage
4.00 pm – coffee
7.00 pm – soup, (not good)

If anybody wants to take their weight down, I strongly advise the above rations. There is not sufficient to feed a new-born baby. We often talk about the dog's supper at home and would give anything for it. This place as a whole is simply bloody!

We were in wooden huts, twenty-four to a hut, each hut divided into two compartments, twelve in each and a stove in each compartment. The beds were the best part of the camp and we make the most of it, going to bed about 9.30 pm and getting up around midday.

By 5 December, there were signs their incarceration was nearing its end. Danish Red Cross officials and parcels were expected. The representative duly arrived. The promised manna from heaven did not. By early afternoon rumours were buzzing that they would soon be repatriated, sailing from Danzig within days.

This news was received with great applause. On 5th December I was invited out by a Captain Robertson. This dinner was the first substantial meal I'd had since I was made prisoner. We had sausages, a tin of pork & beans, boiled potatoes, sultana pudding and a cup of cocoa, a few English cigarettes and a pipe of Players Medium; bliss.

On December 8th we received orders to entrain; we paraded at 4.00 pm and arrived in Danzig at 7.00 am. The first thing we saw when we got off the train was the white ensign flying on HMS Coventry. As soon as we stepped on the gangplank, we knew we were prisoners no more. We were free; it was hard to believe. The band played 'Rule Britannia'.

He finally returned home on 14 December 1918.

Daisy and Armorer were married on 15 January 1919. As they left Hexham by train for their honeymoon in Cumberland, the Abbey bells rang out in celebration.

Wounded

Armorer came back whole, in body at least. Some did not. By May 1917, Pat Beauchamp was driving a different lorry. 'Little Willie' was a Willis-Overland: far less responsive and in worse condition that her previous vehicle, Pat mourned for Susan.

The next day was Wednesday ... I had been up since 5 and was taking a lorry-full of stretchers and blankets past a French Battery

... It was about midday and there was not a cloud in the sky. Then suddenly my heart stood still. Somehow, instinctively, I knew I was 'for it' at last. Whole eternities seemed to elapse before the crash.

I felt myself being hurled from the car into the air, to fall and be swept along for some distance, my face being literally rubbed in the ground. I remember my rage at this, and even in that extreme moment managed to seize my nose in the hope that it at least might not be broken![190]

I tried to move and found it impossible. 'What a mess I'm in,' was my next thought, 'and how my legs ache!' I tried to move them too, but it was no good. 'They must both be broken,' I concluded. I put my hand to my head and brought it away all sticky. 'That's funny,' I thought, 'where can it have come from?' and then I caught sight of my hand. It was all covered with blood. I began to have a panic that my back might be injured and I would not be able to ride again. That was all that really worried me. I had always dreaded anything happening to my back, somehow.

The French soldiers were down from their Battery in a trice, all great friends of mine to whom I had often thrown ration cigarettes. Gaspard gave a cry and was on the ground beside me, calling me his 'little cabbage,' his 'poor little pigeon,' ... presently he half lifted me in his arms and cradled me as he might a baby.

I remained quite conscious the whole time. 'Will I be able to ride again?' kept hammering through my brain. The pain was becoming rapidly worse and I began to wonder just where my legs were broken. As I could move neither, I could not discover at all, and presently I gave a gasp as I felt something tighten and hurt terribly. It was a boot lace they were fixing to stop the hæmorrhage (bootlaces are used for everything in France).

The men stood round, and I watched them furtively wiping the tears away that rolled down their furrowed cheeks. One even put his arm over his eyes as a child does. I wondered vaguely why they were crying; it never dawned on me it had anything to do with me. 'Complètement coupée' (completely cut). I heard one say, and quick as a shot, I asked, 'Où est-ce que c'est qu'est coupé?' Those tactful souls, just rough soldiers, replied without hesitation, 'La jaquette [jacket], Mademoiselle.' 'Je m'en fiche de la jaquette, [I don't care about the jacket!]' I answered, completely reassured.

The little French doctor from the Battery, who had once helped me change a tyre, came running up and I covered the scratched side of my face lest he should get too much of a shock. 'Je suis joliment dans la soupe,' (I'm nicely in the soup) I said, and saw him go as white as a sheet. 'These Frenchmen are very sympathetic,' I thought, for it had dawned on me what they were crying about by that time ... 'So this is what the men go through every day,' I thought.

I was carried into the big hall and there my beloved Wuzzy found me. I heard a little whine and felt a warm tongue licking my face – luckily he had not been with me that morning.

'Take that – dog away, someone,' cried the Colonel, who was peevish in the extreme. 'He's not a – dog,' I protested, and then up came a Padre who asked gravely, 'What are you, my child?' Thinking I was now fairly unrecognisable by this time with the Frenchman's hanky round my head, etc., I replied, 'A F.A.N.Y., of course!' This completely scandalized the good Padre. When he had recovered, he said, 'No, you mistake me, what religion I mean?'

She had been due to go home in four days.

...I asked after 'Little Willie,' and heard his remains had been towed to camp, though being a Hun he would of course manage to escape somehow!...

She had lost her leg.

Captain C. stayed a long time and the evening drew on but still he sat there and talked to me quietly in the darkness. I wondered why I couldn't cry, but somehow it seemed to have nothing to do with me at all. I was not the girl who had lost a leg. It was merely someone else I was hearing about. 'Jolly bad luck on them,' I thought, 'rotten not to be able to run about any more.'

While still in hospital Pat was awarded the Croix de Guerre. She describes the moment with great emotion as well as her usual degree of humour. Returning to Britain, she underwent a long convalescence. Her memoir notes her difficulties in obtaining a suitable artificial leg (the system was rather better at dealing with the prosthetic needs of wounded men) but by 1918 she had succeeded in obtaining a suitable device. As is so often the case, that was not the entire solution. Even today wearers of artificial limbs find themselves aching to take them off:

Half an hour's fitting was enough to make the leg too tender for anything more that day, and I discovered to my joy that I was quite well able to drive a small car with one foot. I was lent a sporting Morgan tri-car which did more to keep up my spirits than anything else. The side brake was broken and somehow never got repaired, so the one foot had quite an exciting time. It was anything but safe, but it did not matter. One day, driving down the Portsmouth Road with a fellow-sufferer, a policeman waved his arms frantically in front of us. 'What's happened,' I asked my friend, 'are we supposed to stop?' 'I'm afraid so,' he replied, 'I should think we've been caught in a trap.' (One gets into bad habits in France!)

As we drew up and the policeman saw the crutches, he said: 'I'm sorry, sir, I didn't see your crutches, or I wouldn't have pulled you up.' The friend, who happened to be wearing his leg, said, 'Oh, they aren't mine, they belong to this lady.' The good policeman was temporarily speechless. When at last he got his wind he was full of concern. 'You don't say, sir? Well, I never did. Don't you take on, we won't run you in, Miss,' he added consolingly, turning to me. 'I'll fix the stop-watch man.' I was beginning to

enjoy myself immensely. He regarded us for some minutes and
made a round of the car. 'Well,' he said at last, 'I call you a couple
o' sports!' We were convulsed!

At that moment the stop-watch man hurried up, looking very
serious, and I watched the expression on his face change to one of
concern as the policeman told him the tale…

'What were we doing?' I asked, as he looked at his stop-watch.
'Thirty and a fraction over,' he replied. 'Only thirty!' I exclaimed,
in a disappointed voice, 'I thought we were doing at least forty!'…

'Well,' said the stop-watch man, lifting his cap, 'we won't keep
you any longer, Miss, a pleasant afternoon to you, and (with a
knowing look) there's nothing on the road from here to Cobham!'

Pat Beauchamp Waddell went on to become FANY adjutant after
the war. She married Peter Washington, a British officer whom she
had met while convalescing and who had also been badly wounded.
In 1939, turned down for active service because of her disability,
Pat was sent by FANY to work with the Free Poles. She was to
be awarded her third decoration, (she had received the Elizabeth
medal from the Belgians as well as the French Croix de Guerre) and
from the commander-in-chief of Polish forces, the grand Cross of
Merit (military class).

Remembrance

On 12 November 2005, Durham's regional newspaper *The Northern
Echo*[191] reported on the story of two forgotten sweethearts, Hannah
Harling and James 'Jigger' Buddin. Hannah was the daughter of
Thomas Harling, who worked in Thrislington Colliery. He was a
mining union official and organiser in Co. Durham and would go
on to be a Councillor serving both district and county. His daughter met James Buddin in West Cornforth Methodist Chapel. She
was twenty-one and he twenty-six. Jim was one of six children,
his family itinerant workers who had arrived in West Cornforth, a
typical Durham mining settlement, referred to locally as 'Doggy'.
Jim and Hannah wished to marry but he had first to make his way

in the world. Opportunities in Durham were scarce in the pre-war years so he travelled to Australia in search of work.

Jim arrived in Corrimal, New South Wales, another boom mining township. He sent letters and postcards to Hannah. And wrote of the local chapel, 'this is a view of Corrimal Methodist Church with Broken Nose [Mountain] in the distance ... you will see it is a wooden chapel. They have the Endeavour meetings and Sunday school in there and sometimes social evenings.' Perhaps a place to be married... Jim did not enlist at the outbreak of war – he volunteered early in 1916. He served as a sapper, photographed astride a camel in Egypt as the vortex of war gradually dragged him westwards. On 12 September, now on the Somme, he met up with his younger brother Joseph. The siblings had not seen each other since Jigger headed to Australia. Joy at the reunion was short-lived as Joseph was killed in action a mere eleven days later.

Hannah's birthday fell on 1 October and, that year, she received a hand-embroidered card from Picardy, the words 'to my dear sweetheart' stitched boldly across the front. He wondered if she would dare add this to her album. Such an overt message might be considered rather too bold for 1916 and sensibilities in 'Doggy'. At Christmas that year he wrote: 'my dear, dear girl once again I have to wish you the old, old wish. May your Christmas be very happy and the New Year bring you all the best and brightest things you can wish for.'

On 14 April 1917 Jigger wrote from No. 6 General Hospital; 'I'm going on well now and quite comfortable or, at least as comfortable as I can expect to be. Thank Annie [Hannah's sister] for her contribution.' He went on, 'I did not sample it but I came to the conclusion it was soap.' This may have been a wry reflection on the girl's efforts at cooking! 'I have a wound in the left side. It is practically on the buttock. It was a good job it was no higher up or it would have greatly upset Jimmy's internal arrangements!' This was his final letter. Jigger had been hit on 9 April. On the day he wrote, his condition worsened and within a week he was dead.

Hannah mourned for a long time, not marrying until she was

thirty-nine. James, Joseph and their four sisters, Hannah, Jane, Louise and Edith – all died young. The brothers are both commemorated on the West Cornforth War Memorial. Also named on the memorial are the names of William Laverick (died in Flanders) and William Laverick, a flight engineer killed over Berlin in 1943. These were the uncle and brother of Mary Laverick (one named after the other, perhaps), who married Jigger's younger brother Robert in 1934. A family who paid a high price in service to their country.

The poignant saga of Hannah and Jigger lay dormant for eighty-seven years and was not discovered till a collection of postcards and letters were found by Hannah's daughter after her death.

A local researcher, investigating the names on the West Cornforth memorial and aware of Jigger's time in Australia, made contact with the Methodist chapel in Corrimal. The old wooden building Jigger wrote of is now gone, rebuilt in brick. The local war memorial had been hidden away behind the stage in this new church. It has twenty-one names. Residents could identify all but one of the men, and this, of course, was Jigger. Now he is remembered in both County Durham and New South Wales.[192]

Even when the war was over, it was not over. It is fashionable now to observe that the final shot of the First World War was the first of the Second and there is truth is this. Versailles, savage and vindictive, retribution rather than conciliation, sowed the seeds of further conflict, one even more cataclysmic than the first. Of those proud empires which stepped so nobly into the ring in 1914, only Britain and France, much diminished, were still upright four years later. Germany, Turkey, Austria and Russia were crushed and what arose in the wake of the Romanoff's fall changed the face of world politics. The blast from the Russian Revolution lingered till the collapse of the Berlin Wall threescore years later and we continue to live with the fallout which exploded into fresh violence in the Balkans and Chechnya.

The toast of 'a land fit for heroes' very quickly turned sour. Survivors came back to unemployment, indifference, hunger, humiliation and despair. Their sufferings and their scars, they carried to the grave. So many wrecked in body and mind, achieved no solace. The 'war to end all wars' in fact ushered in another generation of conflict and a world war even more terrible than the last. Now, a century later, with the last known veterans gone, only the monuments remain; 'the crosses row on row'. Each town and village from Nova Scotia to New South Wales with its inscribed list of the fallen, crumbling testimony to a generation who, when the bugles sounded did not flinch nor fail the test. They poured out their blood in torrents for a cause they believed was just and right. In that, whether history may judge right or wrong, there is honour indeed.

Their memory must endure forever.

The Last Word

From Charles Moss:

Sir,

I wonder how many of the lads who volunteered as I did during the golden autumn of 1914 still remain to talk over the pleasures and rigours and discipline of those intensive training periods? One of them has just has the poignant experience of revisiting the well-remembered localities around Salisbury Plain and, for the moment, to shed the weight of the years and wounds, as memory brought back those boisterous and hard-driven days.

In our spare time, when not on parade or manoeuvres we busied ourselves by cutting copies of our regimental cap badges through the turf, giving each one a setting as white as that of the famous horse. It was a moment of deep emotion when this old Durham Pal came after forty-five years and found so many of the badges clear and well-tended.

Those who had lived through that war of foul trenches, wiring patrols and attacks over no man's land which were the dire and hellish responsibility of the PBI, could forget those grand autumn days of 1915 when they gathered juicy blackberries as big as cherries from the tall hedges and munched apples dropped on the road from overladen trees.

– *Durham Advertiser*, 10 November 1961

NOTES

1   Trustees of the Green Howards Museum Richmond, MA 364.
2   Authors' collection.
3   *Daily Mail*, August 1923, Trustees of the Green Howards, MA 364.
4   Hewitson, T. L., *Weekend Warriors from Tyne to Tweed* (Tempus, Gloucs, 2006) p. 60.
5   Ibid., p. 64.
6   Wilfred Owen, 'Disabled'.
7   Hewitson. p. 63.
8   Ibid.
9   Pease, H., *The History of the Northumberland (Hussars) Yeomanry 1819–1923* (Constable, London, 1924) p. 60.
10 Sadler, J., *The Field Gun Run* (Royal Military Tournament, London, 2010) p. 5.
11 TWAM: DF.WF/22/1.
12 TWAM: DF.WF/22/1.
13 Stewart, G., & Sheen, J., *Tyneside Scottish* (Pen & Sword, Barnsley, 1999) p. 27.
14 Ibid., p. 26.
15 Ibid., p. 28.
16 Ibid., p. 22.
17 Ibid.
18 Ward, S. G. P., *Faithful: The Story of the Durham Light Infantry* (Thomas Nelson & Sons, London, 1962) p. 319.
19 Trustees of the Fusiliers Museum of Northumberland.
20 Ibid.
21 Anonymous and undated document in author's possession, forming part of a dated autograph book.
22 Trustees of the Fusiliers Museum of Northumberland.
23 Ibid.
24 Ibid.
25 Ibid.
26 Ibid.
27 TWAM: DBC.1845/362.

28 Extracts from J. B. W. Pennyman sourced from the Trustees of the KOSB Museum.

29 TWAM: DF.WF/22/1.

30 Trustees of the Green Howards Museum, MA 342.

31 Trustees of the Green Howards, MA 364, the words, by Charles Jeffrys are set to the tune of the 5th Battalion Green Howards marching song, music by Sidney Nelson. The 'Rose' referred to is Queen Alexandra herself.

32 D/DLI 7 813(52).

33 Quoted in Ellis, J., *Eye Deep in Hell* (Crook Helm, London, 1976) p. 84.

34 Northumberland Hussars, 28 June 1915.

35 Unofficial periodical of 'B' Squadron, Northumberland Hussars.

36 This extract and those that follow throughout 'The 1st Battle of Ypres' (unless stated otherwise) sourced from Pease, H., *The History of the Northumberland (Hussars) Yeomanry 1819–1923*.

37 TWAM.

38 Heugh Gun Battery Trust Limited.

39 Ibid.

40 Extracts from Charles H. Moss sourced from D/DLI 7/478/ S (17).

41 Heugh Gun Battery Trust Limited.

42 D/DLI 7/478/ S (17).

43 Heugh Gun Battery Trust Limited.

44 D/DLI 7/478/ S (17).

45 Ibid.

46 This extract and those that follow throughout 'Winter' sourced from Pease, H., *The History of the Northumberland (Hussars) Yeomanry 1819–1923*.

47 Pease, H., *The History of the Northumberland (Hussars) Yeomanry 1819–1923* (Constable, London, 1924) pp. 103–4.

48 Ibid., p. 103.

49 Ibid., p. 104.

50 Authors (1915).

51 D/DLI 2/5/17.

52 Ibid.

53 Extracts attributed to George Hilton sourced from the Trustees of the KOSB Museum.

54 D/DLI 2/5/16.

55 This extract and those that follow throughout 'Baptism of Fire' sourced from the Trustees of the Fusiliers Museum of Northumberland, unless otherwise stated.

56 Primary, undated document in author's own collection.

57 D/DLI 2/5/17.

58 This extract and those that follow throughout 'Attrition' sourced from NRO 00329/F/4/2/1/10 – 11.

59 TWAM.

60 D/DLI 2/5/17.

61 D/DLI 7/137/5.

62 Ibid.

63 Ibid.

64 Extracts attributed to John Walcote Gamble sourced from D/DLI 7/238/1.

65 D/DLI 14/3/ 27 – 35 A.

66 Trustees of the Green Howards Museum – MA369.

67 Trustees of the Green Howards Museum.

68 Extracts attributed to Charles Moss are sourced from D/DLI 7/478/4(1).

69 TWAM.

70 NRO.

71 Trustees of the Fusiliers Museum of Northumberland.

72 *North Durham Advertiser,* 27 July, 1916 (D/WP/2/61).

73 D/DLI 7/577/2.

74 D/DLI 7/560/4.

75 D/DLI 7/137/5.

76 Ibid.

77 D/DLI 7/115/15.

78 D/DLI 7/115/16.

79 D/DLI 7/115/17.

80 NRO 1783(1–4).

81 Ibid.

82 Ibid.

83 D/DLI 7/478/5.

84 Trustees of the Fusiliers Museum of Northumberland.

85 Moses, H., *The Fighting Bradfords* (County Durham Books, 2003), pp. 64–5.

86 Ibid., p. 65.

87 Hart, P., *The Somme* (London 2006), pp. 489–91.

88 Moses, p. 66.

89 Ibid., p. 68.

90 Ibid.

91 Ibid., p. 69.

92 Trustees of the Fusiliers Museum of Northumberland.

93 Ibid., ALNFM 2008:44.

94 Ibid.

95 Trustees of the Green Howards Museum, MA 364.

96 Extracts attributed to Arthur Terry are sourced from the Trustees of the Fusiliers Museum of Northumberland.

97 DCRO.

98 Extracts attributed to John Carr are sourced from the NRO.

99 Roberts, A., *As Good As Any Man* – unpublished memoir.

100 Extracts attributed to Arthur Roberts are taken from his unpublished memoir.

101 References to and by Norman Gladden are sourced from Gladden, N., *Ypres 1917* (New Kimber, London, 1967).

102 Extracts attributed to Ernest Greenwood are sourced from DX668/1/1-2.

103 Authors' collection.

104 This extract and those that follow until chapter end are sourced from Moses, H., *The Fighting Bradfords* (County Durham Books, 2003).

105 D/DLI 14/3/27 – 35 A.

106 Ibid.

107 References to and by George Harbottle sourced from Harbottle, G., *Civilian Soldier* (Newcastle, 1981).

108 Harbottle, p. 87.

109 D/DLI 14/3/27 – 37 A.

110 Quoted in Farrell, J. G., *Troubles* (Penguin, England, 1975), p. 119.

111 D/DLI 14/3/23 – 35 A. (official press despatch).

112 D/DLI 7/347/2 (short article in DLI papers).

113 D/DLI 14/3/27 – 35 A.

114 Extracts throughout 'Sergeant McGuffie wins the Victoria Cross' sourced from the Trustees of the KOSB Museum.

115 D/DLI 7/813 (1 – 6).

116 D/DLI 14/3/31 – 34.

117 D/DLI 7/417/3.

118 Extracts attributed to George Purvis are sourced from the Trustees of the Green Howards Museum.

119 Trustees of the Green Howards MA 317. Amongst the items held by the Green Howards Museum (RICGH 1962.150 and RICGH 1962.150) are framed fragments of stained glass from churches in the Arras area collected by Major J. B. Purvis (who spent fourteen months at the Front, divisional gas officer for 50th Division) and Lieutenant J. S. Purvis with another frame of stained glass fragments from churches in the Ypres salient. Both Purvis brothers left numerous pencil, pen and ink and watercolour sketches.

120 Trustees of the Green Howards, MA 317.

121 Trustees of the Green Howards, MA 363.

122 D/DLI 7/478/5.

123 D/DLI 7/929/3.

124 D/DLI 7/929/1.

125 Ellis, J., *Eye Deep in Hell* (Crook Helm, London, 1976)

126 Extracts attributed to Jack Wilson are sourced from the Trustees of the Fusiliers Museum of Northumberland.

127 Quoted in Jones, E. & Wessely, S., *Shellshock to PTSD: Military Psychology from 1900 to the Gulf War,* Volume One of the Maudsley Series, Issue 47 of Maudsley Monographs, Psychology Press, 2005.

128 Field Punishment replaced flogging in 1881, the offender was shackled or restrained and then strapped to say, a gun wheel, often in a spread position, hence the nickname 'crucifixion'.

129 D/DLI 14/3/27 – 35 A.

130 Hesketh-Pritchard, Major H., *Sniping in France 1914–1918* (Hutchinson, London, 1920), p. vi.

131   All references to and by Major Pemberthy sourced from Pemberthy, Major E., 'An account of the training and organisation of snipers in the British armies in France' in *The English Review*, September 1920.

132   Gilbert, A., *Sniper: One on One* (Sidgwick & Jackson, London, 1994) p. 60.

133   Pemberthy, Major E. in *The English Review*, 1920.

134   Ibid.

135   Quoted in Gilbert, p. 40.

136   Pemberthy, Major E. in *The English Review*, 1920.

137   Ibid.

138   Ibid.

139   Ibid.

140   Extracts attributed to Hesketh-Pritchard are sourced from Hesketh-Pritchard, H., *Sniping in France* (Hutchinson, London, 1920)

141   D/DLI 14/3/27 – 35 A.

142   Hart, P., *Falling Aces* (Weidenfield & Nicholson, London, 2007), pp. 9–10.

143   All references to and by George Elder are sourced from Elder, G. W., *From Geordie Land to No-Man's-Land* (Author House, Indiana, 2011) p. 4.

144   http://www.dublin-fusiliers.com, last accessed 15 March 2013.

145   D/DLI 14/3/27 – 35 A.

146   All references to or by John Norton-Griffiths and Frederick Mulqueen are sourced from Re A.231.2.RE A.231.2.

147   Krippner, Monica, *The Quality of Mercy* (David & Charles, London, 1980)

148   All references to or by Potter Daggett sourced from Potter Daggett, Mabel, *Women Wanted: The Story Written in Blood-Red Letters on the Horizon of the Great World War* (G. H. Doran, 1918).

149   All references to or by Pat Beauchamp are sourced from Beauchamp, Pat, *Fanny Goes To War* (London: John Murray, 1919)

150   Anonymous, *Diary of a Nursing Sister on the Western Front 1914 – 1915*, (William Blackwood, 1915). Now attributed to Katherine Evelyn Luard. All further references to or by K. E. Luard from the same source.

151   Frances Cluett: Romkey, W. & Riggs, B. G. (eds), *Your Daughter Fanny: The War Letters of Frances Cluett, VAD* (Flanker Press, St Johns, 2008)

152   Potter Daggett, p. 42.

153   All references to George Thompson's diary are sourced from D/DLI 7/700/11.

154   Potter Daggett, Mabel, *Women Wanted: The Story Written in Blood-Red Letters on the Horizon of the Great World War* (G. H. Doran, 1918).

155   Purvis, Stanley, 5th Battalion Green Howards, *Diary 1916* (Green Howards).

156   Luard, K. E., p. 227

157   Beauchamp, Pat, p. 119

158   Williams, Albert Rhys, *In the Claws of the German Eagle* (E. P. Dutton & Co., 1917).

159   http://www.spartacus.schoolnet.co.uk/SSthomson.htm last accessed 18 March 2013.

160   Luard, K. E., p. 160

161   Ibid., p. 228

162   Beauchamp, Pat, p. 78.

163   http://www.edithappleton.org.uk/default.asp last accessed 18 March 2013.

164   Sue Light, http://greatwarnurses.blogspot.co.uk/ and http://www.scarlet-finders.co.uk both last accessed 18 March 2013.

165   Sue Light, http://www.scarletfinders.co.uk

166   Luard, K. E., p. 53.

167   Ibid., p. 231.

168   Ibid., p. 129.

169   NRO 1783(1–4).

170   Humphries, S. and van Emden, R., *All Quiet on the Home Front: An Oral History of Life in Britain during the First World War* (Headline, London, 2004).

171   Luard., K. E., p. 148

172   Beauchamp, Pat, p.33

173   Luard, K. E., p. 153

174   Ibid., p. 133

175   Ibid., p. 131

176   Ibid., pp. 1–97

177   Ibid., p. 236

178   Beauchamp, Pat, p. 202

179   Ibid., p. 198

180   Luard, K. E., p. 88

181   D/WA 5/3/5(9).

182   Corns, C. and Hughes-Wilson, J., *Blindfold and Alone: British Military Executions in the Great War* (Phoenix, London, 2005) p. 173.

183   Walter G., ed., *In Flanders Fields* (Penguin, London, 2004), p. 160.

184   Trustees of the Fusiliers Museum of Northumberland.

185   Ibid.

186   All references to W. W. Hall sourced from NRO 2332/4.

187   All references to or by J. T. Milburn sourced from NRO 07338/2.

188   http://ashington.journallive.co.uk/20/11/07/the-milburns-ashingtons-footba.hmtl last accessed 2 July 2012.

189   All references to or by Isaac Armorer Patterson soured from TWAM.

190   *Northern Echo*, 12 November 2005.

191   Durham Record Office, 25/4/12 D/X 1785/ 1 – 21, 23 – 47: Hannah, born 26 October 1893, died 14 November 1968; widow of William Evans, Coal Mines deputy, nearly twenty years her senior. They lived at 4 Lilburn Crescent, Newton Aycliffe. Her daughter, Mary Williams, found the box of cards and letters after her death. There is the photograph of Jigger in Egypt and others showing him in uniform on his way home, of Hannah and Jigger together and of his grave and of Hannah when she married, together with a copy of the newspaper article on the unveiling of the West Cornforth Memorial. Jigger volunteered for 3rd Field Company, Australian Engineers, (service no 7105). There are also studio portraits of Jigger taken before he left for Australia. Photo D/X 1785/47 shows the cross making his

grave in the field near Rouen Hospital: D/x 1785/46 shows him standing
with two other men in uniform. The inscription on the back says 'have you
ever seen anything like this?' D/x 1785/42 shows him in Australian uniform.
On the back is written, 'one for Mother as I heard her say yours would
never leave her place – Jim.'

GLOSSARY

AA: Anti-aircraft
ADS: Advanced Dressing Station
A&SH: Argyll and Sutherland Highlanders
ATS: Auxiliary Territorial Services
Bde: Brigade
BEF: British Expeditionary Force
CIGS: Chief of the Imperial General Staff
C in C: Commander-in-Chief
CO: Commanding officer
Coy: Company
CP: Command post
Cpl: Corporal
CRA: Commander, Royal Artillery
CSM: Company Sergeant-Major
CWGC: Commonwealth War Graves Commission
DCLI: Duke of Cornwall's Light Infantry
DCM: Distinguished Conduct Medal
DCRO: Durham County Records Office
Di':   Division
DLI: Durham Light Infantry
DSO: Distinguished Service Order
Enfilade: flanking fire
FANY: First Aid Nursing Yeomanry
FAP: Forward Aid Post
FOO: Forward observation officer
HE: High explosive
IO: Intelligence officer

IWM: Imperial War Museum
KOSB: King's Own Scottish Borderers
KRRC: King's Royal Rifle Corps
L/Cpl: Lance-Corporal
LOB: Left out of battle
MC: Military Cross
MG: Machine gun
MM: Military medal
NA: National Archive
NAM: National Army Museum
NCO: Non-commissioned officer
NF: Northumberland Fusiliers
NRO: Northumberland Records Office
OP: Observation Post
ORs: Other ranks
PBI: Poor bloody infantry
QM: Quartermaster
RA: Royal Artillery
RAMC: Royal Army Medical Corps
RAP: Regimental Aid Post
RASC: Royal Army Service Corps
RE: Royal Engineers
RFC: Royal Flying Corps
Regt: Regiment
RHA: Royal Horse Artillery
RN: Royal Navy
RND: Royal Naval Division
RSM: Regimental Sergeant-Major
RTR: Royal Tank Regiment
Sgt: Sergeant
TWAM: Tyne and Wear Archives & Museums
WD: War department
WO: Warrant officer
W/T: Wireless telegraphy
Uhlan: German lancer
VAD: Voluntary Auxiliary Detachment
VC: Victoria Cross
YLI: Yorkshire Light Infantry

BIBLIOGRAPHY

Unpublished sources

Heugh Battery Trust Limited, *Heugh Battery*

Charles H. Moss, 18th Battalion DLI

George Purvis, 5th Battalion Green Howards, Diary 1915 (Green Howards)

Stanley Purvis, 5th Battalion Green Howards, Diary 1916 (Green Howards)

Herbert Waugh, 4th Battalion NF, *St Julien, a Soldier's Diary* NF, ALNFM: 6916/1

Drummer Joseph Dawson, 2nd Battalion NF, POW Diary 1915, Northumberland Fusiliers

Shuttleworth family letters, NF, ALNFM: 2008. 48

Corporal Percy Alcock, 19th Battalion NF, Northumberland Fusiliers

Captain Stanley Moffat, 5th Battalion NF, Diary 1916, Northumberland Fusiliers

Tyne and Wear Archives, *Is There Someone I've Forgot* DF.WF/22/1

Wor Contemptible British Army & *The Big Push* DBC 1845/362

Ernest W. Greenwood, *Memoir 4th–9th October 1917* DX668

Liddle family, sundry correspondence 517

R. E. Lumsden Nurse, 1915 Diary DX101

William Falcus, Canadian Expeditionary Force, Diary and Papers 1915–1919 DX668

Captain Peacock, medical papers and cartoons 1915 – 1918 DX250

The authors have attempted to secure copyright permissions in all cases and if there are any omissions they will rectify these accordingly upon being informed.

Published sources

Arthur, M., *Forgotten Voices of the Great War* (London, 2002)

Bailey, Brigadier J. B. A., *Deep Battle 1914–1941: The Birth of the Modern Style of Warfare* in 'British Army Review' no. 120

Bailey, Brigadier J. B. A., *The Century of Firepower* in 'British Army Review' no. 120

Barton, P., *The Somme: A New Panoramic Perspective* (London, 2006)

Baynes, J., *Morale* (London, 1967)

Beauchamp, Pat, *Fanny Went to War* (London, 1919)

Beech, Dr J., MBE, *The Division in the Attack 1918* – SS135, T/1635, 40/WO/7036 (Strategic and Combat Studies Institute, 'The Occasional' no. 53)

Blunden, E., *Undertones of War* (London, 1965)

Brittain, V., *Testament of Youth* (London, 1978)

Chandler, D. G., (ed.) *The Oxford Illustrated History of the British Army* (Oxford, 1994)

Clarke, A., *The Donkeys* (London, 1991)

Clayton, A., *The British Officer* (Harlow, 2007)

Corns, C. and Hughes-Wilson, J., *Blindfold and Alone – British Military Executions in the Great War* (London, 2005)

Corrigan, Major G., *Mud, Blood & Poppycock* (London, 2003)

Dunn, J. C., *The War the Infantry Knew* (London, 1988)

Elder, G. W., *From Geordie Land to No-Man's-Land* (Indiana, 2011)

Ellis, J., *Eye Deep in Hell* (London, 1976)

Falls, C., *The First World War* (London, 1960)

Ferguson, N., *The Pity of War* (London, 2006)

Giddings, R., *The War Poets* (London, 1988)

Gilbert, A., *Sniper: One on One* (London, 1994)

Gladden, N., *Ypres 1917* (London, 1967)

Glubb, Sir J., *Into Battle: A Soldier's Diary of the Great War* (London, 1978)

Graves, R., *Goodbye to All That* (London, 1969)

Hart, P., *The Somme* (London, 2006)

Hart, P., *Falling Aces* (London, 2007)

Hesketh-Pritchard, Major H., *Sniping in France 1914–1918* (London, 1920)

Hewitson, T. L., *Weekend Warriors from Tyne to Tweed* (Gloucester, 2006)

Holmes, R., *The Western Front* (London, 1999)

Hussey, J., *Between Somme and Ancre; 35th Division's Troubles, 26th March 1918*, in 'British Army Review' no. 118

Jones, E. and Wessely, S., *Shellshock to PTSD: Military Psychology from 1900 to the Gulf War*, Volume 1 of the Maudsley Series, Issue 47 of Maudsley Monographs, Psychology Press, 2005.

Junger, E., *The Storm of Steel* (London, 1929)

Keegan, Sir J., *The First World War* (London, 1978)

Keegan, Sir J., *The Face of Battle* (London, 2004)

Laffin, J., (ed.) *Letters from the Front* (London, 1973)

Luard, K. E. (attributed to), *Diary of a Nursing Sister on the Western Front 1914–1915* (William Blackwood, 1915)

MacArthur, B., (ed.) *For King & Country* (London, 2008)

Macmillan, H., *The Winds of Change* (London, 1966)

Marrion, R. J. and Potten, D. S. V., *The British Army 1914–1918* in Osprey 'Men-At-Arms' no. 81

Martin, B., *Poor Bloody Infantry: A Subaltern on the Western Front* (London, 1987)

Moses, H., *The Fighting Bradfords* (County Durham Books, 2003)

Pease, H., *The History of the Northumberland (Hussars) Yeomanry 1819–1923* (London, 1924)

Potter Daggett, Mabel, *Women Wanted: The Story Written in Blood Red Letters on the Horizon of the Great World War* (G. H. Doran, 1918)

Pound, R., *The Lost Generation* (London, 1964)

Sadler, D. J., *The Field Gun Run* (Royal Tournament, 2010)

Samuels, M., *British Tactical Experiments in 1915* in 'British Army Review' no. 119

Sheen, J., *Tyneside Irish* (Barnsley, 1998)

Sheen, J. and Stewart, G., *Tyneside Scottish* (Barnsley, 1999)

Sheffield, G., *Leadership in the Trenches* (London, 2000)

Thompson, Major-General J., *Setting the Record Straight – the Douglas Haig Fellowship Lecture*, 21 June 2010

Walker, G., (ed.) *In Flanders Fields* (London, 2004)

Ward, S. G. P., *Faithful: The Story of the Durham Light Infantry* (London, 1962

Wylly, Co. H. C., *The Green Howards in the Great War 1914–1918* (Richmond, 1926)

INDEX

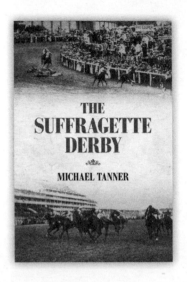

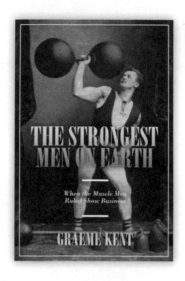